CW01090916

PATWANT SINGH (1925–2009) v
worked in the family construction
New Delhi in the 1930s. In 1957 he
Design, devoted to architecture and wider aesthetic concerns, which he published and edited in Bombay and later New Delhi for thirty-two years. He was well known both inside and outside India for his books and articles on India, international affairs and the environment. His books include *India and the Future of Asia* (1967), *The Struggle for Power in Asia* (1971; French edition *Le Jeu des Puissances*, 1974); *The Golden Temple* (1989), *Gurdwaras in India and Around the World* (1992), *Of Dreams and Demons: An Indian Memoir* (1994), *Garland Around my Neck: The Story of Puran Singh of Pingalwara* (2001), *The Sikhs* (1999), *The World According to Washington* (2004) and *The Second Partition: Fault-Lines in India's Democracy* (2007). His articles appeared in the *New York Times*, the Toronto *Globe and Mail*, the London *Independent* and many leading Indian newspapers.

JYOTI M. RAI, from a distinguished Maratha family, was educated in London and New Delhi. She is married to a Sikh. From 1980 to 2000 she lived and worked in New York, becoming a numismatist of international reputation. On the American Numismatic Society's Standing Committee for Central and South Asian Coins for many years, she made its Sikh collection one of the world's finest. She has also built up an important personal collection of Sikh coins, with related rare books and historical documents. She has published numerous articles and papers on Sikh coins and on Maharaja Ranjit Singh, as well as a biography of her father, Air Chief Marshal H. Moolgavkar, PVSM, MVC, entitled *Leading from the Cockpit: A Fighter Pilot's Story* (2010). She is President of the Delhi Coin Society.

THE MAHARAJA DULEEP SINGH CENTENARY TRUST was established in 1993 by a group of British Sikhs in order to commemorate the centenary of the Maharaja's death and to promote a wider appreciation of Sikh heritage and culture. It has collaborated with the Victoria and Albert Museum in the mounting of the exhibition 'The Arts of the Sikh Kingdoms' in 1999 and the establishment of the annual 'Portraits of Courage' lectures at the Imperial War Museum. The Anglo-Sikh Heritage Trail has also been recognized as an important and groundbreaking initiative of the Trust.

There could be no more vivid encounter with the roots from which Duleep Singh was so cruelly torn than an account of the life and times of his father, Maharaja Ranjit Singh, one of the most original and charismatic figures in Indian history, whose achievements have hitherto been denied full appreciation by British and Indian historians alike. Patwant Singh and Jyoti M. Rai have set the record straight at last in this definitive biography.

It is fitting that the publication of this revised edition falls in 2013, the year in which we mark twenty years of our work to make the enthralling story of the Sikhs more widely known.

PATWANT SINGH AND JYOTI M. RAI

EMPIRE *of the* SIKHS

THE LIFE AND TIMES OF
MAHARAJA RANJIT SINGH

PETER OWEN PUBLISHERS
LONDON AND CHICAGO

PETER OWEN PUBLISHERS
81 Ridge Road, London N8 9NP

Peter Owen books are distributed in the USA and Canada by
Independent Publishers Group/Trafalgar Square,
814 North Franklin Street,
Chicago, IL 60610, USA

ISBN 978-0-7206-1483-1

A catalogue record for this book is available from the British Library

Printed and bound in Great Britain by
CPI Group (UK) Ltd, Croydon, CR0 4YY

For Pritam Singh Chahil,
an extraordinarily gifted scholar
and exemplar of Sikh values,
Champa, his lifelong inspiration,
and Satjiv, a cherished friend

Contents

Illustrations

Maps

Illustration Credits

Plate pages *i, ix* (below): Lahore Fort Museum, Lahore Fort, Pakistan; *ii* (above and below), *xii* (above): Victoria and Albert Museum, London; *iii*: © Naresh Singh; *iv* (top right and bottom), *v* (below): Wallace Collection, London; *vi* (top left), *viii, ix* (above), *xviii* (below), *xx* (above and below): Imperial Hotel, New Delhi; *vi* (top right, bottom left and right), *vii* (bottom): *Paintings of the Sikhs* by W.G. Archer (HMSO, London, 1966); *xi* (below): © Julie W. Munro; *xiii*: Musée du Louvre, Paris; *xvii*: Central Sikh Museum, Darbar Sahib, Amritsar; *xviii* (above), *xxi* and Maharaja Ranjit Singh's family tree from Peter Bance's book *The Duleep Singhs* (Sutton Publishing, Stroud, 2004); *xix, xxiv* (top right): Collection of Satinder and Narinder Kapany. The maps on pages 54, 197 and 250 are from *The Sikhs* by Patwant Singh (John Murray, London, 1999).

Acknowledgements

More often than not, to undertake to write a book is far easier than actually to write it. But it is rare so thoroughly to enjoy a task after reluctantly agreeing to do it that an unexpected sense of loss sets in as the work nears its end, and all the vital, valorous, colourful, conspiring, violent and wilful persons whom we encountered in it every day are no longer around. So we cannot thank our friend enough who wishes to remain nameless but who compelled us to write this book. The very idea of writing about a larger-than-life figure like Ranjit Singh was in fact a challenging and alluring prospect that was difficult to turn down. So, in the end, although it took time to finish the biography of this very exceptional man, it was more than worth it.

Our understanding of his true genius was made possible by knowledgeable men and women and those many friends who generously shared their insights with us. Some, alas, are no more, and the one among them who stood out for his intellect and impressive scholarship was Lieutenant General Joginder (Jogi) Singh Dhillon. Ranjit Singh's life and times were one of Jogi's fields of interest, and he had the ability to cut incisively through accounts of him that were hyperbolic, churlish, inaccurate, or which failed to gauge his real worth. His analysis was stimulating, instructive and inspiring, because of his endorsement – as an outstanding soldier himself – of Ranjit Singh's military genius. Jogi also had a knack for analysing and exposing the extent to which

9

the colonial powers would go to achieve their imperial goals. Their misdeeds come through with startling clarity in the later stages of this book. The East India Company's subversive strategies against the Sikh empire after Ranjit Singh's death were base beyond belief; especially since few colonial powers in their heyday have so persistently proclaimed their own virtues as the British have. Nobody could dismantle their specious and deceptive arguments as convincingly as Jogi could. It was his conviction that nations conspire at events and no level is too low to stoop to for achieving their ends, no lie too outrageous if it serves the larger national interest. As George Bernard Shaw said: 'You will never find an Englishman in the wrong.'

As he always has in the past, Jasdev Singh rose magnificently to the occasion by opening up for us the archives of the Imperial Hotel, New Delhi, which have some fine paintings, drawings, sketches and prints of the Sikh period. But it would be an unforgivable oversight not to acknowledge first our deep gratitude to Jasdev's mother, Bibi Nirlep Kaur, an exceptionally gifted person whose profound admiration and respect for the founding Gurus of the Sikh faith sowed the seeds of Jasdev's increasing interest in his own heritage. The veritable treasure house he is creating for it is a tribute to her. The invaluable help of Chowdhary Ominder Singh Mander, the archivist of Jasdev's collection, in putting together the information we needed is gratefully acknowledged.

Four other friends who gave unstintingly of their time and were generous and forthcoming all the way were Harbinder Singh Rana, Hon. Director of the Maharaja Duleep Singh Centenary Trust, Indarjit and Kanwal Singh and Indar Singh Uppal.

The coinage illustrated in this book comes from the Jyoti M. Rai Collection, a private collection of the rarest Sikh coins. Another friend, Narinder Singh Kapany, who has gradually built up a superb collection of Sikh artefacts, very generously allowed us to reproduce whatever we wished out of his collection in

California. As in the past, Susan Stronge responded magnificently
each time we asked her for her insightful advice and comments.
Bhupinder Singh Bance (Peter Bance), Robert Scoales and
Sukhbinder Singh Paul were generous with their time and the
wealth of information they shared with us, as also were Ros Savill
and Jeremy Warren who were most helpful when we visited
London's Wallace Collection. Martin Lutyens was no less generous
in setting aside an entire morning to show us around Sir John
Soane's Museum. Each of these goodwill gestures helped us locate
material for further enriching this book.

We are equally indebted to Rasil Basu and Deidi Von Schaewen
and to Rewa Singh who generously loaned us for an indefinite
period the very rare (1840) edition of W.G. Osborne's book *The
Court and Camp of Runjeet Sing*. We gratefully acknowledge
the many insights that were provided by Harjit Partap Rai and the
Judge family of Kapurthala, Prabeen Singh, Bubli Brar, the Mool-
gavkars, and thank Pat Rai for his consistent encouragement,
guidance and wise counsel.

Warmest thanks are also due to Dr Michael Bates, the Curator
of Islamic Coins of the American Numismatic Society, and the
society's wonderful members who so willingly shared their wisdom and knowledge.

As always, Antony Wood rose heroically to the occasion and
read the manuscript with a sharp and critical eye from the first
to the last page. The book has benefited enormously from his
editorial advice, despite some rather tense moments over some of
his suggestions, which actually helped further strengthen our
friendship!

The wizardry of Jagjit Singh Anand, the librarian at Bhai Vir
Singh Sahitya Sadan, New Delhi, was much in evidence as he produced with ease books that were impossible to lay hands on
elsewhere.

While on the subject of wizardry, Jaya Nair, too, worked

miracles with her computer, with her unending secretarial responsibilities and her occasional forays into research. She took on every
task confidently and performed it convincingly each time.

We reached port because it was Meher who steered the ship –
as she always has in the past. No matter how difficult the task, she
was not only there to share the burden but would help us cross yet
another hurdle with effortless ease. This book could not have been
written without her wondrous interventions.

Preface to the 2008 Edition

Historians, for reasons of their own, have often done grave injustice to outstanding historical figures by refusing to accord them their rightful place in history. But when even convincing evidence of greatness was overlooked because the political culture of the time required it, it becomes necessary to correct oversights and falsifications, no matter how long after the event.

Ranjit Singh was one such colossus who bestrode the Indian scene but who never received the credit due to him as one of the outstanding figures of India's history. He created the altogether extraordinary empire of the Sikhs, the borders of which extended beyond India and into the thresholds of Kabul and Tibet. He also held the British in check for forty years to the south of his realm and closed the Khyber Pass through which plunderers had for centuries poured into India.

Just as Alexander the Great in 333 BC is said to have fulfilled King Midas's prophecy that whoever untied the Gordian knot would rule Asia, Ranjit Singh and Napoleon Bonaparte, two outstanding visionaries and military commanders who were contemporaries, laid their claims to fulfilling this prophecy by untying the knot and establishing empires in the most divided parts of the world. They each shared a deep mistrust of the British, because they had no illusions about the degree to which their common adversary was driven by its own ambitions of empire.

Even though many books have been published on Ranjit Singh,

we felt that a definitive biography of this rare man had still to be written, to cover not only the entire range of his military achievements but also the just and humane rule he provided during turbulent times when barbarism was the order of the day. The task we set ourselves was to bring out the essence of the man, his daily routine, his likes and dislikes and his dealings with people in every walk of life. Equally important to establish were his relationships with the many women in his life and the courtesies and decencies which he extended to them without exception. Yet another side of Ranjit Singh was reflected in the grandeur of his Lahore Durbar, equal to any European or Mughal court, his jewels, *objets d'art* and the precious artefacts which he collected all his life.

In order to draw upon as many different accounts as we could, we went to original sources with eyewitness accounts by Europeans and Indians alike; court diaries during Ranjit Singh's time; reports of Maratha spies at the Lahore Durbar; British parliamentary papers; Lahore political diaries; British–Indian archives and the libraries of Columbia, New York, Punjab and Chandigarh universities.

What we discovered was that the civilized rule of Ranjit Singh was entirely different from the way many other rulers have treated their people in India. The question that has remained unanswered until now is what made him the man he was – a man who shunned the flagrant violations of humanitarian principles so very common throughout history? What made him adhere so scrupulously throughout his life to the goals he set himself? And what inner resources did he draw upon that enabled him to abide by the ethical and exemplary rules he so diligently observed?

In our efforts to find answers to these questions we were drawn ever deeper into a better understanding of the intense beliefs that helped Ranjit Singh achieve all that he did. His most compelling quality was his total commitment to the religious faith into which he was born. If secularity – or equal respect for other religions – was the founding principle of Sikhism, then he was determined never to deviate from it.

Proof of this was the fact that no other ruler in the sprawling subcontinent had ever had in his cabinet as many men owing allegiance to other religions as Ranjit Singh. At the peak of his power, there were only seven Sikhs in his cabinet of fifteen ministers, and the rest were Hindus and Muslims. Many others of different religions, such as Jains, Buddhists, Christians and the bewildering subdivisions of these faiths, were accommodated according to their talents.

How was this leader able to achieve the seemingly impossible goals he set himself? The answer lies in his veneration of the ten founding fathers of the Sikh faith and the ethos of decency and discipline they preached. A part of the answer also lies in the fact that at the age of nine he had to assume the chieftainship of his father's *misl* or confederacy which was one of the more powerful in Punjab. To take on the chief's mantle was an awesome responsibility. But Ranjit Singh, by handling it with energy and *élan*, gained the self-confidence that never left him.

The achievements of his grandfather and his father before him, who were warriors and leaders of great repute, were of fundamental importance to his own career. But the distinctive quality that makes Ranjit Singh truly exceptional was his humanitarianism, his respect for other faiths and his total disgust for the inhumane treatment which rulers of the day inflicted on their defeated adversaries. As the British writer Sir Lepel Griffin observed in *Rulers of India: Ranjit Singh* (1911), 'Ranjit Singh was not cruel or bloodthirsty. After a victory or the capture of a fortress he treated the vanquished with leniency and kindness however stout their resistance might have been, and there were at his Court many chiefs despoiled of their estates but to whom he had given suitable employ.'

Another fascinating aspect of this multi-faceted man was his refusal to allow any cities, towns, forts, highways, gardens, statues, archways, monuments and such to commemorate him. Most extraordinary of all was that, even though he established many mints which produced fine coins, there is just one coin of very small dimensions with his image on it, which shows Ranjit Singh kneeling before Guru Nanak with folded hands. If any one thing highlights his self-effacing qualities and his total rejection of the time-worn ways of self-aggrandizement, this is it.

It is also worth recording that even after he had wrested control of Amritsar from the chiefs of the Bhangi *misl* in 1802, Ranjit Singh arrived at the Harmandir, the Golden Temple, not as a victorious military leader or the monarch of a Sikh state but as a devotee – among countless others – come to pray at the holiest of Sikh shrines. This was his way of demonstrating his conviction that within the precincts of the Durbar Sahib there was no place for the self-important or arrogant.

Equally significant is the fact that the Harmandir Sahib in the centre of the pool of the Durbar Sahib in Amritsar has an inscription of a few lines at the entrance to the shrine, acknowledging Ranjit Singh's contribution towards making the Golden Temple one of the world's great religious places. The inscription, translated from Gurmukhi, reads: 'The great Guru in his wisdom looked upon Maharaja Ranjit Singh as his chief servitor and Sikh, and in his benevolence bestowed upon him the privilege of serving the Durbar Sahib.'

There could be no more telling acknowledgement of Ranjit Singh's lasting legacy than these lines at the entrance of the fountainhead of the Sikh faith. To this day they inspire Sikhs the world over, no matter where they have put down their roots, since Sikhs now live in all corners of the world – confident, purposeful, productive and proud of their incomparable heritage.

Patwant Singh and Jyoti M. Rai
2008

Postscript to the Preface

Sardar Patwant Singh and I first met at his residence in Delhi in 1998. I had been asked to get his book *The Gurdwaras* autographed for a relative's sixtieth birthday. His secretary gave me an appointment, warning me not to be late and to have the details written down as I would be given precisely five minutes, no more. So I went to meet the great Sikh historian. Locked away in his study sat a very dapper Patwant, immersed in writing. He looked up briefly from his sloping writing desk, took the book and signed it. Casually he asked me what I did. I replied that I was a numismatist, specializing in Sikh coinage in eighteenth- and nineteenth-century Punjab. The change in his demeanour was incredible. His eyes brightened; sitting up straighter, he started firing off a barrage of questions at me. I stayed for two hours and was invited to dinner the next evening.

Patwant and I became friends, and from time to time he would ask me to write articles on Sikh coinage for various publications as he felt little was known on this topic. Residing in New York for over twenty years researching Sikh mints and coinage, I had managed to unearth a good number of little-known facts. Patwant and I enjoyed going into lengthy discussions on my latest findings; and he valued the fact that I – a Hindu – was so immersed in Sikh history.

As ardent admirers of Maharaja Ranjit Singh we both felt very strongly that a book should be written that not only spelled out his achievement in establishing a Sikh state but also described what he was like as a person, his likes and dislikes, the details of his daily life. In 2006 we met to discuss the preparation of a definitive biography of this very complex man. I was thrilled when Patwant asked me to co-author this book with him.

The labour was to be divided; the writing to be his and the research mine. I moved my collection of over 200 books and papers on the subject to his house; this, together with his library, made an extensive base from which to work. And work we did! No holidays or sick leave; at one point Patwant even worked from his hospital bed, much to the annoyance of his doctors. Each morning I would enter his study and say, '*Sat Sri Akal, Ji*' ('Truth is God'), and he would reply to my greeting with '*Wahe Guruji Ka Khalsa, Wahe Guruji Ki Fateh, Jyotiji*' ('The Khalsa belong to God, and God's truth will always prevail'). We had the words *Ik Onkar* ('God Is One') written on every sheet of paper we used.

We enjoyed putting the book together, discussing which first-hand accounts to use and hunting for unpublished pictures. There was much we had to leave out. Deciding on what was relevant and what was not created a few heated arguments, but on the whole we were in agreement. Never having written a book before, I had much to learn. As the book progressed, my confidence grew. After the fourth chapter some of the text was written by me; on the arts, coins, women, pageantry and betrayals.

Sardar Patwant Singh passed away in 2009, after his return home from having this book launched at the Library of Congress, Washington. He had missed the earlier launch at the Victoria and Albert Museum, London, in 2008 as a result of ill health. With his passing, we lost a great individual and an extraordinary man. And I lost a dear and irreplaceable friend.

Jyoti M. Rai
April 2013

1

The Legacy That Made the Sikhs Proud

History is not a calculating machine. It unfolds in
the mind and the imagination, and it takes body
in the multifarious responses of a people's culture,
itself the infinitely subtle mediation of material
realities, of underpinning economic fact,
of gritty objectivities.

BASIL DAVIDSON

Over the centuries many invaders from far-off lands, lured by India's untold wealth in gold, diamonds, pearls and gems and its bountiful earth, followed the footsteps of Alexander the Great into India. One quality the Macedonian showed soon after he crossed into India through the Khyber Pass in 327 BC, his magnanimity towards the vanquished, Ranjit Singh shared in abundance. It was not a quality frequently found either in classical times or since.

Defeating King Porus, ruler of Paurava, through which flow two of Punjab's great rivers, Jhelum and Chenab (Hydaspes and Acesines in Greek), Alexander, deeply impressed by the dignified bearing of the vanquished king, asked him what he could do for him, to which Porus replied: 'Treat me like a king.' Alexander said: 'I would do that for my own sake, but tell me what I may do for thee.' 'All my wishes,' said Porus, 'are summed up in my first reply.'[1] The pride and noble bearing of Porus led to a friendship that resulted in the fallen king's ascension once again to his ancestors' throne and the restoration of not only his old territories but many more as well. Porus was not the only one of his fallen foes to be treated royally by Alexander. There were many others who, impressed by his civilized behaviour towards them, brought their own levies of troops to fight alongside the Macedonians.

And among testimonies of Ranjit Singh's generosity towards foes may be cited this from Major H.M.L. Lawrence, political agent in charge of British relations with Lahore, during Ranjit's rule: 'While those of the royal blood are all but begging their bread in Delhi and Kabul, he [Ranjit Singh] almost invariably provides for the families of his conquered enemies.'[2] Such behaviour had not been known on the subcontinent since the days of Alexander the Great. More familiar experience was the general three-day massacre during Tamerlane's sack of Delhi in 1398 and the similar savagery of the invading Nadir Shah of Persia in 1739 and the Afghan ruler Ahmad Shah Abdali in 1748.

On the departure of Alexander the Great from India in 323 BC there was comparative peace in the subcontinent for a century under the Mauryans. But in the course of the next two millennia of Indian history repeated conflicts on Indian soil continued to weaken it. While each new period enriched the culture of the land, it also brought a further proliferation of religious pressures, languages, creeds and customs which inevitably led to big and small wars. The various regional, linguistic and other divisions so very obvious in India today go far back, and they have only increased with time. The clash of arms and relentless bloodshed over the centuries inevitably facilitated the gradual colonization of the country by forces which came to the subcontinent to plunder but ended up ruling it.

The first Muslim invaders entered the subcontinent at the beginning of the eighth century, but the main Islamic assault came with the appearance of Sabuktigin from the Afghan kingdom of

Ghazni on the northern plains of the Punjab with his Central Asian horsemen in 986. His and then his son Mahmud's annual expeditions over several decades set a model for hordes of future invaders who systematically looted the sacred and secular treasures of northern India and decimated its inhabitants. Most of the next millennium saw eight successive Muslim dynasties in India, the last of these, the Mughals, establishing an empire that brought all of India under its rule until the British took over after the suppression of the Indian Mutiny in 1858.

It was the people of the Punjab, the land of the legendary five rivers – the Jhelum, Chenab, Ravi, Sutlej and Beas[3] – who bore the brunt of centuries of invasions, and their rugged character was honed in the unceasing clash of arms. 'From the remotest antiquity,' an Indian historian has written, 'an interest has attached to the land of the five Rivers unequalled by that attaching to any other land of this great Peninsula'; it is 'placed [...] by nature in a locality which gives it a crowning position, and serving as the gateway to India' and 'every invader from the North has, by its possession, sought the road to fame'.[4]

For hundreds of miles to the north of Punjab lie the Himalayan and Sub-Himalayan ranges, and nestling in them are the ancient centres of Nahan, Chamba, Mandi, Suket and Simla, which was the summer capital of British India. Then there are the flowering valleys of Kulu and Kangra, the upland herding towns of Lahaul and Spiti and the hill town of Dalhousie. To the west lie the Sulaiman and Safed Koh ranges, to the east the River Jamuna, and to the south are the deserts of Sind and Rajasthan and the River Sutlej. Covering an area of 100,436 square miles, well defined by its natural boundaries, amply watered by its five rivers, with extensive areas of rich alluvial soil deposited by them, the Punjab has always held rich agricultural potential. And when to all these natural assets are added the indomitable character of its people this region has been justifiably considered a priceless jewel in the crown of whichever ruler sat on the throne of Delhi.

Ranjit Singh's accomplishments, his consolidation of the territories he conquered, the diverse backgrounds of the men he chose as his political advisers, military generals and ministers, can be fully appreciated only in long historical context: against the backdrop of India's self-destructive pressures rooted in religion, class, caste and customs and, above all, in the context of the actions and ethical, philosophical, spiritual and social goals of the founding fathers of Sikhism.

✑

Nanak, founder of the Sikh faith, was born in times when wars, terror, turbulence and periodic invasions were savaging the subcontinent, although at the time of his birth on 15 April 1469 India was experiencing a spell of rare stability under the benign rule of Bahlol Khan, founder of the Lodhi Dynasty (1451–1526). Nanak's life coincided with the religious renaissance in Europe, and by an interesting coincidence Martin Luther (1483–1546) and John Calvin (1509–64) were his contemporaries.

Nanak, too, felt very early in life that the divisive and destructive trends which had been tearing his country, the Punjab, apart – and the very village of his birth, Talwandi near Lahore, on the direct route of invading armies that had not so long ago poured in through the Hindu Kush – could only be met by the resoluteness and impetus provided by a new religion which would revitalize people to meet these destructive forces. His resolve to give shape and form to such a movement led him to lay the groundwork for Sikhism. The new faith, he was determined, must give a new life, add a new cultural dimension and a wholly new dynamic to India's religious mosaic.

Nanak was born into a Hindu family and a very happy one at that.[5] At a very young age he astonished his parents and the family's Brahmin priest with some forthright statements and

questions. 'There is no Hindu. There is no Mussulman,' he pronounced.[6] And at the age of eleven he baffled a gathering of family,
friends and relations when he refused to wear the *janeu* or sacred
thread of the Hindus which all male offspring are enjoined to wear
from that age onwards, which consists of strands of cotton woven
into a thin cord looped from the left shoulder around the right
hip. Nanak asked the priest presiding over the ceremony to explain
to him what difference wearing the thread would make to his life.
If he was unconvinced it could make any real difference, he would
prefer not to be a party to the ceremony. He then recited his own
composition to him and the assembled guests:

> Out of the cotton of compassion
> Spin the thread of contentment
> Tie the knot of continence, and the twist of virtue;
> Make such a sacred thread,
> O Pundit, for your inner self.[7]

When he took his father's cattle out to graze he would spend
hours listening to the sages and mystics who have always been a
part of India's human mosaic. Although he was most attentive to
what they had to say, he usually drew his own conclusions which
were, more times than not, at odds with theirs.

At the age of sixteen, on the persuasion of his adoring sister
Nanaki, he moved to the town of Sultanpur, a hundred miles away
from the parental home, to live with her and her husband, who
worked for Nawab Daulat Khan Lodhi, the region's powerful governor and a relative of the ruler of Delhi, Bahlol Khan. A refined
and scholarly man, Daulat Khan was so impressed by Nanak that
he offered him a job, which he accepted, even though a job wasn't
exactly what he was looking for in life.

During his eight years in Sultanpur Nanak married at nineteen
and became the father of two sons, Srichand and Lakhmidas.

When he was barely in his twenties word spread about his saintliness and scholarly insights into the purpose and meaning of life and the code by which it should be lived. This drew people – even from distant places – to him, and they listened to him with growing reverence. But Nanak knew that he still had much to probe, question and absorb before he could meaningfully communicate with the disciples who had begun to gravitate towards him.

At this stage he took an extraordinary decision: to visit all the centres of religious learning in his country that he could and to travel to those of far-off countries as well, to see and understand the essence of their beliefs and what helped to sustain them. He himself believed in the concept of one god and was increasingly of the view that only this could help a war-ridden, conflict-prone and utterly divided world in which millions of weak and demoralized victims of aggressors were left to their fate. He wished to meet the scholars and sages at the great religious centres and learn their view of these critical human concerns.

Starting in 1496, Nanak's travels lasted twenty-eight years. His journeys were a remarkable feat for those times. But Nanak's gentle and saintly appearance belied his iron will. His travels in India took him from Hardwar to Benares, Kamrup (Assam), Jagannath (Orissa) and to southern India and Ceylon. In the next phase of his travels he visited Tibet, Kabul, Mecca and Baghdad. Each new encounter with men of learning and philosophical bent helped him to define more sharply the contours of the faith he was shaping in a number of newly composed hymns, in which he drew on the basic compassion of Hinduism and the essential brotherhood of Islam, rejecting the demeaning role of the caste system which, in his view, was no less pernicious than the destruction of temples and places of worship.

The word 'Sikh' comes from the Sanskrit word *shishya*, which means a devoted follower. It was very much in tune with the new faith. After Nanak's return from his travels he settled in a peaceful spot by the River Ravi, where he spent the last fifteen years of his life. There he built a village which he called Kartarpur, where his devoted disciples gathered in increasing numbers. Its idyllic setting, the easy flow of the community's daily routine in which all participated, Nanak's reading of his own hymns – he composed 974 in all – and the philosophical discourses he initiated, all helped to establish a daily format which Sikhs have followed, with some variations, ever since.

This man of extraordinary vision, exemplary concern for fellow humans and a resoluteness which helped him achieve the seemingly impossible died a peaceful death in Kartarpur on 7 September 1539.

∽

The founder of Sikhism was succeeded as Guru by Angad, who had been chosen by Nanak in preference to his two sons. He began the task of assembling all Guru Nanak's hymns – and sixty-two of his own – in a book. The script he chose was the Gurmukhi (which is also used for modern secular writing and printing); the hymns were composed in medieval Punjabi, in Hindi and other languages of the time. This book would be the precursor of the Guru Granth Sahib, the holy book of the Sikhs. On his death in 1552 his chosen successor and close disciple Amar Das succeeded him.

Amar Das gave priority to organizationally strengthening the Sikh faith by meeting the many needs of the *sangats* or assemblies of Sikhs which were beginning to be formed in many parts of India. Guru Amar Das organized these into twenty-two *manjis* or districts, which brought a much-needed cohesiveness and continuity to the faith. He also institutionalized the concept of *langar*, a community kitchen where all, no matter what their caste or religion, could eat.

Guru Amar Das's major reform was the emancipation of women. He allowed widows to remarry and broke the tradition of not appointing women preachers. He prohibited followers of the Sikh faith from practising *sati* – the self-immolation of widows on their husband's funeral pyres – and made clear that they were no longer obliged to wear veils. These decisions and others introducing equality between men and women were unprecedented in the subcontinent.

A scholar and thinker, Guru Amar Das also wrote 907 hymns which are included in the Guru Granth Sahib. Many of them emphatically reiterate Sikhism's unbending opposition to caste, cults, clergy and idols while expressing firm belief in one god.

> There were no divisions of caste or rank,
>   no sectarian antagonisms,
> No idols nor temples, nor creeds of particular nations,
> There were no clashing forms of prayer and worship,
> Nor any to worship or pray.
> There were no mullas or qazis or hadjis;
> No Sufis and no disciples of the Sufis,
> No proud Kings, nor their subjects,
> Nor Masters either, nor slaves.
> There did not exist either the cult based on adoring
>   worship of Vishnu,
> Nor that based on Siva, the passive male,
> And Sakti, the active female:
> There was neither friendship nor sexual appetite;
> God was both creditor and debtor then,
> Such being His pleasure.

GURU GRANTH SAHIB, *Rag Maru*, p. 1035

Guru Amar Das also took the first steps to construct the holiest of all Sikh shrines, the Harmandir, which later came to be known as the Golden Temple, by choosing a site with a beautiful clear pool surrounded by a terrain of trees, flora and fauna. The actual construction of the building destined to become the emblematic core of Sikhism would take several decades and owed much to the fourth and fifth Gurus, Ram Das and Arjan Dev.

When Amar Das died in 1574, the leadership of the faith passed to Ram Das, who had created a lasting impression on the third Guru by totally identifying himself with the principles and purposes of Sikhism. He took the development of the Golden Temple's site under his personal direction. None of the Sikh Gurus, it should be noted, used his position to lead a privileged life but worked alongside the congregation on everyday duties and anything else that needed to be done.

Guru Ram Das chose to live in a modest structure by the pool that had appealed to his predecessor. The site was between the rivers Ravi and Beas and about a hundred miles east of Lahore. The first step Ram Das took was to buy the pool and much of the land around it for building the Harmandir, to which Sikhs from far and near were to travel for the great joy of seeing their beloved shrine in the middle of the immortal pool. Around this place rose a holy city, which eventually came to be known as Amritsar. The name derives from the words *amrit*, which in Sanskrit means the elixir of life or water sanctified by the touch of the sacred, and *sarowar*, which means a lake or pool.

In the construction of the Harmandir and its surroundings Sikhism's enduring principles of voluntary labour and self-reliance were considered sacrosanct, which is why Guru Ram Das declined Emperor Akbar's offer to gift land for the Harmandir.

❧

The fifth Guru, Arjan Dev, succeeded Ram Das at the age of eighteen. What he achieved in the twenty-five years of his stewardship proved of fundamental importance for the course of Sikhism. In keeping with the basic Sikh belief that there are no Hindus or Muslims, all being one in the eyes of God, he invited an eminent

Qadirite Muslim saint from Lahore to lay the foundation stone of the Harmandir, probably in 1588.

The siting, scale, design and construction of the Harmandir were strikingly at odds with the trends of those times. While the design and scale of the religious and secular Renaissance buildings of Europe were meant to reflect the power and wealth of a particular faith, or to glorify the monarchs and merchant princes who helped build them, the Harmandir, a single-storeyed structure, was built lower than the surrounding land so that its modest size would stress the faith's enduring ability, strength and confidence, not through extravagant architectural grandeur but by allowing the appeal of that faith irresistibly to draw people to it – the nobility of the idea it enunciated, that all human beings are equal in the eyes of God.

The Harmandir was to have four entrances to demonstrate the fact that its doors would be open to all four castes, Kshatriyas, Brahmins, Sudras and Vaisyas, equal partners in divine instruction. Its location in the centre of the pool, or *sarowar*, was to symbolize the synthesis of *nirgun* and *sargun*, the spiritual and temporal realms of human existence. The *sarowar* was lined with steps for the devout to enter the immortal pool, in which they would come over long distances to bathe.

The materials used for the Harmandir's construction were simple: a solid brick and lime foundation and on it supporting walls of burnt bricks and lime. The gold, marble inlays, mirror work and other embellishments came much later as generations of Sikhs lavished their wealth on increasing the magnificence of their place of worship. The nineteenth century was the 'golden' era thanks to the spectacular rise of the Sikhs under Ranjit Singh and his patronage of artists and craftsmen.

As more sites of sublime significance were developed around the Harmandir, the complex came to be known as the Darbar Sahib. In time the Harmandir or Golden Temple itself was identified as the

Darbar Sahib, until the two became indistinguishable from each other, although the magnetic draw the Harmandir proper exercises on the minds of the devout has not been equalled by any other building in the complex. With the development of the Darbar Sahib and its environs, the city of Amritsar grew in importance to become more than a pilgrimage centre; it became the rallying point for Sikhs everywhere, a complete realization of Guru Arjan Dev's vision of a place of permanence and self-renewal for the community.

In addition to the creation of the Darbar Sahib and the holy city of Amritsar, Guru Arjan Dev's unique contribution to the faith was in compiling the Sikh scriptures in the form of the Adi Granth[8] – later known as the Granth Sahib. This anthology of the thoughts, verses, hymns and teachings of the first five Sikh Gurus and of Hindu and Muslim scholars and saints such as Kabir, Namdev, Ravidas, Sheikh Farid, Jaidev, Surdas and others contains the best that men of wisdom and rare inspiration had to offer and enshrines the 'secular principle' enunciated by Nanak: that all great faiths must be respected for their nobility of purpose, which will always remain the faith's cornerstone.[9]

It is doubtful if any major religion had until this moment allowed the thought of sages of other faiths to be expressed in its own scriptures. Yet the Sikhs listen every day, with veneration and respect, to the viewpoints of all in the Granth Sahib as unvarnished truth. In the words of the Muslim weaver Kabir:

> What makes you a Brahmin
> And I merely a Sudra?
> If blood runs in my veins
> Does milk flow in yours?

> GURU GRANTH SAHIB, *Rag Gauri*, p. 324

Guru Arjan Dev's prodigious efforts produced a holy book of 1,948 pages containing more than 7,000 hymns, 2,218 of them his own. The scriptures are set to thirty-one *ragas* (the classical system of Indian music), so that the rationality of thought is rendered lyrically. None of this could have been achieved without the meticulous editing standards he set himself and the minutest attention he paid to the style, syntax and rhythm to ensure a natural flow of the text.

The Adi Granth was installed in the Harmandir in 1604, and the sanctity accorded to the Harmandir has come to focus on it, fulfilling Guru Arjun Dev's aim of providing those who visited the Harmandir with a profound experience that an empty structure could never have provided. It became the practice for passages to be read from it every day (and now throughout the day), alternating with verses sung to the sound of music played on traditional instruments for the nourishment of those coming to listen to the words and thoughts of the sages.

It has been common throughout history for men of saintly character to be viewed with disfavour by those resentful of their spiritual stature and authority. Guru Arjan Dev was no exception. The Mughal emperor Jahangir, who had succeeded his enlightened father Emperor Akbar, now became the instrument of a brutal act that was to change the course of Indian history. Unlike his father, who had been greatly impressed by observing what the Sikh religion stood for, the shallow and self-indulgent Jahangir listened to the advice of envious and bigoted men who wanted to put an end to the Guru and the Sikhs whose number was increasing every day from the ranks of both Hindus and Muslims.

Within two years of the first copy of the Granth being reverently placed in the Harmandir, and seeing the electrifying effect this had on Sikhs everywhere, the fanatics who had Jahangir's ear made their first move. They persuaded him to act by playing on his jealousy of his liberal and scholarly eldest son Khusru, who had been sympathetically received by Guru Arjan Dev. He turned on the Guru in demonic fury. He ordered the confiscation of all his property and his death by torture. His anger was further fuelled when Guru Arjan Dev brushed aside Jahangir's offer to commute his death sentence if he paid a fine of 200,000 rupees and deleted certain verses in the Granth Sahib.[10]

Even by Jahangir's standards the torture was exceptionally sadistic. Guru Arjan was made to sit on a red-hot iron sheet and burning sand was poured over him, followed by immersion in near-boiling water before his burnt and blistered body was thrown into the Ravi. His fortitude and serenity in face of this torture was unlike anything the Mughals had seen before. To his son Hargobind he sent this parting message: 'Not to mourn or indulge in unmanly lamentations, but to sing God's praises.'[11] He also advised him to 'sit fully armed on his throne and maintain an army to the best of his ability'.[12]

The example of each Guru's life has inspired and welded together generations of Sikhs. The bravery of the saintly Guru Arjan Dev during his torture became a touchstone by which the Sikhs would test their own courage. This senseless deed sent the Sikhs into a towering rage which carried them into bitter battles with Mughal and other Islamic forces for over 150 years and strengthened their resolve to take an implacable stand against tyrants. The extraordinary leaderly qualities of Ranjit Singh and the goals he set himself and his men are best understood in the context of the certainties, self-assurance and rational thinking of the Sikh Gurus.

Hargobind was eleven when he donned Guru Arjan's mantle in 1606. Despite his young age, he rose to the occasion with remarkable self-assurance. Challenging though the task was of converting a community conditioned from the beginning to peaceful and spiritual goals into one now confronted by the harsh reality of an inhuman world, Hargobind was nevertheless to succeed. One of the reasons he did so was because Sikh rage would not be contained until Guru Arjan Dev's martyrdom was avenged.

As the numbers of volunteers increased, Hargobind sent men far and wide to buy outstanding breeds of horses and new and effective weapons which had been developed and battle-tested elsewhere. He also opened training camps to teach physical fitness, archery, horsemanship, swordsmanship, hand-to-hand combat, lancing and other techniques of combat. In a far-sighted move he introduced the concept of *meeri* and *peeri*, meaning that equal time was to be devoted to temporal (*meeri*) and spiritual (*peeri*) concerns. The appeal of this to the Sikhs was immediate, offering a way of following their faith and its ideals and at the same time being prepared to take on religious fanatics who opposed it. For those disinclined to accept people who prayed to a different god, the Sikhs now had an answer. If *peeri* was attacked they would hit back with the razor-keen edge of *meeri*. The distinction between *meeri* and *peeri* would ensure that the supreme authority of the Harmandir would never be compromised by worldly concerns. And the Sikhs were willing to sacrifice their lives for the source of their inspiration.

To help deal with these worldly matters representatives of the Sikhs started meeting at the Akal Takht – the literal translation of which is 'the Almighty's Throne'. The temporal power of the Sikhs was now exercised from here and not from the spiritual sanctity of the Harmandir. The Akal Takht in its present-day form was built much later. In the beginning it was a raised platform of bricks on an earthen embankment across from a wide open space facing the causeway to the Harmandir. Guru Hargobind would usually sit on the platform as people came to him to seek guidance, offer their advice and suggestions and talk to him about their aspirations and concerns. The republican tradition of the faith was clearly evident here, as no decisions were forced on those assembled but accepted only after reaching a consensus. This was a wise practice, since increasingly bloody encounters with the Mughals would soon commence.

After Jahangir's death in 1627 his successor Shah Jahan proved no less hostile to the Sikhs. Within a year of his ascending the throne he precipitated the first armed encounter with them. Its cause was a rare white hawk. Not far from Amritsar, where they were hunting on the same day, Shah Jahan's and Guru Hargobind's followers clashed over the hawk to which each side laid claim. When told of this the irate emperor sent a contingent of troops under Mukhlis Khan to arrest the Guru. In the encounter that followed Mukhlis Khan was killed and his force defeated. The two antagonists fought again at Lahira in 1631 and Kartarpur in 1634, the Mughal forces being heavily defeated in both battles. The Sikhs' casualties were also high, but their morale was even higher, as they had proved that the Mughal writ could be stopped on the battlefield and that a defiant force had been created within the empire.

By now Hargobind was on the move most of the time. He had wisely decided to absent himself from Amritsar, aware of Shah Jehan's penchant for destroying the shrines of other religions and sensing that he might have attempted to destroy the Harmandir in a vengeful attack on Hargobind. As he brought home the philosophy and essence of his faith to different people around the Punjab, the numbers of those converting to Sikhism swelled, and, in the tradition set by Guru Nanak, Hargobind, too, travelled far and wide and established *sangats* from Kabul to Dacca. During the last years of his life he settled down in a beautiful place in the foothills of the Himalayas where he built a small settlement called Kiratpur. This place would later become immortalized for the Sikhs as Anandpur Sahib.

A unique legacy Guru Hargobind left behind is the gurdwara, Sikhism's house of prayer, which plays a defining and unifying role among Sikhs everywhere. The congregation enters a gurdwara to listen to passages from the Granth Sahib, alternating with the *shabads* (hymns) from it, sung by singers known as *ragis* in voices full of resonance and reverence. The experience cannot be described but only felt by the faithful, who enter a large – or small as the case may be – interior with lofty ceilings and lime-washed walls and the ever-present fragrance of marigolds, roses and many other flowers brought as offerings to the Granth Sahib. The holy book lies open on a raised pedestal in pride of place. Draped on its sides and placed below it are beautiful silks whose colours vibrantly alternate with those of the flowers. There is always a priest seated before the Granth Sahib to read passages from it. The congregation sits on the floor covered with carpets and white sheets at a level lower than the Granth Sahib.

Guru Hargobind, the soldier-saint who gave the Sikhs the reputation of being among the world's best fighters, died in 1644. He had ignited a spark in the Indian character which would in time remove the passivity drilled into it by centuries of brutal invasions. His example, like those of Guru Nanak, his father Guru Arjan Dev and, later, Guru Gobind Singh, went into the formation of a legacy that was to give Ranjit Singh his confidence and his inspiration.

❧

Har Rai, who succeeded his grandfather at the age of fourteen, was scholarly, meditative and immersed in the scriptures. But he had a core of steel as well. This man of peace took an inflexible stand against the Mughal emperor Aurangzeb who would soon bring the entire Indian subcontinent under his rule.

Aurangzeb was a cruel, iron-fisted man, incapable of forgiveness. To secure the throne for himself, he showed no compunction in finishing off his own brothers and imprisoning his father Emperor Shah Jahan. He was pursuing his brother Dara Shikoh to eliminate him as a contestant to the imperial throne. The Guru, who liked Dara for his liberalism and philosophic bent, sent a Sikh contingent to divert the imperial troops so that Dara could escape – which he did; although he was captured soon afterwards and put to death.

An irate Aurangzeb, now securely installed on the throne, summoned Har Rai to his presence. Har Rai replied: 'I am not a King who payeth thee tribute, nor do I desire to receive anything from thee, nor do we stand in the relation of priest and disciple to each other, so wherefor hast thou summoned me?'[13] Rather than go himself, he sent his son Ram Rai to meet Aurangzeb. When reading a passage from the Guru Granth Sahib to the emperor, Ram Rai knowingly misinterpreted a passage he felt would be seen as derogatory to Islam. When his father learnt of this, he refused to see his son again for his temerity in altering a verse by Guru Nanak. Even though Ram Rai was his eldest son, Guru Har Rai chose his youngest, Har Krishan, aged five, to succeed him when he died at Kiratpur in 1661. Har Krishan died himself three years later.

The ninth Guru, Tegh Bahadur who now succeeded Har Krishan, born in 1621, was the youngest of Guru Hargobind's five sons. Although he had retired to lead a mystic's life, he had impressed his father with his conduct in the Battle of Kartarpur. He was an inveterate traveller in the cause of rallying people to the Sikh faith. It was in the easterly town of Patna that his son Gobind – the tenth and last Guru – was born. His return to Chak Nanaki in Punjab in 1672 saw the end of his travels. Chak Nanaki later earned renown at Anandpur after he built a redoubtable stronghold there on a high promontory in the foothills of the state of Bilaspur. But by then the outlines of a major tragedy were beginning to emerge, fuelled by the religious intolerance of Aurangzeb.

In April 1669 the emperor had ordered the governors of all the Mughal provinces to stamp out the practice of any religions other than Islam.[14] In Kashmir this foolhardy policy was carried out with exceptional cruelty by the governor of that province, Iftikhar Khan. The persecuted pandits sent a delegation to Tegh Bahadur in Anandpur to ask his help to save the Hindu religion in Kashmir. After long and careful thought, Guru Tegh Bahadur offered to inform the emperor that if he could make him convert to Islam the Kashmiri pandits, too, would convert. He explained to the pandits that it was necessary to bring home to bigoted heads of state the inherent right of citizens to practise their faith despite the vagaries of wilful rulers.

Aurangzeb, incensed, ordered the Lahore governor to fetter and detain the Guru. Tegh Bahadur had already left for Delhi of his own free will but was arrested near Ropar and brought to Delhi in an iron cage on 5 November 1675. His message to the Mughal did little to calm him: 'The Prophet of Mecca who founded your Religion could not impose one religion on the world, so how can you? It is not God's will.'[15] Aurangzeb responded by ordering that for the next five days Guru Tegh Bahadur's treatment should alternate between inducement to convert to Islam and torture if he refused. The Guru's three close companions were put to death in his presence: one was sawn in two, one placed in a cauldron and boiled to death and the third burnt alive. Since Guru Tegh Bahadur was unmoving in his stand, he was publicly beheaded the same day. On the very spot of his beheading the Sikhs, when they captured Delhi a century later, built Gurdwara Sis Ganj to commemorate his sacrifice. It stands today, in the heart of the Delhi built by Shah Jahan.

During the night that followed the beheading a loyal follower, Bhai Jaita, recovered the Guru's head and carried it all the way to Anandpur where his nine-year-old son Gobind received it. It was cremated on a sandalwood pyre before an assembly of Sikhs. In Delhi on the very same night, a man called Lakhi Shah Lubana, with his companions, carried off the Guru's body and cremated it in Rakabganj on the outskirts of the city. But because an open-air cremation would have invited suspicion Lakhi Shah placed the body in his own house and set it on fire. On this site the gurdwara of Rakabganj Sahib was later built.

His father's sacrifice for the upholding of religious freedom would indicate the direction of Guru Gobind Singh's own life over the next thirty-three years. His ode to the sword left no doubt about how he would deal with the perpetrators of the atrocities to his father and great-grandfather:

> The sword which smites in a flash,
> Which scatters the armies of the wicked
> In the great battlefield;
> You symbol of the brave.
> Your arm is irresistible, your brightness shines forth,
> The blaze of the splendour dazzling like the sun,
> O Sword, you are the protector of saints,
> You are the scourge of the wicked;
> Scatterer of Sinners I seek your protection.
> Hail to the world's creator,
> Hail to the saviour of creation,
> Hail to you O sword supreme.

BACHITTAR NATAK

In the Anandpur area and along the long range of the lower Himalayas the several independent hill rajas had one thing in common – their jealousy and resentment of the Sikhs' increasing military power. In the ten years of peace he was fortunate enough to get after succeeding his father, Gobind Singh worked intensively on honing the fighting skills of the Sikhs while also finding time to study Sanskrit, Braj, Persian, Arabic and Avadhi along with astronomy, geography, metaphysics and botany; and he composed a number of literary works, including the celebrated *Bachittar Nata* and *Akal Ustat*. He also completed the Granth Sahib by adding Guru Tegh Bahadur's works to it.

Three concerted attacks by the Hindu hill chieftains on the Sikhs settled in Anandpur were heavily defeated. Gobind Singh knew that these victories would not go down well with Aurangzeb, already furious at the growing Sikh ascendance in the area, and prepared his defences by building a chain of forts around Anand- pur, at Anandgarh, Lohgarh, Keshgarh and Fatehgarh. He was able to secure a further decisive victory over a combined Mughal and Hindu force in 1690 at Nadaun on the River Beas. Aurangzeb now ordered all military commanders in Punjab to prevent Guru Gobind Singh from any further assemblies of his followers.[16]

This was more easily said than done. Gobind Singh's response was to ask Sikh *sangats* from all over India to converge on Anand- pur for Baisakhi (New Year's Day) at the end of March 1694. They were to come fully armed and with their beards uncut so that the imperial forces along the way were fully aware of their identity. When the huge gathering at Anandpur – in direct defiance of the imperial edict – was reported to the emperor, a sizeable force was immediately sent to Anandpur to take the Guru to task, but the sound of Sikh battle drums and war cries so rattled the imperial contingent during its night advance that it preferred to flee the field without joining battle. After further defeats, including one sustained by Aurangzeb's son Prince Muazzam, the imperial forces preferred to leave the Sikhs alone for the time being.

During a period of comparative peace from 1697 to 1700 Guru Gobind Singh created the fellowship of the Khalsa or 'purified ones', giving followers of the Sikh faith a distinctiveness which fol- lowers of no other religion in India had had until then. The first requirement was baptism. The second was that members of the Khalsa should be easily identifiable through five distinctive sym- bols they would always wear. The baptismal ceremony was simple. To a bowl of clear water would be added some sugar and the mix stirred with a double-edged sword as passages were recited from the Granth Sahib. This mixture of sweetness and steel, which the Guru called *amrit*, would then be administered to any person wishing to belong to the Khalsa fellowship.

Each of the five personal symbols emblematic of the Sikh faith would start with the letter K: *kesh* (long hair), *kanga* (comb), *kara* (steel band around the wrist), *kachh* (short breeches) and *kirpan* (short sword). *Kesh* set the tone for the other four by making members of the Khalsa instantly recognizable. The long hair was meant to put iron in the spine. The confidence instilled in them by their appearance was vital for a people whose courage and convictions would be repeatedly tested in the battles ahead. The *kanga* emphasized the importance of cleanliness. The *kachh* stressed the need for continence and moral restraint. The *kara* safeguarded the wrist that wielded the sword, while the *kirpan* symbolized the Khalsa's commitment to giving wrong-doers short shrift. To convey the psychological purpose of these symbols still further, the *pagdi* or turban – six yards of muslin tied around the head in an impressive manner – would set Sikh men apart from all others. Finally, each man without exception would use the surname Singh (Lion), while women would have the surname Kaur (Princess).

The creation and baptism of the Khalsa on Baisakhi Day, 1699, taking place against the backdrop of Keshgarh fort and the soaring mountain ranges, was attended by over 80,000 Sikhs. Gobind Singh, standing on high ground, drew his sword and demanded of the stunned audience that one of them step forward to prove his willingness to sacrifice his head for his faith. Some quietly slipped away, but one individual stood up and walked up to the Guru who led him into a tent and emerged a few minutes later with his sword dripping blood. The same exercise was repeated with more volunteers, from whom Gobind Singh selected four, and each time the Guru emerged from the tent with still more blood on his sword.

The terrible suspense ended when the Guru walked out of the tent with the five Sikhs, each now attired in saffron-coloured robes and turbans. Lamb's blood had served to drive home the point that what the Guru had been testing was the courage and resoluteness of the assembled Sikhs, which he had found lacking in those who had fled in fear. The new martial community which emerged that day on India's multi-religious landscape would be a race apart, sustained by its religious faith, its strong convictions and its fearlessness. The bedrock of its beliefs would be equality among all and an unbreakable commitment to the secular principles defined by the nine Sikh Gurus who had preceded Gobind Singh.[17]

The tenth Guru's message to the assembled Sikhs was: 'You will love man as man, making no distinction of caste or creed . . . you will never worship stock, stone, idol or tomb . . . In each of you the whole brotherhood shall be reincarnated. You are my sons, both in flesh and spirit.'[18] The proof of Gobind Singh's own commitment to 'making no distinction of caste or creed' was provided by the caste composition of the *panj piyare* or 'five loved ones' whom the Guru had selected from the volunteers who had come forward for the surprise ceremony. One was a Khatri of higher caste, the second a Jat, a step lower, and the remaining three were Shudras, untouchables or those belonging to a low caste. The most convincing proof of the Guru's opposition to the caste system became obvious to the assembled gathering when he first baptized each of the five himself, then knelt before them and asked them to baptize him. By taking *amrit* from them the Guru put an end to the pernicious hierarchical customs that had long bedevilled the Sikhs just as other societies. As Guru Gobind Singh put it on that Baisakhi Day: 'Your previous race, name, genealogy, country, nation, religion, customs, beliefs and sub-conscious memories are completely burnt and annihilated. Believe this to be so without a doubt, for you now start a New Birth in the House of Guru – Akalpurkh.'[19] And in kneeling before the 'five loved ones' he also stressed the republican spirit of the faith.

The creation of the Khalsa proved a turning-point for Sikhism because of the dynamic it injected into it by making every individual Sikh feel responsible for upholding Sikhism's stature and prestige. If a man in a turban and wearing the other symbols of his faith disgraced himself, he would disgrace all Sikhs. So it was obligatory on him to conduct himself in a manner conducive to the principles to which Sikhs were pledged.

Inevitably, the success of the conclave at Anandpur – where around 50,000 persons were baptized – made the hill chieftains uneasy. They sent a message to Emperor Aurangzeb informing him of the creation of the Khalsa and telling him that Gobind Singh had suggested general rebellion against the emperor. They asked for his assistance to expel the Guru from Anandpur, with the warning 'Should you delay his punishment, his next expedition will be against the capital of your Empire.'[20]

This representation to Aurangzeb illustrates how India's people – perpetually resentful of each other – have so often helped aggressors get a stranglehold on the subcontinent. These same chieftains had often come to the Guru for help but were not averse to betraying him when it suited them. Aurangzeb needed no persuasion. Although their plea reached him as he campaigned in the south, he sent an expeditionary force against the Sikhs, which was joined by the *pahari* (hill) rajas. Once again it was routed.

After yet further humiliating military defeats, Aurangzeb now tried a different strategy. He laid siege to the entire Anandpur area, diverting the only stream on which Anandpur depended for its water. He offered the Guru and his party safe passage if he vacated Anandpur for good. A wrenching dilemma faced Guru Gobind Singh. Acceptance of Aurangzeb's offer would violate everything he had learnt from the exemplars of his faith. Equally unthinkable was to witness the slow death of his family and fellow men. At the end of 1704 he took the decision to leave his beloved Anandpur.

Despite their pledge of safe passage, the Mughals and their camp followers attacked the Sikhs no sooner had they left their fastness in the hills and reached the plains to cross the River Sarsa. The attack, and the swollen river after the winter rains, separated many of the party from each other, which included Gobind Singh's mother and two sons. With a handful of men left out of an initial 500, the Guru, with his two elder sons Ajit Singh (seventeen) and Jujhar Singh (fifteen), fought his way to Chamkaur village with a Mughal force close on his heels.

Here a fierce battle was joined between forty Sikhs and the heavily armed Mughal force. The Guru's two elder sons were killed in hand-to-hand combat. Only Gobind Singh and three others survived. As they evaded the enemy's formations at night and headed for a place more conducive to regrouping the Khalsa, the Guru was separated from his companions in the heart of Machhiwara Forest. Continuing his journey on foot, however, he was fortunate enough to be reunited with his three companions. Aside from other Sikhs who rallied round them, when they reached the village of Jatpura they experienced a gratifying reception from the Muslim chief of the area, Rai Kalha, who was deeply appreciative of the uncompromising stand the Sikhs had taken against the intolerant and oppressive policies of Islamic rulers. What Rai Kalha and his fellow Muslim chiefs of a liberal bent proved once again was that, even in dire situations, human decency between men of different faiths need never be forsaken. Even 'the Caliph of Mecca had shown disagreement with Aurangzeb's religious policy, while the Caliph of Baghdad had even refused to receive Aurangzeb's envoy'.[21]

One of those evil men with primitive instincts who are always at hand, Aurangzeb's governor of Sirhind, Nawab Wazir Khan, had Guru Gobind Singh's two younger sons Zorawar Singh (aged eight) and Fateh Singh (six) killed in the most gruesome manner when they fell into his hands. They were first bricked up alive up to their necks, then extricated and beheaded when they would not convert to Islam. It was following this tragedy that Guru Gobind Singh wrote the celebrated letter to Aurangzeb known as the *Zafarnamah*. This was an open letter to him in Persian that bluntly accused him of deceit and inhumanity. 'If the Prophet himself was present here, I would inform him of your treachery,' he wrote.[22] History offers few other instances of a sovereign of a major empire wielding absolute authority being so indicted by the representative of a tiny minority group.

Astonishingly, instead of being outraged at Gobind Singh's open accusations, Aurangzeb expressed a desire to meet Gobind Singh, to see and talk to the man who had such nerve. Despite the emperor's proven perfidiousness and the blood of the Guru's sons on his hands, Gobind Singh was confident enough to travel to the south to meet him. Their meeting, however, never came about as the ninety-year-old emperor died while Gobind Singh was still travelling.

Following Aurangzeb's death, his son Prince Muazzam sought the Guru's help in his power struggle with his brother Azam. The same Muazzam had once been sent by his father to assault Anandpur and put Guru Gobind Singh down once and for all, but Muazzam, reputedly a man of rectitude, preferred not to do so. The Guru had not forgotten this and sent a contingent of Sikh troops to fight alongside Muazzam's in the Battle of Jajau near Agra. Azam was killed, his force routed, and Muazzam ascended the Mughal throne as Emperor Bahadur Shah.

He and Gobind Singh had their first meeting in Agra. It was cordial, and they discussed at length how things could be set right in Punjab. The two continued their discussions while journeying together to the south, where Muazzam wanted to deal with his other brother Kambakhsh who had also risen against him. By the time they reached Nander, however, Gobind Singh had realized that the new emperor had little intention of ending the tyrannical ways of Mughal rule, and so in September 1708 he parted company with him.

During his short stay in Nander, Gobind Singh converted a Hindu *sadhu* or ascetic, Madho Dass Bairagi, to Sikhism. Bairagi

was an assertive man of some standing in the area with a following of his own. His initiation into the Sikh faith as Banda Singh
Bahadur was to prove of profound historical significance.

First, however, a cataclysmic event overtook the Sikh camp at
Nander. Wazir Khan of Sirhind, the murderer of Gobind Singh's
two younger sons, fearful that Bahadur Shah's closeness to
Gobind Singh might adversely affect his own fortunes, sent two
Pathans to kill him. One of them stabbed the Guru in the chest as
he lay on his bed after evening prayers. Although wounded near
the heart, Gobind Singh ran him through with his sword, while
his followers decapitated the second. While the wound seemed to
be healing well, his over-exertions a few days later reopened it,
and excessive bleeding ended the life of this remarkable man at
the age of forty-two.

But before the end he drew on his willpower and inner reserves
to tell his followers who had assembled in large numbers around
him that the tradition of living Gurus would end with him and
that after his death the Granth Sahib would be the Guru of the
Sikhs for all time. This was a far-sighted move reflecting a clear
understanding of human loyalties which can waver when familiar
conditions give way to new and stressful demands. The Guru
Granth Sahib, as it would thenceforth be known, was not only a
repository of the supreme insights of the Sikh Gurus but a com-
pendium of the wisdom of scholars and sages of all faiths. These
unique scriptures would ensure that Sikhs would always be open
to every thought that respects reason, compassion and just social
structures.

As a modern Sikh historian has pointed out: 'When a Sikh bows
before and seeks guidance from the Holy Granth, he offers his
devotion as much to Farid, the renowned Muslim Sufi, and Jaidev,
a Hindu *bhakta* of Krishna, as to Guru Nanak or Guru Arjan, the
compiler of the Granth. It is a commonwealth of the men of
God.'[23]

So when Sikhs bow before the Guru Granth Sahib they bow before knowledge and wisdom, not before an idol or deity.

༺

With unerring instinct Guru Gobind Singh had sensed in Banda Singh the qualifications of a future leader. Banda, believed to have been born in Kashmir, was at ease everywhere, which is how he had come to settle in Nander in the remote south. He had been a farmer and a hunter and had won a reputation as a formidable fighter; at the same time he possessed the willpower and the discipline to practise yoga and the ascetic life. In converting this seemingly pacific *sadhu* to the Sikh faith Guru Gobind had released his white-hot inner nature.

Burning with hatred for those who had perpetrated such crimes against a man like Guru Gobind Singh and his family, Banda was determined on vengeance. He set out for Punjab almost 1,500 miles away with just twenty-five armed followers, But he was also armed with Gobind Singh's *hukamnamahs* (directives) to all Sikh *sangats* to rally round his banner. The Guru had given him five arrows from his own quiver, a *nishan sahib* (flag) and a *nagara* (war drum) as symbols of authority. Banda's tiny force soon swelled with the addition of warriors eager to strike back at their Mughal tormentors.

After many armed clashes on the way Banda and his men eventually arrived at the gates of the heavily fortified town of Samana, home of Sayyed Jalal-ud-Din, Guru Teg Bahadur's executioner, and Shashal Beg, who had executed Guru Gobind Singh's two younger sons. Helped by a previously oppressed peasantry, the augmented Sikh force took the town in a surprise dawn attack. Other Punjabi towns towns fell before Banda's men and finally Sirhind. Given the extent to which Sikh anger would boil over at the very mention of Sirhind and its governor, Wazir Khan, the outcome of the first savage battle that took place over it outside the city was never in doubt. Wazir Khan's well-armed army of 20,000 men fought a far smaller Sikh force, but he was killed.[24] Sirhind itself was taken after a two-day siege but at high cost to the Sikhs, who lost 500 men before the fort's heavy guns were silenced. The destruction of the town was not permitted following a fervent appeal by its Hindu population. Because of its notorious past, however, it was not to be spared half a century later when Jassa Singh Ahluwalia's forces invested it.

A six-year roll of victories brought Banda to the gates of Lahore, a city symbolic of Mughal and Afghan authority in India. In one of his most audacious campaigns the Sikh leader captured the fortress of Mukhlispur built on a promontory on the lower reaches of the Himalayas, renamed it Lohgarh and flew the flag of the Khalsa over it. He announced that Lohgarh would henceforth represent Sikh authority over the regions now under their control, and seals and coins were struck to celebrate Sikh rule.

An incensed Emperor Bahadur Shah, with a force of 60,000 horsemen, laid siege to Lohgarh. The majority of a combined Sikh force of around 3,000 horsemen and foot soldiers held the enemy at bay while Banda and a few of his men escaped. Inevitably, however, the vastly superior Mughal forces prevailed. When Banda Singh was finally taken in a siege of the town of Gurdas Nangal on 17 December 1715 the Mughals outdid themselves in barbarity. Three hundred Sikhs were summarily executed and their heads stuffed with hay, mounted on spears and carried in a victory procession to Lahore and then on to Delhi. After spells of torture alternating with attempts to buy him off, Banda was finally taken to the Qutb Minar (a thirteenth-century stone tower 239 feet in height) where 'they had him dismount, placed his child in his arms and bade him kill it. Then, as he shrank with horror from the act, they ripped open the child before the father's eyes, thrust his quivering flesh into his mouth and hacked him to pieces limb by limb.'[25]

❧

The Sikhs now faced the most savage persecution in their history. With the death of Bahadur Shah in 1712 and the accession of Farrukh Siyar to the throne in 1713, the Mughal Empire came to be headed by a man who outstripped all his predecessors in gratuitous cruelty. His governors and commanders curried favour with him by sending him severed Sikh heads 'for his pleasure'.[26] When once Zakariya Khan, for example, who was later to become governor of Lahore under him, called on the emperor in Delhi and presented him with a particularly large number of Sikh heads, the overjoyed emperor raised Zakariya's rank and loaded him with presents. Zakariya ordered his men to arrest Sikhs wherever they saw them and bring them to Lahore for daily public executions. He announced a reward of 50 rupees for every Sikh head brought to him.

But the head-hunters' policies made the Sikhs even more determined to make the administration pay for its misdeeds. Zakariya Khan, disconcerted by the unending plunder of his treasuries and arsenals and the loss of a number of his men, now tried appeasement. In 1733 he offered the Sikhs a large *jagir* or gift of land, which they willingly accepted. This proved a major error from the Mughal point of view. The Sikhs saw an opportunity for rigorous institutionalization of their activities that concerned the larger purpose of safeguarding the faith and its followers from genocidal Mughal attacks. Kapur Singh was the man chosen to head this programme. A tough, self-assured and experienced warrior, he was also deeply devout and dedicated to building solid institutions that would protect the Sikhs.

He organized the Sikhs into different groupings or *dals*, which would later be merged into the Dal Khalsa. The *dals* had responsibilities ranging from armed resistance against the Mughals and guarding Sikh places of worship to attending to conversions and baptisms. The Taruna Dal, composed of younger men, relished the opportunity of dealing with the Mughal military; the years of

Mughal oppression had hardened Sikh farmers into a motivated potential soldiery, able-bodied men keeping lance and sword by them as they worked on their land. As its membership increased to 12,000, it was further divided into five sections, each having its own commander with his banner, drum and administrative control of the territories annexed by him.

These five sections, along with several more that would be formed as time went on, were to lead to the formation of the Sikh *misls*. The word *misl* in Arabic means 'equal'; the term was first used by Guru Gobind Singh in 1688 when he organized the Sikhs into a battle formation of groups each under its own leader, with equal power and authority. These groups eventually took the form of twelve *misls*, which derived their names from their villages or leaders: Ahluwalia, Bhangi, Ramgarhia, Faizullapuria, Kanaihya, Sukerchakia, Dallewalia, Shahid or Nihang, Nakkai, Nishanwalia, Karorsinghia and Phulkian. The *misl* chiefs, the Sardars, who have been compared to the barons of medieval times, had complete control over their territories, and their military units were able to discourage any defiance of their authority. They had absolute autonomy, but in times of war they pooled their resources to take on the enemy. In times of peace they often fought each other.

The *misl* warrior was a soldier of fortune, a horseman who owned his own mount and equipment, armed with matchlock, spear and sword. Infantry and artillery were virtually unknown to the Sikhs for serious purposes before the days of Ranjit Singh. Sikh soldiers despised 'footmen' who were assigned the meaner duties – garrison tasks, provisioning, taking care of the women. 'The Sikh horseman', according to Bikrama Jit Hasrat, 'was theoretically a soldier of the Khalsa, fired by the mystic ideals of Gobind which he little understood, and he had no politics. He was also a soldier of the Panth [Sikh community], out to destroy the enemies of the Faith in all religious fervour and patriotism. Above all, he was a free-lance, a republican with a revolutionary impulse . . . The

48

armies of the Dal Khalsa, unencumbered by heavy ordnance, possessed an amazing manoeuvrability. [They] were sturdy and agile men who could swiftly load their matchlocks on horseback and charge the enemy at top speed, repeating the operation several times. They looked down upon the comforts of the tents, carrying their and their animals' rations of grains in a knapsack, and with two blankets under the saddle as their bedding, they marched off with lightning rapidity in and out of battle.'[27] At the height of their power in the latter part of the eighteenth century, the *misls* could muster around 70,000 such horsemen.

The Sikhs at this time accounted for only 7 per cent of the population of the Punjab, as against 50 per cent Muslims and 42 per cent Hindus.[28] Before their golden period they had to face huge and continuing adversity. To start with, Zakariya Khan, having given them a *jagir* as a peace offering, sent a force two years later to reoccupy it. He took Amritsar by siege, plundered the Harmandir Sahib, filled the pool with slaughtered animals and desecrated its relics.

When Zakariya Khan died in 1745 and his son Shah Nawaz Khan succeeded him as governor of Lahore, the progeny proved even worse than the parent. Nawaz Khan's favourite pastime appears to have been to watch the bellies of captive Sikhs being ripped open and iron pegs stuck into their heads. In June 1746 the first of the two so-called *ghalugharas* (disasters) took place: a large body of Mughal troops under Yahiya Khan massacred 7,000 Sikhs while an additional 3,000 were captured and taken to Lahore for public execution. The *wada ghalughara* or great disaster – to be described – took place in February 1762, perpetrated by the Afghan invader Ahmed Shah Abdali.

The sixteen years between the two *ghalugharas* saw copious bloodshed in the Punjab, with the forces of the Khalsa continually set upon by one or another of their three principal enemies – the invaders Nadir Shah of Persia, the Afghan leader Ahmed Shah Abdali and the Mughal emperor. Abdali invaded India eight times between the years 1748 and 1768. Punjab now became the setting for a triangular struggle between the Afghans, Sikhs and Mughals. Abdali and the Mughals wanted to see the end of the Sikhs, but the Khalsa was willing to take on both. Jassa Singh Ahluwalia, head of the Ahluwalia *misl*, liberated the Golden Temple from Mughal control and restored the shrine to its former glory. In 1752 the new governor of Lahore, Mir Mannu, a particularly duplicitous and sadistic man who had defected from the Mughals to the Afghans and who was keen to curry favour with Abdali, now officially declared Punjab an Afghan province, in defiance of the declared Sikh sovereignty over several regions and towns of Punjab dating from Banda Singh's time.

When in 1757 the Sikhs waylaid Abdali's baggage train full of the wealth he had plundered from Delhi, Mathura and Vrindavan, rescued hundreds of captive Hindu girls and returned them to their homes, it was the last straw for him. He ordered his son Timur Shah, now governor of Lahore, to eliminate the 'accursed infidels' and their Golden Temple once and for all.

Attacks and counter-attacks between the Sikhs and their persecutors formed a continuing dance of death on the landscape of Punjab, culminating in the *wada ghalughara* on 5 February 1762. In a surprise attack on a large assembly of Sikhs at Kup near Sirhind, Abdali's army, having covered 110 miles in two days, killed from 10,000 to 30,000 Sikhs (estimates vary), a very large number of whom were women and children who were being escorted to a safer region. In the ferocious fighting the odds were heavily loaded against the Sikhs.

Abdali now headed for the Golden Temple and struck on 10 April 1762, at a time when thousands had gathered there for the Baisakhi celebrations. The bloodbath was horrific. The Harmandir was blown apart with gunpowder. The pool was filled with the debris of destroyed buildings, human bodies, carcasses of cows and much else, and topping it all a pyramid of Sikh heads was erected. Within a few months, however, early in 1763, Charat Singh, head of the Sukerchakia *misl* – whose grandson Ranjit Singh was to be born one and a half decades later – managed to wrest back control of the Golden Temple.

The very next year, however, Abdali was back in India and once more bore down on the Sikh shrine. Each of the thirty Sikhs present died defending the sacred edifice, which was yet again demolished and defiled. But this was the last time the Afghans or the Mughals would ever set foot in it. In a swift military action the Sikhs not only annexed Lahore on 16 April 1765 but declared their sovereignty over the whole of Punjab. To make absolutely clear that political power in the region now rested with them, they struck coins and declared Lahore the mint city, *Dar-ul-Sultanate* (Seat of [Sikh] Power).

With their control of Punjab, in addition to large parts of what is now Pakistan, plus the present-day states of Jammu and Kashmir, Himachal Pradesh and Haryana, the Khalsa now emerged as a territorial power of significance and substance. The process was helped by the economic activities of the twelve *misls* which were beginning to prosper as major cultivators of crops such as wheat, rice, pulses, barley, sugar cane, cotton, indigo and jaggery, in addition to a wide variety of fruit. Nor were manufacturing, crafts, construction of townships or internal and external trade neglected. Exports were sent to Persia, Arabia, Yarkand, Afghanistan, Chinese Turkestan, Turfan and Bokhara. Lahore and Amritsar between them also produced increasingly fine silks, shawls, woollen materials, carpets and metalware. The Sikhs, with their entrepreneurial drive and inclination to spend well and indulge themselves fully, were changing the character of the Punjab.

❧

In March 1783 an event took place that would have been inconceivable a few years earlier. A combined *misl* force under Jassa Singh Ahluwalia, outstanding among Sikh chiefs for his qualities of leadership, entered Delhi, the imperial seat of the once mighty Mughals. Some of the *misl* leaders arrived at the Red Fort which represented Mughal power and walked into the emperor's audience hall, and Jassa Singh Ahluwalia had himself installed on the imperial throne. It was a symbolic move, but its meaning was clear to all. The Khalsa withdrew only after the emperor agreed to an annual tribute, but when he broke his promise in 1785 the Sikhs returned to Delhi and subjugated it once again. They had no wish to take permanent possession of it, but they made the emperor agree to the construction of eight gurdwaras, each built on a site with a special significance for the Sikhs, one of them being Gurdwara Sisganj, on the spot where Emperor Aurangzeb had had Guru Tegh Bahadur, father of Guru Gobind Singh, tortured and beheaded in November 1675.

The Sikh contingents entering Delhi scrupulously maintained the secular and civilized principles of their religious teachings. No orgy of bloodshed was indulged in despite the number of revered Sikhs who had been brought to Delhi over the years to be barbarically put to death by successive Mughal rulers.

The *misls* contributed significantly to the Sikh vision, with its moral underpinnings. Each of them consolidated Sikh power in the Punjab by imaginatively developing their territories and providing just administration. 'In all contemporary records, mostly in Persian,' one modern historian points out, 'written generally by Muslims as well as by Maratha agents posted at a number of places in Northern India, there is not a single instance either in Delhi or elsewhere in which Sikhs raised a finger against women.'[29] And as we have seen, with Sikh rule now established over large parts of the Punjab, its people now experienced a sense of security and a rapid increase in prosperity to a much greater degree than over the past half-century.

Two Afghan rulers, however, were still forces to be reckoned with for the Sikhs: Abdali's son Timur Shah who succeeded him in 1772 and Timur's son Zaman Shah who succeeded him in 1793.

While Timur Shah avoided the Sikhs as far as possible, Zaman Shah during one of his invasions briefly occupied Lahore before being thrown out. But events of this period belong to the young Ranjit Singh's first years of leadership and will be described later.

The eighteenth century was a costly one for the Sikhs. It has been estimated that Guru Gobind Singh, in his battles with the Mughals, lost about 5,000 men and Banda Singh at least 25,000; that after Banda Singh's execution Abdus Samad Khan, governor of Punjab (1713–26), killed not less than 20,000 Sikhs and his son and successor Zakariya Khan (1726–45) an equal number; that Yahiya Khan (1746–7) accounted for some 10,000 Sikhs in a single campaign after the *chhota ghalughara*, the first disaster; and that his brother-in-law Muin-ul-Mulk, indulging his sadistic instincts between 1748 and 1753 as governor of Punjab by putting a price on Sikh heads, dispatched more than 30,000. Adeena Beg Khan, a Punjabi Arain, put to death at least 5,000 Sikhs in 1758; Ahmad Shah Abdali and his Afghan governors killed around 60,000 between 1753 and 1767; Abdali's deputy Najib-ud-Daulah, also an Afghan, slew nearly 20,000. 'Petty officials and the public' may have killed 4,000.[30]

To this total of around 200,000 Sikhs killed over the first seventy years of the eighteenth century must be added the casualties of the clashes with Timur Shah and Zaman Shah.

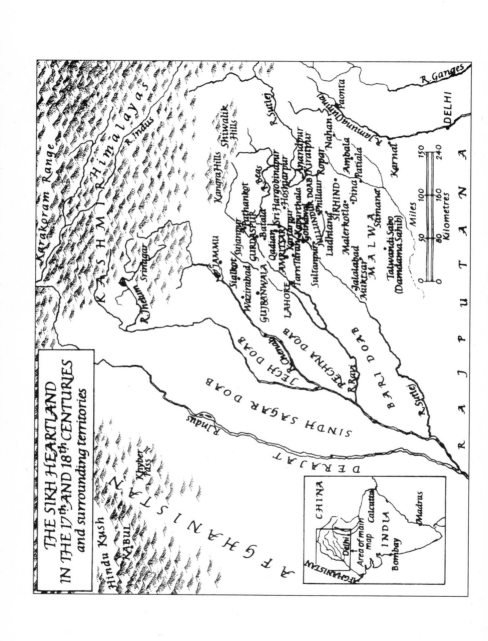

THE SIKH HEARTLAND
IN THE 17th AND 18th CENTURIES
and surrounding territories

2

Drumbeat of a School Drop-out

'The Maharaja [Ranjit Singh] has no throne.
"My sword", he observed, "procures me
all the distinction I desire."'

BARON CHARLES HUGEL

Into this bloodied landscape of Punjab, Ranjit Singh, only son of Mahan Singh Sukerchakia and Raj Kaur, daughter of Raja Gajpat Singh of Jind, was born on 13 November 1780. He seemed an unlikely prospect as the founder of a kingdom. The people of the Punjab belonged to the tall, large-boned type settled in northern India since the Aryan migrations of around 1500 BC, physically distinctive in the region to this day. Ranjit Singh conformed to this type not at all. He was small of stature and slight of build, and in childhood his face was scarred by smallpox, which left him blind in one eye. In his early years he was nicknamed Kana, 'the one-eyed one'. As C.H. Payne, a chronicler of the Sikhs, put it: 'The gifts which nature lavished on Ranjit Singh were of the abstract rather than the concrete order. His strength of character and personal magnetism [were to be] the real sources of his greatness.'[1] A Western observer of the time wrote of 'the splendid mental powers with which nature had endowed him'.[2]

As a child the boy does not seem to have occupied himself with any of the pursuits in which children of privileged circumstances are apt to indulge or be indulged. Instead of giving his child play-things, his father is said to have handed him a sword. While he could never find the time to learn to read and write beyond the Gurmukhi alphabet, he eagerly learnt musketry and swordsman-ship. The stories of the daring feats of his father, grandfather and others before them greatly influenced him and helped shape the course of his life.

The most colourful of his ancestors was a figure from the seventeenth century, Desu, a cultivator, his father's great-great-grandfather. Desu's earthly possessions consisted of twenty-five acres of land, a well, three ploughs and two houses for his family and cattle. The Sukerchakia *misl* took its name from that of his village, Suker Chak, which was located near the town of Gujran-wala, about forty miles north of Lahore.

An accomplished cattle-lifter, Desu was also known for his courage and derring-do; he was a giant of a man and a fearless fighter. The great love in his life was his piebald mare Desan, on which he would swim all the five rivers of Punjab when in flood. According to one account, he and Desan did this fifty times. At the age of fifty, Desu decided to go and see Guru Gobind Singh at Anandpur with the request that he baptize him. After the baptism his name was changed to Budha Singh, and, greatly inspired by the Guru, he stayed with him to participate in the many battles fought by the Khalsa. When he died in 1715 at Gurdas Nangal fight-ing alongside Banda Singh, there were twenty-nine scars of sword cuts on his body, seven bullet wounds and seven wounds from spears and arrows.

The two sons of this colourful man, Nodh Singh and Chanda Singh, were much less spectacular in their military exploits. But Nodh Singh's eldest son Charat Singh, Ranjit Singh's grandfather, stood out as a man of great stature both on the battlefield and because of the extent to which he expanded the territories of the Sukerchakias. His daring exploits attracted Abdali's attention, and in clashes in 1761, 1764 and 1766 he tried to eliminate Charat Singh, but the indomitable *misl* chief emerged stronger than ever, making sure after each engagement to annex still more territories.

In his brief lifespan of forty-five years, he acquired the entire districts of Gujranwala, Sheikhupura, Jhelum, Shahpur, Fatehgunj, the salt mines of Khewra and Pind Dadan Khan and the much fought-over northerly fort of Rohtas. He also captured Chakwal, Jalalpur, Rasulpur, the towns of Kot Sahib Khan, Raja Ka Kot, parts of Chaj and Sind Sagar Doab and took many other territories under his control, such as parts of Rawalpindi, but in some cases he was content merely to receive revenue. By means of many other such arrangements he established his suzerainty, the Sukerchakia *misl*, over a considerable area. His power was won and consolidated not only by force of arms but through alliances entered into by marrying his sons, sister and daughters into families of consequence. The broad base he created was without doubt the springboard that was to enable his grandson to establish an empire of the Sikhs. Had it not been for his untimely death at forty-five, caused by the accidental firing of his own gun, this energetic man would have achieved much more.

Of his three children, his two sons Mahan Singh and Sahaj Singh and their sister Raj Kaur, it was Mahan Singh, born in 1760, who headed the *misl* and proved a worthy successor to his father who died when the boy was just ten. Until he took charge of the *misl* just five years later, his purposeful and able mother, Mai Dessan, handled its affairs and its extensive territories with exemplary skill, self-confidence and courage. She provided Mahan Singh with invaluable lessons in the management of his complex inheritance, lessons he put to good use. The problems she dealt with ranged from a revolt by senior officials appointed by the *misl* to winning the army's support of her stewardship and rebuilding Gujranwala Fort, the seat of the Sukerchakia *misl*, which had been destroyed by Ahmed Shah Abdali. Mai Dessan finely exemplified the tradition by which Sikh women took on crucial responsibilities in critical times.

Married four years earlier (1774) to another Raj Kaur, later known as Mai Malwain, daughter of Raja Gajpat Singh of Jind, Mahan Singh soon set about expanding the territories of the *misl* still further. From the Bhangi *misl* he annexed Issa Khel and Mussa Khel, then went for the Chatha Pathans of Rasulnagar whose territories lay along the River Chenab and who were briskly building fortifications and townships there. To tame Pir Muhammad, who headed the Chatha tribe, Mahan Singh laid siege to Rasulnagar, which held out for several months but eventually gave in to him. The Pathan Chathas at that time were highly respected for their fighting qualities, and in the strong base they were creating for themselves along the River Chenab Mahan Singh saw a future threat to his *misl*'s interests. Fortunately for him Pir Muhammad and his brother Ahmad Khan were bitter enemies, which enabled Mahan Singh to subdue them both, capturing their forts at Sayyidnagar and Kot Pir Muhammad as well as Rasulnagar.

Mahan Singh was on his way home after the siege of Rasulnagar when he received news of the birth of his son Budh Singh on 13 November 1780. The first thing the father did on reaching home was to change the boy's name to Ranjit – which not only meant 'the victor of battles' but was also the name of Guru Gobind's war drums: a prophetic change.

Mahan Singh was soon on the march again – this time to Jammu, in the Kashmir foothills. Through manipulative politics, inter-*misl* rivalries and clash of arms, Mahan Singh made his way to Jammu and ransacked it. Although he had agreed on a joint operation with the Kanhayia *misl* and an equal share in the booty, he left the Kanhayias out on both these counts. In their rapidly deteriorating relations the two *misls* frequently took to the battlefield, but in the end Mahan Singh's forces prevailed, and the

Kanhayia *misl* chief's son Gurbaksh Singh was killed in one of their battles, although at the hands of the Ramgarhias.

It should be noted that while the *misl* chiefs as a rule pooled their resources to fight an enemy they fought each other with equal zest if there was no enemy to take on. There are no known instances of a *misl* chief combining forces with a hostile regime or an invader to settle scores with a fellow *misl* chief, but conspiracies and changing alliances between the *misls* were constant, and in Mahan Singh's time he emerged the victor wherever he intervened. Whether he prevailed over his adversaries in an entirely upright manner or through deceit has been endlessly debated. Many chroniclers say he often resorted to treachery against those who opposed him, starting with Pir Muhammad and Ghulam Muhammad of the Chathas, Raja Brij Raj Singh Deo of Jammu and another member of the Kanhayia *misl*, Haqiqat Singh, and convincing reasons have been provided in support of their criticism. But much has been written in his favour, too. It does seem, however, that he was less principled than his father Charat Singh and his son Ranjit Singh.

What cannot be denied is that in his short span of twenty-nine years – he was felled by a sudden illness – he achieved far more than most other chiefs in those turbulent times. In addition to his legacy of expansion and consolidation, he set up an administrative structure for his *misl*, which was an overdue move few chiefs had attempted before. The first step he took was to appoint a *diwan* (minister) to handle everyday administration along lines specifically laid down. For his soldiery, for instance, he made a beginning by doing away with the spoils system, strictly enforcing the rule that whatever was plundered or seized as booty during a battle would be the property of the *misl* and not of individuals. All tributes and fines received would also accrue to the *misl* chief, not the officer in charge of operations. Records would also be maintained of all such income. In the same way, administration of territories acquired was also thought of for the first time, although it was Mahan Singh's son who would establish a sound and enduring system of administrative control of the territories he added to his ever-expanding empire.

⤴

While some historians are of the view that Ranjit Singh was born in Gujranwala (now in Pakistan), one of the towns newly developed by the Sikhs, others are convinced he was born in Badhrukhan near Jind, his mother's home, about 250 miles southeast of Gujranwala. In the view of the historian Sir Gokul Chand Narang, who was an official in the British administration of Punjab in the years 1926–30, Ranjit Singh was 'born in 1780 in Gujranwala at a spot in the Purani Mandi near the office of Gujranwala Municipal Committee, marked by a date-palm tree and a slab put up there probably by the Municipal Committee'.[3] Several other British historians affirm Gujranwala as his birthplace. It has been claimed that up until 1947 a cradle was preserved in the room where Ranjit's mother was confined, an annual holiday being traditionally observed in Gujranwala on the date of her son's birthday.[4] The historian Hari Ram Gupta, on the other hand, categorically rejects this assertion and claims Badhrukhan as his place of birth. A pre-Independence British gazetteer of undivided Punjab states that 'Ranjit Singh . . . was born at Gujranwala and he made it his headquarters during the years which preceded the establishment of his supremacy and his occupation of Lahore in AD 1799.'[5]

There may be different views about the birthplace, but there is agreement among numerous accounts of the wild rejoicings that followed the news of the heir's arrival. Spectacular feasts and distribution of large sums of money among the poor continued for days on end in a city festooned with lights and alive as never before.

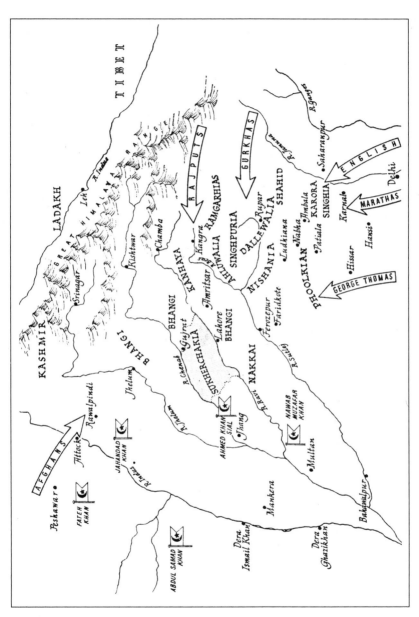

SIKH MISLS IN THE LATE EIGHTEENTH CENTURY

Of Ranjit's earliest years little detail has survived, but there is ample confirmation of the fact that he was adored and indulged by his doting family. He was sent to Bhagu Singh Dharamsala (centre of learning) in Gujranwala, where he learnt no more than a few numerals and acquired some knowledge of how to follow maps and charts, which was to stand him in good stead throughout his life. He showed no interest in the arts, mathematics or book-keeping but was instinctively drawn to agriculture and other disciplines that required physical input. After just one year he left the Bhagu Singh Dharamsala. He zestfully set about learning the martial arts – especially how to fight with sword and spear. He also loved to swim, wrestle, shoot and hunt, perhaps sensing that these were not the times in which scholarly pursuits would get him far. He revelled instead in the acquisition of the skills he knew he needed to be a warrior and to lead troops into battle. A Brahmin, Amir Singh, an expert with guns, taught him how to handle a musket.

At the age of six, in 1786, he nearly lost his life to an attack of smallpox when, according to some accounts, he was with Mahan Singh at Jammu who, despite his high fever, took him back to Gujranwala Fort. But this version of events is contradicted by some historians who hold that Mahan Singh was campaigning in Jammu when he was informed of his son's illness in Gujranwala. Be that as it may, it took twenty-one days for the fever to abate and several more days for the boy to open his eyes. When he did it was found that he had lost all sight in his left eye. Throughout his illness his father had prayers read out for him day and night from the Granth Sahib, the Hindu scriptures and the Koran. Money was distributed to the poor and donations for followers of all three faiths were sent to Sitla Devi (Goddess of the Smallpox Temple), Jawala Mukhi and the Kangra temples.

The age of six seemed to have a special significance in Ranjit Singh's life because his first marriage also took place in 1786 soon after he recovered from his illness. His bride Mehtab Kaur was five.

The dating of this event, too, is a matter of controversy, some records stating that he was sixteen when he married. Most of the evidence, however, points to the earlier date. Marriages in those days were usually arranged for political or dynastic reasons, and the practice was to book them early lest other parents with similar concerns stole a march in the marriage market. The Sukerchakia and Kanhayia *misls* being among the foremost of the twelve, Ranjit Singh's marriage to the daughter of the Kanhayias promised to forge an enviable alliance. No one was more aware of this than Mehtab Kaur's mother Sada Kaur, who would take over the leadership of the Kanhayias in 1789 on the death of her father-in-law Jai Singh, her husband Gurbaksh Singh having been killed earlier in a battle with the Ramgarhia *misl* in February 1785 when she was twenty-two.

Most accounts agree that when Ranjit Singh's mother Raj Kaur went to the Hindu shrine of Jawalamukhi in the hilly region of Kangra to pray for the recovery of her son, Sada Kaur followed and persuaded her to agree to the marriage of her daughter with Ranjit Singh. After the boy's recovery his father organized a grand feast at Gujranwala to which Mehtab Kaur's grandfather, Jai Singh Kanhayia, the *misl* chief, was also invited. It was on this occasion that he formally asked Mahan Singh for his son Ranjit Singh's hand in marriage to his granddaughter. The betrothal and marriage were, as was to be expected, celebrated on a spectacular scale.

The special nature of the boy may be grasped from the fact that within three years of his attack of smallpox he took over the siege of Sodhran, in 1789 at the age of nine, when his father was suddenly stricken by a serious illness. It was an amazingly young age to take on such a task, even in a period when major responsibility could often come considerably sooner than in modern times. The town of Sodhran, lying some twenty-five miles south-east of Gujranwala, belonged to the Bhangi chief's son Sahib Singh, Mahan Singh's brother-in-law. In an engagement typical of the time Mahan Singh laid siege to it after Sahib Singh had refused to pay him tribute in acknowledgement of his suzerainty. The Bhangi *misl* chieftains, seeing in Mahan Singh's illness an opportune moment to help their besieged kin in Sodhran, headed for the town in force in order to annex it permanently. But they were ambushed and decisively defeated by young Ranjit Singh's quick thinking and actions which would become characteristic of him throughout his life. His father did not live to see his son's Sodhran victory over the Bhangis; by the time he arrived back in Gujranwala Mahan Singh was already dead.

In a brief *pagri*- or turban-tying ceremony, Ranjit Singh became the chief of the Sukerchakia *misl*. 'When he first stood in his father's place,' wrote a British author nearer to Ranjit Singh's time than our own, 'everything was against him. He was beset by enemies, by doubtful friends, false allies and open foes.'[6] Yet he overcame them all with an unflinching sense of purpose which again became evident within a year of his father's death, in April 1790. Resolved to put an end to his new young rival, Hashmat Khan of the Chathas, smarting from the defeats his *misl* had suffered at Mahan Singh's hands, waylaid young Ranjit Singh when he was out hunting and made a slash at him with his sword, which was deftly evaded. Ranjit Singh's return blow proved fatal for Hashmat Khan.

There was no set pattern to Ranjit Singh's life during the years in which he grew to adulthood. His time was almost entirely taken up not with the customary occupations of boyhood but with military campaigns, which left him with no option but to be on horseback most of the time, often covering over fifty miles a day in the saddle. During these years of unending battles, which ranged from taking some of the Sikh *misl* chiefs head-on to warring with India's Muslim rulers in addition to the Pathans, Afghans and other invaders who had always considered India fair game, his headquarters were at Gujranwala Fort.

There is a story of Ranjit Singh's mother, Raj Kaur, asking him to be wary as their enemies were trying to snatch away their lands. His reassuring reply was: 'Don't be impatient, Mother, I shall not only take back my own lands but will also finish off the intruders.'[7]

❦

The notorious Afghan Ahmed Shah Abdali, founder of the Durrani dynasty, had repeatedly ransacked India before Ranjit Singh's time, but his grandson Zaman Shah was no less enthusiastic in pillaging and plundering India and even had an ambitious plan to found an Indian empire. The Afghans had long been held in considerable awe on the subcontinent. Ranjit Singh's first brush with Zaman Shah's army occurred when he invaded India for the second time in 1795; the first had been in 1793. In December 1795 Zaman Shah headed for Hasan Abdal, a place which, as Panja Sahib, has hallowed memories for the Sikhs since Guru Nanak sojourned there in the late fifteenth century. While Zaman stayed behind in Hasan Abdal, his general Ahmad Khan Shahanchibashi marched from Attock on the River Indus 200 miles to the town of Rohtas, which belonged to Ranjit Singh.

To confuse Zaman and draw his force from its base in Hasan Abdal, Ranjit Singh withdrew his men from Rohtas to Pind Dadan Khan in the salt ranges. When the Afghans attacked Ranjit Singh he crossed the River Jhelum, reassembled on its southern bank and sent his messengers to the regional Maratha chief, Daulat Rao Sindhia, at Aligarh, inviting him to join the Sikhs and expel the Afghan invader. There was, however, no response from the Maratha chief.

As fate would have it, Zaman had to return home in a hurry on hearing news of a revolt at Herat, but he was back again by October 1796, for the third time, camping in Peshawar for a month. Ranjit Singh's rapid manoeuvres once again had the Afghans baffled. He established himself with a force of 10,000 men across the Jhelum not far from Peshawar, then moved to Pind Dadan Khan, then on to Miani, then suddenly crossed the Jhelum for a surprise attack on the Durranis at Pind Dadan Khan before recrossing the river once again. At this point Zaman Shah addressed a letter to Ranjit Singh asking him to desist from opposing him. Ranjit Singh's reply is celebrated. 'Through the grace of the Guru every Sikh is bound to be victorious.'[8]

Still on his third invasion, Zaman Shah entered Lahore in January 1797 with a formidable force. Lahore had been officially made an Afghan province in 1752 after the Abdalis had wrested it from the Mughals. Zaman did not want to waste time in Lahore because he was keen to reach Amritsar to settle the Sikh problem once and for all. Ranjit Singh could barely wait to take him on. When a detachment of the Afghan army first took the offensive and attacked Amritsar on 11 January 1797 it suffered a humiliating defeat with much loss of blood. A furious Zaman Shah, beside himself with rage, now took personal command and arrived in Amritsar the next day. He, too, was not only vanquished but was chased all the way to the gates of Lahore by the Sikh army.

To make certain that the Durrani hordes would never again set foot in India, Ranjit Singh invited Sahib Singh to join him in expelling him. Sahib Singh was chief of the Phulkian *misl*, whose great-grandfather, Ala Singh, had been made Raja of Patiala by Ahmed Shah Abdali during a previous invasion of India in 1763, the same Abdali who a year before that had blown the Harmandir Sahib apart, filled the sacred pool with human bodies and carcasses of cows, killed thousands of pilgrims and made a pyramid of Sikh heads on the site. Not surprisingly, Ranjit Singh received no reply from Sahib Singh. Most of what the Patiala family owned had come to it through Abdali's largesse.

Zaman Shah, still smarting from his defeat at the gates of Amritsar, left Lahore in February 1797 for Peshawar *en route* for Afghanistan. His general Ahmad Khan Shahanchibashi, left behind at Rohtas to take care of the Sikhs, was finished off there on 29 April 1797. With India still very much on his mind, Zaman launched his last invasion in September 1798, eager to drive the Sikhs out of Punjab and put a decisive end to Ranjit Singh's power. The various battles and skirmishes that took place during this visit took him no further towards ending Sikh power, and when he received news from Afghanistan of a serious threat to his throne in Kabul he hastened back to his capital. Taking advantage of his absence, the Iranians had invaded Khorasan in Afghanistan and were making their way to Kabul. In his precipitate departure, Zaman lost twelve of his prized cannon in the Jhelum river which was in spate. The loss of these guns in fact proved a turning point in his relations with Ranjit Singh who, on receiving an urgent plea for his help in retrieving the guns, magnanimously complied. Zaman Shah then assured Ranjit Singh that he would not oppose his taking over Lahore.

On returning home, Zaman Shah was soon in the thick of rampant court intrigues and fateful events which will be related later.

It may be asked at this point what help and guidance was available to Ranjit Singh during his formative years, who was close to him and may have influenced him. One friend in particular deserves mention: Gurmukh Singh, eight years older than Ranjit Singh, who came into the family around the time Ranjit was born. The story goes that 'In the summer of 1780, as Sardar Mahan Singh was passing through the little town of Kheora on his return from an expedition in the neighbourhood of Pind Dadan Khan, Gurmukh Singh, then a boy of eight years, was presented to him by his uncle Basti Ram, the Toshakhania [Treasurer]. The Sardar was pleased with the bright eyes and intelligent looks of the boy and kept him with himself. Later in the same year Ranjit Singh was born, and Gurmukh was appointed his companion.'[9] An enduring friendship developed between Ranjit Singh and Gurmukh Singh, who was to be by his side when he captured Lahore in 1799. Because of his trust in him the Sukerchakia chief not only put him in charge of all the treasures of Lahore that fell into his hands but made him paymaster of his victorious army.

Ranjit Singh's learning of Gurmukhi and his grounding in the beliefs, ethics and tenets of the Sikh faith at a very early age played a key role in the shaping of his humane character and of the state's even-handed policies under his rule. The extent of his commitment from a very young age to secular ideals, that is, his open-mindedness to other religions and cultures besides his own,[10] is borne out by the fact that while he loved composing verses in Punjabi, which was an integral part of his being, he made Persian the official language of the Lahore Durbar. Although he did not know it at this age – the only other language he knew besides his own was Gurmukhi – he was as attracted to Persian as he was to Urdu, Kashmiri, Sindhi and many other regional languages.

While there is no denying his fascination throughout his early years with horsemanship, hunting, shooting and swordsmanship, another side of him drew inspiration from the spiritual under-pinnings of his faith; an inspiration that could have come only from the environment of the household in which he grew up. He was, after all, a great-great-grandson of the legendary Desu (Budha Singh), who had gone to Guru Gobind Singh at the age of fifty to be baptized into the Khalsa at Anandpur and who had died at Gurdas Nangal in 1715 fighting by the side of Banda Singh Bahadur. There can be little doubt that having the blood of this larger-than-life figure in his veins must have been more influential in shaping his leaderly qualities than any formal education could have been and that in his formative years there was more going for him than even he could have realized.

Among other influences working on Ranjit Singh in those years up to early adulthood were two strong-willed women – his mother

Raj Kaur (also known as Mai Malwain) and his mother-in-law Sada Kaur. His marriage to her daughter Mehtab Kaur was a complete failure, not only because of his abiding interest in other women – he was ultimately to have twenty wives in all besides a very sizeable harem – but because of Mehtab Kaur's deep and continuing conviction that Ranjit Singh's father Mahan Singh had had a hand in her father Gurbaksh Singh Kanhayia's death in battle, although he had died in a clash with the Ramgarhias. Sada Kaur's view was more pragmatic. She hoped to repair the rift between the two *misls* through this marriage, with the aim of creating a grand alliance with far bigger goals in mind.

Sada Kaur played a major role in Ranjit Singh's life. It was, however, preceded by his mother Raj Kaur's more modest but nevertheless significant contribution. She was only twenty-four years old when Mahan Singh died in 1790, but despite her young age she was of considerable help in holding the *misl* together for seven years through a form of regency which included Diwan Lakhpat Rai and Dal Singh, who was Mahan Singh's maternal uncle and Chief of Akalgarh. But her regency was the cause of strife between the two power camps around Ranjit Singh, with Raj Kaur and Diwan Lakhpat Rai being opposed with increasing bitterness by Sada Kaur and Dal Singh, each trying to bring young Ranjit Singh under its influence.

In this face-off Sada Kaur and Dal Singh, the more aggressive of the protagonists, were determined not only to undermine Raj Kaur's effectiveness as an administrator but to tarnish her personal reputation as well. Aside from an ongoing smear campaign against her over her relationship with Lakhpat Rai, many intrigues well beyond the bounds of decency were hatched to destroy her in the public's esteem. In 1797 her seventeen-year-old son took over the *misl*'s affairs because, according to some reports, he had grown impatient with her control of things.

The death of Raj Kaur was a mysterious and controversial

episode. The most vicious rumours soon circulated suggesting that Ranjit Singh had a hand in the killing of his mother and were believed by many. One British army officer, writing nearly half a century later, gives a distinctly novelettish version of events. Ranjit Singh, his story goes, entered his mother's chamber early one morning and, finding a man there, quietly left, summoned some followers, took up a sword and returned to his mother's room where he now found her alone. In an increasingly heated argument Raj Kaur is said to have upbraided her son for casting a slur on her moral character and Ranjit, 'stung to madness by her reproaches', to have dispatched her 'as she was sitting up on her bed half naked and with dishevelled hair'.[11]

The historian Hari Ram Gupta, a specialist in the period, comments as follows:

> Some writers accuse Ranjit Singh of having killed his mother with his own hands . . . Kushwaqt Rae, Sohan Lal, Amar Nath and Bute Shah [writers and chroniclers of distinction whose judgments are based on first-hand observation or on a serious study of events of the period] do not mention this event. Kushwaqt Rae wrote his book in 1811, and he was not in Ranjit Singh's service. Bute Shah was an employee of the British Government at Ludhiana. He says that Ranjit Singh took charge of his *misl* in consultation with his mother . . . N.K. Sinha says the story is based on 'mere gossip'. Sita Ram Kohli considers the charge entirely false and baseless. In our view, by any stretch of imagination, Ranjit Singh cannot be called a matricide. The story is purely malicious and absolutely unfair and unjust.[12]

There would seem to be no justification for the charge of matricide against a man whose patent decency throughout his life is especially striking seen in a historical context so replete with the most extreme examples of cruelty and bloodthirstiness on the part of rulers not only towards persons defeated by them but even towards the innocent. A British historian comments: 'Ranjit Singh was not cruel or bloodthirsty. After a victory or the capture of a fortress he treated the vanquished with leniency and kindness, however stout their resistance might have been, and there were at his court many chiefs despoiled of their estates but to whom he had given suitable employ.'[13]

Eventually it came to be accepted that Raj Kaur had been poisoned at the instigation of her adversaries.

~

Sada Kaur was on an altogether grander scale of ambition than Ranjit Singh's mother Raj Kaur and possessed of both courage and ability in abundance. On several occasions she proved herself a valuable ally to her son-in-law. Lepel Griffin describes her as 'a widow of great ability and unscrupulousness [who] took command of the confederacy and held her own against her son-in-law successfully till 1820'.[14] After Raj Kaur's death Diwan Lakhpat fell in an expedition against the Chatthas, and with both her rivals removed from the field Sada Kaur had ample scope to pursue her ambitions. The alliance between the Sukerchakias and the Kanhayias, the two most eminent of the twelve *misls*, created by the marriage between her daughter Mehtab Kaur and Ranjit Singh was a formidable starting-point, and Sada Kaur planned to establish her writ over the entire Punjab by drawing on their combined military strength and material resources. But despite her sharp intellect and understanding of the centrality of war and political intrigue in getting what she wanted, she failed to gauge her own limitations with regard to her son-in-law who was already thinking far beyond her vision of the future. He envisioned not only all of Punjab under his control but also territories well beyond India's boundaries which belonged to those who had savaged the country for centuries. He was clear in his mind that without first bringing the different *misls* under his control he would lack a sound power base.

Bikrama Jit Hasrat pinpoints the political situation in the Punjab at the time when Ranjit Singh took over the Sukerchakia *misl* in 1797. 'The *misl* system born out of a sense of national unity to combat foreign aggression had foundered on the rock of personal ambition and lust for power. The carving out of several principalities by the powerful Bhangis, the Ramgarhias, the Ahluwalias and the Phulkians had struck a blow at the mystic ideal of the Commonwealth of Guru Gobind Singh . . . The unity of action or concerted will in the name of the Khalsa had become a thing of the past.'[15] Ranjit Singh's vision of where and how far he wanted to go to recreate the Commonwealth – although he ended up creating an empire – was beyond Sada Kaur's powers of conception. And his mother-in-law, able and sharp-witted as she was, could not have been more wrong in believing that she could bring Ranjit Singh under her tutelage.

In the first years after Raj Kaur's untimely end, however, and while Ranjit Singh was still coming to grips with running his extended *misl*, he gained a good deal from Sada Kaur's decisiveness, as when, for example, Zaman Shah appeared in Punjab on his fourth invasion of India in September 1798 and crossed the River Indus at Attock in October. Ranjit Singh prepared to oppose him at Ramnagar on the River Chenab but headed back for the Amritsar–Lahore region when some of the Muslim landlords of the area along with the Afghan governor of Kasur, Nizam-ud-din, prepared to occupy some of the Sikh forts. In the ensuing action a wounded Nizam-ud-din had to be removed along with dead Afghani soldiers who were more than twice the number of Sikh soldiers killed.

While Sikh contingents under Ranjit Singh continued to attack the Afghans, several Sikh chieftains and their men in Amritsar at this time were most reluctant to combine forces with him, despite his urging. Sada Kaur, also then in Amritsar, promptly made her presence felt. Addressing the Sardars, she said: 'If you are disposed to assist Ranjit Singh, advance and join him, if not, throw off that dress and take mine, give me your clothes and I will march against the enemy.'[16] On 24 November 1798 Zaman Shah, temporarily occupying the city of Lahore, which had been under Bhangi rule since the ousting of the Afghans in 1765, sent a force of 10,000 men to Amritsar to teach the Sikhs a lesson by occupying their holy city, too. Ranjit Singh with 500 horsemen waylaid the advance contingents of Zaman's army and after particularly intense fighting – in which the Sardars from Amritsar with 2,000 of their men joined in – the Afghans retreated to Lahore. These were the same Sardars who had been addressed by Sada Kaur; her taunts had born fruit.

The following year provides another example of Sada Kaur's resourcefulness. The citizens of Lahore had become thoroughly discontented with Bhangi rule and had sent a petition to Ranjit Singh for help, which he agreed to provide. He left Gujranwala with a very small force for Amritsar – ostensibly to visit the holy city (which was shared between the Bhangi and the Ramgarhia *misls*) but with the underlying aim of attacking Lahore from there. For that he needed more troops. When he sent an urgent message to Sada Kaur for help, she promptly arrived with a sizeable force of several thousand and helped him to annex Lahore in July 1799 – except for the city's well-fortified fort, which was left in the hands of the Bhangis. The role Sada Kaur played here had been made possible by the far-sightedness of the third Guru Amar Das (1552–74) in the sixteenth century, who had given complete equality to women in every sphere of life – as radical a change as any ever brought about in India's archaic social customs.

While Ranjit Singh was determined to storm the fort as well, Sada Kaur advised him against it. She argued that the people besieged inside the fort were left with no option but to surrender because of lack of provisions and communications with the outside world. Her assessment was right; the Bhangi chief surrendered the very next day and his stronghold was taken without bloodshed. On other occasions, too, as Ranjit Singh fought on many fronts to consolidate his hold, Sada Kaur was there to lend him a hand.

◦⁀◦

Ranjit Singh's first move on occupying Lahore was to issue an order that his officers and troops were to treat the people of the city with courtesy and consideration and that failure to obey this order – as also any attempt at plunder – would bring severe punishment. He rode through Lahore's streets to assure citizens of their personal safety and the safety of their property and to leave no doubt in their minds that they would be safe under his rule. And, in a gesture reminiscent of Alexander's treatment of the defeated King Porus, he made certain that Sardar Chet Singh, the defeated Bhangi ruler of Lahore, would not only be treated with full respect but given a handsome grant of land.

Lahore, once the prized possession of the Mughals and then of Abdali who after his victories over the Mughals in 1748 had declared Punjab a territory of Afghanistan with Lahore as its capital, was now in the possession of Ranjit Singh. The nineteen-year-old conqueror was master of one of the most historic cities of India. Lying on the banks of the Ravi, one of Punjab's five great rivers, 2,000-year-old Lahore had not only borne wave after wave of Muslim invaders beginning with Mahmud of Ghazni in 1014 but had been home to dynasties established by numerous earlier invaders including the Ghoris, Mongols, Tughlaks, Khiljis, Lodis and Suris. The myths, legends and lore associated with it were age-old, and among the many who made mention of it were Ptolemy and Hiuen Tsang.

When the Mughal emperor Akbar shifted his capital to Lahore

in 1584 he built a strong brick fortress with imposing towers which would intimidate his enemy and within its walls constructed spacious villas for his harem and himself. His successors continued to fortify the walls of Lahore Fort until it was well-nigh impregnable. It had twelve gates, three of which opened on to the river. The elegant buildings inside were decorated with fine paintings, engravings and carved and pierced marbles, some even finer than those in the Taj Mahal in Agra. The Badshahi Mosque and the Moti Masjid (Pearl Mosque) were but two of the imposing structures inside the citadel. Lahore Fort became Ranjit Singh's principal residence, workplace and the Durbar, or court, from which he ruled when he was in his capital.

The Lahore Durbar when fully established has been the subject of many descriptions. The hall where Ranjit Singh received his ministers and dignitaries was of impressive proportions, and its floor was covered with rich carpets. The canopy was an enormous embroidered shawl encrusted with gold and precious stones; it covered nearly the whole hall and was suspended from carved golden pillars. Almost all the carpets and shawls in the Durbar came from Kashmir.

The Lion of Punjab loved colour and bejewelled people around him, although he himself wore white or saffron yellow. 'He is plain and simple in dress', as Henry Prinsep describes, 'but seems to take pleasure in seeing his courtiers and establishments decorated in jewels and handsome dresses, and it is not to be denied that they show considerable taste, for the splendour of the display of his Durbar is very striking.'[17] Prinsep also has a description of him in his later years seated on his famous golden chair, cross-legged, dressed from head to toe in white, sitting upright as men born to the saddle do. His 'countenance, full of expression and animation, is set off by a handsome flowing beard, grey at 50 years of age but tapering to a point below his breast'.[18]

Ranjit Singh's Moti Mandir Toshakhana (treasury) was full

of jewels. But he rejected the more garish and glittering ornaments for his person, wearing only on ceremonial occasions the unrivalled table-cut Golkunda diamond, the Koh-i-noor, surrounded by two smaller diamonds as an armlet, and his famous string of round pearls, perfectly matched in shape and colour, the size of small marbles and around 300 in number, hung around his neck and sometimes his waist.

A magical adjunct to Lahore were the Shalimar Gardens, laid out in 1667 by Shah Jahan's talented engineer Ali Mardan Khan. Spread over eighty acres, with three magnificent terraces rising one after another at intervals of twelve to fifteen feet, 450 fountains fed by a canal especially built for the purpose, cascading waterways, exotic flower and fruit trees and much else, the Shalimar Gardens ('Abode of Love and Joy') lie three miles north-east of the city and may be enjoyed in their full splendour today. From its creation Shalimar was an integral part of Lahore's allure, and Ranjit Singh was to revel in it more than most rulers.

His acquisition of Lahore in 1799 was the first major step towards his vision of the future. He was even more convinced now than ever before of the need to bring all the *misls* under his control; or, better still, do away with them altogether and merge their territories with the others he was acquiring. Some of the *misl* chiefs provided him with the excuse he needed. The first two reckless enough to stick their necks out were the Bhangis and Ramgarhias. Resentful of Ranjit Singh's growing power, they formed an alliance to take Lahore, even after he had dealt magnanimously with the defeated Bhangi Sardar when taking the city.

These two *misls*, like his other adversaries, misjudged him. The Bhangis were the first to suffer one humiliating defeat after another until they not only also lost their share of the sacred city of Amritsar but in due course all their other territories as well. In time they ceased to exist. The loss of their part of Amritsar and the fall of the Bhangis was entirely a self-inflicted tragedy, precipitated by their loss of Lahore. Determined to avenge that humiliation, they hatched a plan to assassinate Ranjit Singh during a meeting to be held at a village called Bhassin about ten miles east of Lahore. The young ruler, although barely twenty, was already well versed in the ways of the world and, coming to know of their plot, arrived at the venue with a formidable force of men. The would-be assassins, realizing the folly of trying to kill him, abandoned their plan. But Ranjit Singh, by now fully informed of their intentions, would exact a heavy price for what they had planned to do. To legitimize his overthrow of the Bhangi *misl* he first asked for the return of the giant Zam Zama gun, the highly prestigious symbol which was now in their hands but which the Sukerchakias had earlier acquired from the Afghans. Quite understandably the Bhangis refused to return it, which was the excuse Ranjit Singh needed to attack and take over Amritsar. By this bold move Ranjit Singh became possessed of the two Sikh capitals, the political and the religious, and was well on his way to the execution of his grand strategy.

After the Bhangis, Ranjit Singh turned his attention to the Ramgarhias. Since the two *misls* had divided Amritsar between them, the Ramgarhia half of the city consisting of the Ramgarh Fort and the lands around it was soon under Ranjit Singh's control, too, after his army had taken over Amritsar. The complete acquisition of the Ramgarhia territories would take longer, because even in the midst of conflict and armed clashes a strange bond of brotherhood had been established between Ranjit Singh and the then chief of the Ramgarhia *misl*, Jodh Singh, who had come to enjoy Ranjit Singh's confidence and even took part in several of his campaigns until his death in 1815 when the territories of the Ramgarhia *misls* eventually went to the Lahore Durbar.

It is important to note that even before Lahore became the seat of Sikh power Ranjit had begun the consolidation and expansion on which he had set his mind. After further annexations, including Gurdaspur and Jalandhar to the east and north-east of Lahore, he set his eyes further north on Jammu, heading for it within a few months of taking Lahore. He first subdued Mirowal and Narowal before taking Jassarwal Fort by siege. On the march again, he was less than four miles from Jammu when its ruler, realizing what lay in store if he resisted the seemingly invincible Ranjit Singh, called on him with gifts and a fervent request for clemency for his city and himself. Ranjit Singh responded handsomely by restoring to him some of his holdings and gifting him a robe of honour. Sialkot and Dilawargarh fell next. Since the latter's chief Bawa Kesar Singh Sodhi had surrendered, Ranjit Singh not only pardoned him but gave him a sizeable *jagir* as well.

With the year 1800 almost entirely taken up by continuous campaigns, it was time for Ranjit Singh to return to Lahore, henceforth to be his home for the rest of his life. And here he announced the setting-up of his rule; something he had thought of for quite some time and for which he had judiciously laid the groundwork by earning considerable goodwill in the conquered territories through humane and generous treatment of his defeated foes.

Historical accounts often make mention, cryptically and without convincing evidence, of the 'cruel treatment' to which Ranjit Singh is supposed to have subjected defeated adversaries. Even a distinguished historian such as Syad Muhammad Latif, describing the fall of Jassarwal Fort to Ranjit Singh in 1800, says that, 'having reduced it, [he] put the defenders to the sword'.[19] But no details are provided as to how many were 'put to the sword' or why. Such reprisals were entirely uncharacteristic of him, and it is difficult to believe that they actually occurred.

Ranjit Singh clearly aimed from a very young age at establishing his own state. But what was unique about him, and makes his life-story so different from that of most other rulers, was that he drew his strength not from the brutal exercise of power but from his humanity, vision, vitality and tolerance and that he never allowed irrational or primitive instincts to interfere with affairs of state. The powerful impulse that drove Ranjit Singh to create a just, secular and cosmopolitan society for his people was his unshakeable faith in the religion into which he was born.

❦

Considering the many religions that existed in the Sikh state he was creating – Hindu, Muslim, Sikh, Jain, Buddhist and Christian, as also the bewildering number of various subdivisions of these faiths – Ranjit Singh made a far-sighted move at the very outset of his reign. He ensured that the religious and social festivals a multicultural society like India observes throughout the year should be celebrated by people of all beliefs. He was convinced that this would provide the necessary impetus to the secularism to which the Sikhs subscribed. And so he made it a rule that his senior ministers, governors and eminent citizens, including himself, should try to attend as many of them as they could.

Hari Ram Gupta points out that there were different days of special significance for the four castes of the Hindus alone: 'for Brahmans, Rakhi, or Rakhri, or Raksha Bandhan or Solunon in July–August; for Kshatriyas (warrior class), Dasahra in September–October; for Vaishyas (trading class), Diwali in October–November; and for Shudras (cultivators and the like), Holi in February–March'.[20]

There was logic in each of these points of the calendar, rooted not just in the religious but in the economic facts of life as well. While the trading classes, cultivators and those engaged in various vocations looked forward to the Diwali festival to celebrate good yields from wheat, sugarcane and other crops, the fighting caste of Kshatriyas chose to herald the coming winter season to plan new campaigns. For the Brahmins Rakhi was a time of thanksgiving for all the offerings they received from the other castes, and for the Shudras the months of February and March seemed the most appropriate to mark the end of rigorous winters and celebrate the onset of spring through the colourful festival of Holi.

There were many other festivals in addition to these, such as the birthdays of the Hindu gods Lord Rama and Lord Krishna. The former, Ram Navmi, was celebrated in early April and the latter, Janam Ashtmi, in August–September. Guru Nanak's birthday, or Gurpurab, in November was an occasion of the utmost significance for the Sikhs and was observed with great fervour.

Many other lesser festivals were also looked forward to with much enthusiasm. Lohri, in January, was especially important in Punjab where the festive mood was highlighted by roaring bonfires around which people sang and danced well into the night. Basant, which fell in January–February each year, heralded the advent of spring, and just as the fields were full of yellow mustard flowers people also dressed in yellow robes to celebrate the good times to come. Baisakhi, in April, was – and still is – a day of great rejoicing because it was harvest time. People in their thousands travelled to Amritsar to take a dip in the holy pool on this day.

The list is a long one because Ranjit Singh well knew how vital it was to make every citizen in his realm feel an integral part of – and entitled to – the best that his country had to offer him and made sure that people of different castes, creeds and religions were encouraged to assemble together to celebrate religious holidays and overcome their differences and prejudices. It was most important for the well-being of his state that its people should develop a sense of fellow feeling and religious toleration and have the right to practise their own religious beliefs in absolute freedom. His aim of creating a spirit of communal harmony was convincingly conveyed by the pomp and gaiety that attended Muslim religious days. Ranjit Singh 'celebrated the Muslim festivals of Id with the same enthusiasm as he showed for Holi and Dussehra. Persian continued to be the court language. Although illiterate, he acquired a speaking knowledge of Persian and Urdu. He married Muslim women and tried to curb the Akalis (independent Sikh warriors fully armed and dressed in deep blue, and wearing tall conical turbans with steel quoits stuck in them) with an iron hand. There were no forced conversions in his reign, no communal riots, no language tensions, no second-class citizens. Any talented man could come to the court and demand his due.'[21] Christmas was also joyfully celebrated, and Ranjit Singh's Lahore Durbar would send big hampers of fruits, sweets, wine and other presents to Europeans living in the Sikh kingdom.

Those accorded sainthood are usually persons venerated for their holiness, spiritual stature and virtuous life. As we shall see, Ranjit Singh was far from virtuous in his personal life. He was unrestrained in his sexual relationships, in the number of times he took marriage vows, in his unconcern for the traditional definitions of morality and in his bouts of drinking from time to time. Since he indulged himself in these whole-heartedly, he was obviously nowhere near sainthood if his life is judged through these self-indulgences. But his passion for ensuring just governance for his people, his dedication to secular beliefs, his respect for god-given life and the uncompromising stand against tyranny enjoined by the Sikh Gurus – these were articles of faith from which he seldom deviated.

The rulers or conquerors of that period were occupied with no such concerns. Appalling atrocities were the order of the day, and it is in this context that Ranjit Singh came close to being a saint. No conqueror ever established a regime as humane as his. He built up his power with a very small percentage of people of the Sikh faith and without the customary barbarities which the victors of that or indeed many another age visited on those of other religious beliefs who were subjugated. He conducted himself civilly as a ruler of a mixed nation, without any cruelty, arrogance or arbitrariness, and in this respect he may well be called a saint at the same time as he was indubitably a sensualist. His strength lay in the versatility with which he combined both fundamental aspects of his nature. If he lived his personal life the way he did, it was not at the expense of his responsibilities as a ruler.

&

One of Guru Nanak's specific injunctions to the followers of his faith was that 'only they are the true Rajas' who can justly and even-handedly carry out their responsibilities to their people. Ranjit Singh's status as a maharaja, resonant and awe-inspiring as it was, was born of no attempt to project himself as larger than life, even though that is the impression conveyed by the well-worn words like 'king', 'kingdom', 'emperor' and 'empire' used by so many chroniclers to describe his assumption of power as ruler of Punjab. Such terms, however, do not indicate how he saw his new role.

What comes through from all the records on Ranjit Singh is that his was a highly complex personality and that he set himself many seemingly impossible goals, most of which he actually achieved. Nor did he aspire to personal aggrandizement or imperial status to boost his ego. Even at the apex of his power, he preferred to be addressed as *Sarkar* or the source of authority. It was not a grandiose title, nor how kings and emperors liked to be addressed.

His goal was not to live in monarchical splendour but to make a just and civilized state out of a Punjab riven with in-fighting, intrigue and instability, where power was dispersed among a large number of fractious constituents. In 1799, a little over a year before he established his rule over Punjab, there were sixty-eight territories quite independent of one another between the Indus and the Sutlej rivers: twenty-five Muslim states, twenty-seven Hindu states and sixteen Sikh states, an amazing medley of chiefs and feudal lords, including some who owed allegiance to nations beyond India's borders.[22] While, for instance, Kashmir, Peshawar and Mul-tan belonged to the Afghans, Kasur, Kunjpura, Bahawalpur and

Malerkotla also owed allegiance to Kabul, and some of the other Muslim territories were tributaries of Afghanistan. A few were run as fiefdoms, such as Jammu, Kangra, Pind Dadan Khan, Muzaffarabad, Jhang and Shahpur. The Hindu chieftains were a divided lot, too, and the Sikhs – including the twelve *misls* – although far fewer in numbers, were as fractious as the rest.

The complexity of Punjab, whether in its religious or its demographic composition, posed problems in the way of even-handed governance. With Sikhs accounting for only 7 per cent of the population as against 50 per cent Muslims and 42 per cent Hindus,[23] Ranjit Singh could neither deny Sikhs considerable authority under Sikh rule nor deny the others a fair representation. He could not have achieved what he did had he not possessed a sure grasp of what constituted just governance, or had he been vindictive, a religious bigot or obsessed with his own exalted status. That he succeeded in creating a prosperous, multireligious, militarily powerful nation, founded on secular principles and rid of predatory invaders and conquistadors, without resorting to the barbarities that have characterized so many conquests and creations of kingdoms and empires, is what makes him such an unusual figure in world history. He exercised supreme power without sacrificing his humanity, decency, civility and resolve to respect his peoples' right to practise their religious beliefs in absolute freedom. He revealed his style of kingship at the very outset of his reign, when he insisted that the investiture ceremony to install him as absolute ruler of Punjab on 12 April 1801 should be simple, low-key and devoid of pomp.

Descriptions of his 'coronation' on that day have used terms such as 'his crowning', 'an able king', 'the Sikh monarchy', 'the Great Maharaja'. But all this is altogether inaccurate. Ranjit Singh never assumed any of these titles, preferring, as we have seen, *Sarkar* to all others. He drew his authority not from titles but from his qualities of leadership. No building or monument ever bore his name. The fort built by him at Amritsar was called Govind Garh, while the palace and gardens were named Ram Bagh, the Park of Lord Ram.

He never possessed either a throne or a crown. In the words of Baron Charles Hugel, 'The Maharaja has no throne. "My sword," he observed, "procures me all the distinction I desire."'[24] His strange oriental chair (*murha*) served him as a throne, on which he often sat cross-legged, and his turban was his crown, which he proudly wore. Quite appropriately, his court was known as Durbar Khalsa ji. There is hardly any mention of Ranjit Singh's coronation in any state archives, in Punjab, Lahore or in the National Archives of India in New Delhi.

Historical distortions not only prevent an accurate assessment of persons whose contributions in the past were most significant but obscure major milestones in a country's evolution. As a British chronicler of the times put it, the Sikhs 'had now reached nationhood . . . [and were] fully equipped with confidence and energy under Ranjit Singh, who, by transforming the Khalsa into a territorial power, decided once and for all whether the Sikh or the Afghan was to rule the Punjab. Thus, after a hundred years of unflinching struggle, was fulfilled the prophecy of the martial Guru Gobind Singh.'[25]

Guru Gobind Singh, forming the brotherhood of the Khalsa, had galvanized his people with the words *Raj Karega Khalsa*, 'The Khalsa Shall Rule'. And now the time had come for the Khalsa to establish its rule over Punjab. So it is no coincidence that the day of the Baisakhi Festival, early in April 1801, was chosen by Ranjit Singh to be formally declared its ruler – the same Baisakhi Day on which the fellowship of the Khalsa had been created by Guru Gobind Singh 102 years earlier. To the 80,000 or so who had assembled on that day in 1699 at Anandpur, the Guru's exhortation had been 'You will love man as man, making no distinction of caste or creed . . . In you the whole brotherhood shall be reincarnated.'[26] This was the mission Ranjit Singh would now fulfil.

The ceremony was simple. Baba Sahib Singh Bedi, a descendant of Guru Nanak, applied some saffron paste or *tilak* (which has a sacred significance) to Ranjit Singh's forehead and confirmed him as the Sikh Sarkar of Punjab, which in the past had been ruled by the Mughals, the Afghans and countless other interlopers. Now at the dawn of the Sikh Age, not only important Sikh Sardars but also Hindu and Muslim chiefs and notables witnessed the religious rites as Sardar Ranjit Singh was pronounced the king appointed as God's humble servant deputed for the service of the people.

From the very outset Ranjit Singh left no doubt in anyone's mind about his adherence to the secular convictions which had been forcefully enunciated by Guru Gobind Singh when he established the Khalsa. There was no ambiguity in his declaration of what people should expect under his rule. Muslim religious laws would be allowed to cover Muslims, and Qazis (judges ruling in accordance with Sharia, the Islamic religious law) would preside over their courts. Nizam-ud-Din was made the head Qazi of Lahore. Nor was the role of *muftis* (Muslim scholars who interpret the Sharia) overlooked. It was also decreed that mosques would continue to be supported by the state. In acknowledgement of the fact that Muslims were in a majority in the capital city of Lahore, he appointed Imam Baksh as its chief of police, who in turn was given a free hand to designate persons of his choice to senior positions in the force. The overarching authority in religious matters relating to Muslims as a whole was vested in Nizam-ud-Din who had the final say in religious disputes among members of his faith. He in turn was advised by Mufti Mohammed Shah and Mufti Sa'dullah Chishti.

The administration of Lahore was a model which Ranjit Singh replicated throughout his extensive territories. He was determined to create an administrative system undiluted by religious prejudices, political affiliations, preference for family connections, regional and caste loyalties or countless other pressures that made a mockery of just governance. Despite the disparate and potentially destructive elements he had to keep in control, his aim was to create a cohesive society out of erstwhile enemies. One study of an early cabinet lists fifteen Hindu ministers and top officials compared with seven Sikhs. The former included the ministers of finance, revenue, the paymaster-general, the accountant-general and the governors of Multan and Kashmir, while the Sikhs were almost entirely generals, some of whom held additional posts as governors. In a later cabinet, in which Hindus, Muslims and Dogras (hill Rajputs from the Jammu area) predominated, the prime minister's portfolio was given to a Hindu Dogra, Dhian Singh, and three of the most important portfolios to Muslims: Fakir Azizuddin was foreign minister, Fakir Nuruddin home minister and Fakir Imamuddin custodian of the treasury at Amritsar. 'Even Akbar who was the most liberal of the Mughal Emperors, who thought so much of expedient considerations, did not go as far as Ranjit Singh did. Whereas Ranjit Singh gave the highest positions, such as prime ministership, foreign ministership, etc., to members of other communities, Akbar could not go beyond associating one or two non-Muslim ministers with his court which thus predominantly remained Muslim in character and composition.'[27]

In a number of 'democracies' around the world today, just representation in upper echelons of government is a rare thing; religious, caste and class considerations matter far more. Ranjit Singh's monarchical practice was more in keeping with democratic principles than democratic functioning in India today.

Neither were non-Punjabis discriminated against in Punjab. Even more significantly, even though in 1606 Chandu Shah, an influential Brahmin in the service of the Mughals (along with a Brahmin lobby, deeply resentful of the independent ways of the Sikhs), had influenced the Mughal emperor Jahangir cruelly to put to death Guru Arjan Dev, builder of the Harmandir and compiler of the Guru Granth, Ranjit Singh appointed Khushal Singh, a Brahmin, as the chamberlain of his court. He later converted to Sikhism. His nephew, Tej Singh from Meerut (he became a Sikh in 1816), was also taken into service and eventually became commander-in-chief of the army after Ranjit Singh's death.

Some of the men Ranjit Singh rewarded with senior positions were to betray the Sikh state after his death. But in his lifetime this worldly-wise ruler, well aware of the inborn human tendency towards treason and religious bigotry, was well able to deal with such people and their propensities and instinctively to use their abilities for the good. He could thus afford not to deviate from the secular principle in the governance of his state, the even-handedness which in such large part underlies his achievements.

The steadfastness of his own beliefs helped him provide a model of good governance to the heterogeneous population of the Sikh nation and to give its constituents the freedom to practise their own faiths. He showed them the way himself by his regular visits to Hindu temples and Muslim mosques towards which he expressed the same reverence as he did towards Sikh gurdwaras.

Even more convincing was his munificence towards different places of worship. This, again, was even-handed as between Hindu and Muslim shrines. After he annexed Lahore in 1799, the Sunahri mosque, which the city's previous *misl* rulers had taken over, was restored to the Muslims, while huge sums were spent on the restoration of the buildings of two Mughal emperors, Jahangir and Shah Jahan. Nor were any funds denied for the upkeep of the tombs of various distinguished Muslims. In the case of the Hindu temple at Jawalamukhi, aside from various other donations in cash and kind he had the roofs of the two main temple buildings – one large and the other smaller – covered in gold as a token of his esteem for the shrine. He also donated fourteen quintals (equal to

225 pounds or 100 kilograms) of pure gold for gilding the Vishwa Nath temple at Benares which Emperor Aurangzeb had converted into a mosque.

Ranjit Singh's impartiality to all religions is acknowledged not only by past and present historians but by British and European observers of the time. There is an account of one Wolff Joseph, who came to Lahore in 1832 and set about putting up posters everywhere propagating Christianity and running down other religions while urging people to look to Christ as the true saviour. He soon received this message from Ranjit Singh: *In sakhun nabayad guft* – 'Such words must not be said.' That his own respect for different faiths raised him in the estimation of his people came through convincingly during his entry into Peshawar in 1818. This city, a few miles from the Khyber Pass, was the gateway through which invaders from Central Asia had poured into India over the centuries and more recently the Durranis from Afghanistan, described as 'remarkable for their cruelty and fierceness', whose great heroism was 'exalted neither by mercy nor resolution'.[28]

When a victorious Ranjit Singh rode into Peshawar after wresting it from the Afghans, he provided a striking contrast to Mohammad Ghori, Timur, Nadir Shah, Ahmed Shah Abdali and all the other blood-shedding armies down the centuries. He made it an ironclad rule that his armies would not indulge in carnage, nor burn holy books, nor destroy mosques. The civilian population could, with confidence, continue its daily activities as usual, and no women would be molested, nor men flayed alive. The people of Peshawar acknowledged this rare quality in this leader, and when Ranjit Singh rode through the streets of the city the holy men of the town blessed the conquerer and prayed for his long life. The rebellious tribesman who saw the spectacle exclaimed: '*Khuda Hum Khalsa Shud*' ('The Almighty is on the side of the Khalsa').

His respect for Christianity again proved not only his abiding interest in other faiths but his deep desire to know what held the followers of those faiths in such thrall. When he asked a European visitor to his court to tell him about the holy book of the Christians and was shown a Bible, he touched it to his forehead with reverence and had passages from it recited to him. He appointed many Christian officers to his army – Italians, Frenchmen, Englishmen, Greeks, Spaniards, Russians, Americans, a German and an Austrian, and some of these he made senior army commanders and governors of provinces. Their numbers have been put between thirty-nine and forty-two.

Ranjit Singh's ongoing interest in other religious beliefs was born out of a genuine desire to broaden his mind and to deal effectively with the extraordinary mix of people under his rule, drawing on the wisdom of knowledgeable men of other faiths, with many of whom he enjoyed having discussions on the subject of divinity. Revering the *kalgi* (plume) of Guru Gobind Singh in his possession, he was respectful of the relics of others – and especially those held to be of the Prophet Muhammad himself, which he found in some of the Muslim principalities he conquered. The latter included a copy of the Koran, a cloak and a pair of shoes kept in the Royal Toshakhana (Treasure House).

3

Emergence of the Sikh Kingdom

'Never was so large an empire founded by
one man with so little criminality.'

HENRY T. PRINSEP

Once the new ruler took up residence in Lahore Fort his days took
on a more discernible pattern. An amazingly early riser for a man
whose days were so full of physical and mental activity, he was
usually up around four in the morning, a habit formed in early
childhood. After he had bathed and dressed, he would with bowed
head make his way to the hall where the Guru Granth Sahib was
installed. It was a beautifully appointed room with a rich array of
carpets, shawls and silks symbolic of the deep regard the Sikhs
have always had for the places in which their scriptures are housed.

Here Ranjit Singh would sit and listen for an hour or more with
deep concentration to words and verses from the scriptures, which
were either read or sung out to him and to all others who might
be there. For in the Sikh house of prayer everyone was equal in
the eyes of God, and all sat on the ground with crossed legs, folded
hands and covered heads to listen to the words of wisdom from
the sacred book of the Sikh scriptures.

After the *path* and *kirtan* (readings and recitations) Ranjit
Singh would respectfully and briefly cover his eyes and forehead
with the *kalgi* of Guru Gobind Singh – a plume the tenth Guru

had worn on his turban, which had always been associated with him and was an integral part of his striking personality. Ranjit Singh had bought this precious relic for 125,000 rupees from the grandsons of Bhai Sant Singh, a Sikh martyr, and the sons of Bhai Hara Singh who had migrated to Peshawar.[1]

After prayers, if he was in a hurry to attend to court matters, take to the field, receive visiting dignitaries, inspect his troops or deal with any of the other demands on his time, he would have a simple breakfast and then attend to what awaited his attention. But if he had time he would go to the wing of the palace where his ladies lived and have breakfast with them, which usually consisted of quail, partridge, eggs, milk products and sweet dishes, with sometimes an exotic drink to wash down the meal.

Attending to matters of court, although unable to read in any language, Ranjit Singh would have papers, correspondence and orders to commanders in the field, state governors and others read out to him, and his comments and criticisms would be duly incorporated and the documents once again presented to him for his approval. His ability to attend to the smallest minutiae of business was astonishing. Henry T. Prinsep, who worked with the British political agent at Ambala and who was a close observer of the Lahore Durbar, leaves this account. 'He transacts business rapidly, is ready with a short and decided order upon any report or representation read to him, and when the draft of his instruction is submitted, after being prepared in due form, he sees at once whether it fully meets his view . . . his memory is excellent . . . his disposition is at the same time watchful and his eye quick and watching, so that nothing escapes his observation; while the perspicacity displayed in his appreciation of character, and in tracing the motives of others' actions, gives him a command and influence over all that approach him, which have been mainly instrumental to his rapid rise.'[2]

Sometimes Ranjit Singh's day would start off with an early-morning ride in the countryside. W.G. Osborne, who was military secretary to the Earl of Auckland, governor-general of India in the later years of Ranjit Singh's life, accompanied him on one such occasion and leaves this account of a conversation with him. (Although Ranjit Singh did not speak English, he developed an understanding of it.)

This morning we rode with him for some miles, gossiping and chatting, and endeavouring in vain to satisfy his insatiable curiosity upon subjects of the most opposite nature. 'Are you fond of riding?' 'Yes.' 'Are you fond of shooting?' 'Very.' 'Have you been out lately?' 'Yes; about two months ago.' 'Where?' 'In the Terai and Dehra Dhoow.' 'What did you shoot?' 'Twelve tigers.' 'Are you married?' 'No.' 'Why don't you marry?' 'I can't afford it.' 'What's the horse you're on?' 'An Arab.' 'Where did you get him?' 'He was given to me.' 'How long have you been out shooting?' 'Fourteen days.' 'Do you like my wine?' 'Yes; but it's very strong.' 'Have you breakfasted?' 'Not yet.' 'Then we will breakfast here.'[3]

Osborne goes on to describe a mouthwatering breakfast. Under a beautiful canopy, promptly pitched up on the Maharaja's orders, in a lovely green setting, rich carpets were spread out and golden chairs for Ranjit Singh and his guests were placed for breakfast which was produced minutes later – trays of curries, rice, sweetmeats, curds and quail which were spiced, seasoned and deboned.

The rest of the morning back at the palace was spent with Ranjit Singh grilling Osborne on a whole variety of subjects, which he would do with most foreign visitors, so that he could keep himself informed about what the rest of the world was up to. His curiosity never left him and his knowledge of a vast range of subjects was phenomenal.

At some time of the day, quite often very early in the morning, he would meet with the Sardars, ministers, viziers and chiefs who would be waiting to have a word with him. Brief though these encounters often were, they gave him a sense of what was on the minds of some of the key figures in charge of important matters, so that he was able to keep his fingers on the pulse-beat of his far-flung state and its functionaries.

What pattern the Maharaja's lunches followed again depended on the workload he faced and on whether he had to entertain visiting dignitaries. These two considerations permitting, his own personal preference was to lunch with the ladies in their wing of the palace, with some of them singing and dancing for him, while others served him food, often feeding him delicately with their fingers. The dishes served were sumptuous: a variety of succulent kebabs, fish, partridge and quail, pulaos, curds and varieties of vegetables curried or cooked in rich spices, followed by an array of sweets and desserts, even though the Maharaja himself was a frugal eater.

The wines he liked were potent beyond belief, the ingredients used running to ground pearls, musk, opium and plants of every kind. While some of the guests were left dazed by the drinks served, Ranjit Singh took them in his stride and seemed to get even more energized and enthusiastic. Such was his soundness of mind and body that when he was in middle age one doctor of the East India Company gave him thirty more years to live provided he controlled his intake of liquor.[4]

At the end of the afternoon meal Ranjit Singh would retire to his own chamber in the ladies' wing for an hour or so of rest, and if there was work to be done he would go back to his office or the audience chamber and attend to it. Or he would go out for a ride or to the Shalimar Gardens.

Despite what some have taken to be appearances to the contrary, Ranjit Singh never allowed himself to be distracted from the pressing problems of state. The degree of his personal day-to-day involvement in the administration of his realm can be gauged

from the fact that officials at every level, from the governor down-
wards, of what were in due course the four provinces (*subas*) of
the Sikh state – Lahore, Multan, Kashmir and Peshawar – were
under strict orders to report to him regularly on matters of
particular importance. The reports he received were carefully
screened for him by a hand-picked team of officials consisting of
a chief minister and a number of senior officials in charge of different departments under him. The departments consisted of
revenues received, state expenditure, the state treasury, levying and
collection of land revenue and taxes on incomes, customs and
transit duties, tributes and other incomings, forfeitures, fines and
such. An estimate of the revenues of Punjab in 1831 placed it at 30
million rupees.

All accounts bring out that Ranjit Singh kept himself constantly
and precisely informed about the affairs of his state. Aside from his
strict instructions on being kept regularly in touch on every matter of importance, one chronicler has recorded in detail 'how after
1823 Ranjit Singh devoted most of his time to visiting different districts and busying himself with the examination of decisions and
hearing complaints against the corruption of officials'.[5] One significant detail that has been recorded is that 'the finances of the Sikh
kingdom were regulated on the simplest basis of keeping the
expenditure within the limit of revenue. If the revenue of the kingdom declined owing to some unexpected circumstances, expenses
were curtailed proportionately. No effort was made to meet such
deficit by means of borrowing, but the simple method of asking
the State employees to accept a voluntary cut was used.'[6]

One of many who witnessed Ranjit Singh's diligence in his
everyday work, Dr W.L. McGregor, a British army surgeon who was
also at hand during the First Anglo-Sikh War, records that 'should
the affairs of the State require his attention, Runjit is ready at all
times during the day and night; and it is not unusual for him to
order his secretary and prime minister to carry the designs on

which he has been meditating during the night into execution before daybreak'.[7] One English traveller based in Kabul, Sir Alexander Burnes, who met the Maharaja in the latter years of his life, records that he 'never quitted the presence of a native of India with such impressions as I left this man. Without education and without a guide he conducts all the affairs of his kingdom with surprising energy and vigour, and yet he wields his power with a consideration quite unprecedented in an Indian prince.'[8]

Equally unprecedented – since most monarchs avoided it – was the enthusiasm with which he personally led his forces. According to a Captain Leopold Von Orlich, 'In battle, he was always seen at the head of his troops and foremost in combat; he twice crossed the Indus with his cavalry, in the very face of the enemy, and gained victory. In energy, will and endurance he was unequalled by any of his people . . . The want of education was covered by the splendid mental powers with which nature had endowed him, and prudence and knowledge of mankind enabled him to maintain himself in his high station.'[9] Charles Metcalfe, the British envoy negotiating the Sutlej Treaty with Ranjit Singh in 1808, noted the impact he made on those he led: 'His command in his army is as implicitly obeyed as perhaps it could be among the best disciplined troops. Every private or footman is compelled to look upon him as his master, whatever Chief he may immediately be attached to, and the Chiefs are as much subject to receive orders as the private soldiers.'[10]

As one chronicler pointed out, 'Ranjit Singh rarely remains fifteen days in the same place.' When he did stay for a stretch of time in Lahore, his evenings could be as unpredictable as the foregoing day. In fact, sometimes his days never ended, for he would go on working late into the night. On days when he was able to break away, however, he would repair to the ladies' quarters for relaxation and revelry. Some of his favourite courtesans would serve his special wine to him as he reclined on his bolsters, while others would dance to the tune of stringed instruments, flutes and drums. It is recorded that once he was so struck by the celebrated flute-player Attar Khan that he spent almost four hours listening to him late into the night.

His own dinner, by all accounts, was a fairly spartan affair; he avoided red meats, venison and such. For guests, on the other hand, a most impressive array of dishes and exotic foods would be served, and his wines would leave many a foreign guest literally unable to keep up. What left foreigners baffled was Ranjit Singh's complete indifference to the drinks they presented him with, such as claret, hock, port and champagne, although he is said to have acquired a liking for whisky. His evenings with his ladies would often extend past midnight, and, since he was accustomed to wake up early in the morning, the total number of hours he slept out of twenty-four customarily numbered four to six.

What greatly helped Ranjit Singh strengthen the nation he had just founded was his statesmanship in handling the British. It is astonishing that someone so young and unversed in the ways of colonial powers should have risen with such aplomb to the challenge of dealing with the British, with their suave ways, boundless ambition and experienced and efficient army equipped with sophisticated weapons.

When in 1801 Ranjit Singh became head of the Punjab State, the British were already firmly ensconced in Delhi. Even though the Mughals still existed in name, they counted for very little by that time. It was Britain's writ that prevailed over most of India up to Delhi. Beyond Delhi Ranjit Singh was the man to reckon with. Even at that early stage, when he was barely twenty-two, his designs for the future were on a grand scale. His intention was to exercise his exclusive writ over northern India, the north-western provinces, the hill states and the mountain ranges up to the

Khyber Pass. This vast territory was outside British control. Nor was it under the control of any single authority, although the Sikh nation was the most powerful in that part of the subcontinent. But the Afghans possessed the most prosperous cities and towns and controlled major trade routes. They also had sizeable armies to enforce their writ. Then there were many other big and small Hindu and Muslim chiefs, aside from the tribes in the north-west who were a law unto themselves – as they have remained up to the present day.

The only obstacle left between the British and their dominance of the whole of India was the land of the five rivers under Sikh rule. They had shrewdly observed the fighting qualities of the Sikhs, fuelled by their religious beliefs and certainties and sustained by their amazing self-confidence. So it was clearly not in the British self-interest to get involved in any military showdown with them at this stage. Ranjit Singh, too, was canny enough to appreciate the importance of creating a well-defined boundary between British possessions and the Sikh state. Both sides were perfectly aware of the advantages of this. But, as so often happens, the twists and turns of fate were to play their part in influencing events.

When contact was established between the British governor-general Lord Wellesley and Ranjit Singh at the beginning of the new century, it coincided with developments that favoured Ranjit Singh. Wellesley, who had taken office in May 1798 at the age of thirty-eight, was the paterfamilias of the colonial expansionists. Aggressive and ambitious as they come, he publicly proclaimed that British rule was undoubtedly in the best interests of the ruled. 'I can declare my conscientious conviction', he wrote, 'that no greater blessing can be conferred on the . . . inhabitants of India than the extension of the British authority, influence and power.'[11] True to form, Wellesley set about adding Mysore, Tanjore, Surat and Oudh to the increasing number of British holdings in India. Because these territories lay in south, central and western

India, no attempt was made to show the flag in northern India or to the ruler of the new Sikh kingdom.

But Wellesley's enthusiasm for expansionism was not received well by the directors of the East India Company in London. They were in India to make money through profitable trading, but with the Company constantly at war because of 'their local Manager's persistent disregard of the spirit of his orders', its treasury was being seriously depleted. After watching its stocks falling steadily with no dividends coming in, the Company decided to eliminate the cause of their problem. Wellesley was accordingly recalled in July 1805.

His successor, Marquess Cornwallis, died within months of taking over his post. It was when the next governor-general, Lord Minto, assumed office in July 1807 that Ranjit Singh's awareness of British designs on India took on a keener edge. He now realized that although their aim in India was to build up their trade, an aim which they had pursued – aside from a few hiccups – with considerable success, they were now moving on to outright conquest.

General Lake, who in 1803 had defeated the Marathas, who had opposed the British under Holkar and pursued them across the trans-Sutlej states, had been persuaded by the Sikh chieftains of that area, jealous of Ranjit Singh's growing power, of the danger he could pose to the Company. Lord Lake seemed receptive to these voices, and one seasoned British administrator of the time reflects what must have been the British army's response to the propaganda of the cis-Sutlej chieftains in his comment that 'the prospect of a big fight was cheering'.[12] Bemused by a long-held belief in their own invincibility, the British administrators and officers were convinced that the wild men on their horses who were opposing them on the battlefield would easily be annihilated by the disciplined white troops. They would soon be wiser.

While Lake in pursuit of Holkar's troops had reached the banks of the Beas and got a feel of the terrain, young Ranjit Singh had not been idle. Through his intelligence network which he had begun to assemble early on in his rule, combined with his common sense, he assessed far more accurately than most the threat the British would eventually pose to the Sikh kingdom. Taking advantage of the presence of General Lake's troops on the Beas, he paid a secret visit to the English camp and noted 'the machine-like drill of the sepoy battalions, the mobility of the Company's artillery, and the solidity of the British regiments, horse and foot'.[13] In all likelihood, it was this secret visit to the British army camp that convinced Ranjit Singh of the need to introduce into his own military formations those weapons, battle tactics, training methods and innovative ideas that had given the Europeans a lead over the armies of Asia and even, in due course, to recruit European officers to help achieve this. He henceforth made a point of assembling material and systematically updating his intelligence about the British in India, which helped him to develop his own insights into their moves, motives and methodology.

It is timely to interrupt the diplomatic story for a glimpse at the military forces Ranjit Singh had at his disposal at this time. His army consisted essentially of irregular cavalry, the Ghorchurras, made up mostly from soldiers from the *misls*, the Misldar Sowars. Distinct from these was a cavalry regiment called the Ghorchurra Khas, the first standing unit that Ranjit Singh formed as Maharaja, composed of leading Sardars and their kinsmen, eventually numbering up to 2,000 men; together with a similar regiment formed later it became known to admiring foreign visitors as 'the Maharaja's bodyguard' and was considered the elite of the Sikh army.

The men of the Misldar Sowars had been taken into the Sikh state's service after the capture of a fort or town or the death of a chief, a process that went on for most of the Maharaja's life. These men were paid by the state – at first entirely in *jagirs*, since they looked on cash payment as the mark of mercenaries; only gradually did Ranjit Singh succeed in his desire to make cash payment the norm, so putting the force on a more regular footing. These Ghorchurras came to constitute the bulk of Ranjit Singh's cavalry, their style continuing the traditions of the Dal Khalsa. Not subject to overall discipline or wearing uniform, resisting the introduction of European drill and methods to which they contemptuously referred as 'harlots' dancing', they retained their local character; they wore mail shirts and a belt from which hung a bag containing musket balls; some wore a steel helmet and bore a shield on their back. Their charges were swift and deadly. Near the enemy they would halt, load, fire their matchlocks and retire, repeating the operation several times.[14]

Besides the state-paid Gorchurras, Ranjit Singh had at his disposal the lower-grade feudal army made up of the forces maintained by the local Sardars – those who held *jagirs*, the *jagirdars* – each of whom undertook to provide, when called upon, a contingent according to the size of his landholding. Until the 1830s, when the Sardars were called upon to provide infantry and artillery as well, these forces consisted entirely of cavalry.

Around 1805 Ranjit Singh was ready to begin to lay the foundations of a regular army, the Fauj-i-ain, alongside his irregular forces, with his first infantry units. By 1808 there were five battalions (1,500 men in all). When Metcalfe saw these units, consisting of only around 300 ununiformed men in each (distinguished only by a scarlet turban), armed with 'swords and a mixture of European muskets and traditional matchlocks', he was not impressed.[15] It took a decade and a half for Sikh infantry to reach any sizeable strength and in larger battalions: around 2,800 men in 1811, 7,750 in 1819, nearly 12,000 in 1823. The total strength of this branch of Ranjit Singh's army stood at just under 30,000 at his death in 1839.[16]

With continuing Sikh aversion to infantry, the ranks were at first filled mainly with Hindus, Muslims, Gurkhas and Afghans. The Hindu Diwan Ganga Ram commanded the infantry until his death in 1826, but Ranjit Singh took a particular pride in it; by 1813 it had become effective enough for a decisive defeat of the Afghans under the leadership of Diwan Mokham Chand at Chuch outside Attock. The Sikh infantryman's powers of endurance were admired by foreign observers; he could subsist on very small quantities of food and could rapidly cover a lot of ground. The 'iron-legged' Sikh infantry in its developed state was distinctly more manoeuvrable than the British.

In Ranjit Singh's first years as head of the Sukerchakia *misl*, only the strongest *misls* possessed artillery of any kind, most often taking the form of camel-mounted swivel-guns, *zamburaks* ('wasps') of one-inch calibre and firing shot of about one pound. Artillery was as generally unpopular as infantry with the Sikhs; it was looked on as an encumbrance to the movement of the horsemen, besides the problem of lack of trained personnel. When Ranjit Singh came to power as ruler of Punjab in 1801, he inherited a battery of six field guns commanded by an Afghan, Ghaus Khan, and immediately realized the importance of artillery. He created an artillery corps in 1804, divided into heavy (bullock-drawn), light (horse-drawn) and camel-drawn artillery. At first this force was built up with guns taken over from captured forts and towns, but in 1807 foundries were established in Lahore and Amritsar which eventually mass-produced copies of British guns received as diplomatic gifts. The largest guns in Ranjit Singh's possession were captured eighteenth-century Muslim pieces firing up to 84-pound shot. Artillerymen were mostly Hindus, with ordnance factories employing a high proportion of Muslim workmen from Delhi.

The most unruly element in Ranjit Singh's army were the Akali horsemen, also known as Nihangs, the 'Immortals', descendants of Guru Gobind Singh's armed guards of the faith and keepers of the Golden Temple, by now fanatical fundamentalists. They lived an itinerant life, existing on charity or simply helping themselves. These irregulars were Ranjit Singh's shock troops, coming to number about 4,000; they were gradually absorbed into his army and used as mounted infantry on the most dangerous missions. Here are two eyewitness descriptions of these ferocious and almost uncontrollable soldiers. According to a Sikh official, the Akali was a man 'whose body is unaffected by pain or comfort. He is a man of firm faith, sexual restraint, meditation, penance and charity, and a complete warrior. In the presence of worldly authority, he remains full of pride. . . [In battle,] having no fear of death, he never steps back.'[17] To W.G. Osborne 'They are religious fanatics, and acknowledge no ruler and no laws but their own; think nothing of robbery, or even murder, should they happen to be in the humour for it. They move about constantly, armed to the teeth, and it is not an uncommon thing to see them riding about with a drawn sword in each hand, two more in their belt, a matchlock on their back, and three or four pairs of quoits fastened round their turbans.'[18] These 'quoits' were sharp-edged steel rings some six to nine inches in diameter, thrown after being spun round the forefinger; it was claimed they could lop off a limb or slice through a neck at sixty to eighty yards, although according to some accounts they were thrown 'with more force than dexterity'.[19]

The Akalis hated Europeans and Muslims and hurled abuse at them whenever they encountered them. Marching past the Maharaja on parades, they would shout insults at him and throw musket balls at his feet, disapproving of his tolerant attitude towards the British. Ranjit Sigh bore this patiently, but if any crime was committed he would see that due punishment was exacted by the removal of a nose, ear or limb according to the seriousness of the crime.[20] These 'military madmen', as Henry Edward Fane, an aide-de-camp to his uncle Sir Henry Fane, Commander-in-Chief of the East India Company's army, described them, even made more than one attempt on their sovereign's life. He always took care to prevent their concentration in large numbers, dispersing them among different regiments when necessary.

❦

While the Maharaja was attending to the state of his army, the East India Company, having solved the Wellesley problem, had another concern – the treaty signed by Napoleon and Tsar Alexander I at Tilsit in July 1807. London viewed this treaty as a threat to the British hold on India, especially as Persia had also been persuaded by the French to grant passage to a French army should Napoleon decide to attack India.

It is held by some that it was around this time that Ranjit Singh began to give serious thought to the need to establish a demarcation line between British territories and the Sikh kingdom. Perhaps the Jamuna or the Sutlej rivers could provide that line. He was not unaware of British concerns about Napoleon's victories in Europe and the distinct possibility of his making plans to annex India. If he was right in his assessment, then the British would prefer a strong Sikh state to hold an enemy at bay. And the Sikhs had proved their ability to expel intruders from India. So he was keen to turn the French threat to his advantage.

The incoming governor-general Lord Minto was as convinced of the likelihood of hostile French moves against India as were the mandarins in London, and soon after he took up office in the summer of 1807 the British opened negotiations for a treaty with the Lahore Darbar. In 1803, while they were debating whether the River Jamuna or the Sutlej should be the dividing line between the British and Sikh spheres of control, Ranjit Singh had already suggested the Sutlej as the natural frontier between them. This boundary had the disadvantage of splitting Punjab, leaving many cities, towns and regions south of the river, such as Ludhiana, Kapurthala, Jind, Patiala, Nabha, and Faridkot, outside the Sikh state. But Ranjit Singh had much bigger plans for his Sikh empire beyond the Punjab.

Wellesley's indecision on which boundary to agree on had given Ranjit Singh the opportunity he needed, and the justification for making the most of it. He crossed the Sutlej in 1806, 1807 and 1808 and each time not only added new territories to his state south of it but redistributed some of the lands to win allies. The British continued to debate treaty terms that would suit them best, and Ranjit Singh complicated the matter for them by being unwilling to sacrifice Sikh interests south of the Sutlej to the British. In 1808, after the governor-general had received intelligence that the French were planning the conquest of Kabul and Punjab, the British government accordingly decided to dispatch envoys to both Lahore and Kabul. Mr Charles Theophilus Metcalfe was chosen to conduct negotiations with Lahore and a rising member of the British political service in India, Mountstuart Elphinstone, with Kabul.[21] Metcalfe was the younger of the two, aged only twenty-three. Born in Calcutta, he was the son of a director of the East India Company, whose service Metcalfe had entered at the age of sixteen. He was assistant to the resident at Delhi, where the British held sway over the blind and infirm Mughal emperor Shah Alam, when he was called to Lahore. He was to develop into an able British administrator, but at this stage he had a lot to learn. The real purpose of the mission he headed was 'to initiate a penetration of the Punjab',[22] although this was disguised as a response to the serious threat Napoleon was perceived to pose to India.

The eight months following Metcalfe's crossing of the Sutlej on 1 September 1808 were stormy so far as his negotiations with Ranjit Singh were concerned. His brief was twofold: to alert Ranjit Singh to the imminent danger of a French invasion from the north and to make him agree to accepting Britain's suzerainty over all the territories south of the Sutlej. Ranjit Singh found this demand impudent and proved himself more than a match for Metcalfe in the art of negotiation. He was not as inexperienced as the British had hoped. Easily seeing through the Napoleon ruse, he expressed his complete willingness to side with the British in the event of a French invasion. But English suzerainty south of the Sutlej was quite a different matter. A rueful British comment on Metcalfe's inability to make full use of the French card aptly summed it up:

'In this wild encampment the bogey of Napoleon could not look so convincing as in the dining rooms of Calcutta and Delhi.'[23]

Ranjit Singh brushed aside the envoy's talk about British commitments to the Sikh chiefs south of the Sutlej. Indeed, he went a step further. After their meeting at Kasur, on the north bank of the river, Metcalfe, on waking up the next morning, found that Ranjit Singh and his force had moved on and left word for him to follow. The highly indignant envoy, left with no option, reluctantly rode after Ranjit Singh and caught up with him the next day. The discussions that followed, although affable, did not serve the British purpose at all. To add to British discomfiture, Ranjit Singh, with Metcalfe following him around, set about straightening out some recalcitrant Phulkian states, starting with Faridkot, which surrendered on 1 October 1808. In the two months or so that Ranjit Singh campaigned south of the Sutlej he annexed not only Faridkot but Shahabad and Ambala. While he shrewdly kept the talks with Metcalfe in progress, he made sure they were held while he was on the move – which was all the time – because the obvious message this sent to the Phulkian chiefs was that the British were a party to Ranjit Singh's designs on them. Why else would their envoy be by his side all the time? In fact the Patiala chief, who now looked on the British as his protectors, was described by the British resident in Delhi as 'labouring at this moment under the most cruel anxiety' lest Ranjit Singh attack him.

Thoroughly exasperated by Ranjit Singh's diplomacy-on-the-run since it made them look quite silly, the British decided they did not want to keep up with Ranjit Singh's momentum but, rather, gain time to find their own feet, especially as their latest assessment showed that the danger of French invasion of India was receding, and having Ranjit Singh as a buffer between British India and possible invaders from the north was now less important to their interests. From a position of 'scrupulous non-intervention' they could not now 'resist the conviction that the interests and security of the British Government would be best promoted by the reduction, if not the entire subversion of [Ranjit Singh's] power'.[24]

To warn Ranjit Singh of their displeasure, and send a signal of their clout to him, a Lieutenant-Colonel David Ochterlony was dispatched with an expeditionary force to a point south of the Sutlej so as to underscore the extent to which the territories between the Jamuna and the Sutlej were now British protectorates. At the same time Metcalfe, too, was withdrawn from Ranjit Singh's side and asked to camp some way off. On returning to Lahore at the end of 1808 and being told of the new aggressiveness in British moves south of the Sutlej, Ranjit Singh ordered General Mohkam Chand to proceed with a force to Phillaur, which lay north of the Sutlej facing Ludhiana on the south bank. The British in turn ordered Ochterlony to Ludhiana.

Suddenly British intelligence reports indicated a renewal of French interest in India. The British commander-in-chief was quietly told to withdraw his military force from its advance position; Ranjit Singh had again become important as the redoubtable defender of northern India. Reflecting this pragmatic view of their self-interest, the British now put forward terms for a treaty of 'perpetual friendship' with the Sikhs, and the Sutlej Treaty was signed on 25 April 1809. According to its provisions the Lahore Durbar would not relinquish its sovereignty over the territories acquired by it south of the Sutlej prior to 1806. The 'perpetual friendship', according to the treaty, would rest on these four main clauses: that the British would leave control of the territories north of the Sutlej to the Sikh state; Ranjit Singh would not maintain 'more troops than are necessary for the internal duties' of his territories south of the Sutlej; he would 'not commit or suffer any encroachments on the possessions or rights of the chiefs in its vicinity'; in the event of a violation of these articles, or a 'departure from the rules of friendship', the treaty would be considered terminated.

THE TREATY WITH LAHORE OF 1809

Treaty between the British Government and the Raja of Lahore (dated 25th April 1809)

Whereas certain differences which had arisen between the British Government and the Raja of Lahore have been happily and amicably adjusted; and both parties being anxious to maintain relations of perfect amity and concord, the following articles of treaty, which shall be binding on the heirs and successors of the two parties, have been concluded by the Raja Ranjit Singh in person, and by the agency of C.T. Metcalfe, Esquire, on the part of the British Government.

Article 1. – Perpetual friendship shall subsist between the British Government and the State of Lahore: the latter shall be considered, with respect to the former, to be on the footing of the most favoured powers, and the British Government will have no concern with the territories and subjects of the Raja to the northward of the river Sutlej.

Article 2. – The Raja will never maintain on the territory which he occupies on the left bank of the river Sutlej more troops than are necessary for the internal duties of that territory, nor commit or suffer any encroachments on the possessions or rights of the Chiefs in its vicinity.

Article 3. – In the event of a violation of any of the preceding articles, or of a departure from the rules of friendship, this treaty shall be considered null and void.

Article 4. – This treaty, consisting of four articles, having been settled and concluded at Amritsar, on the 25th day of April 1809, Mr C.T. Metcalfe has delivered to the Raja of Lahore a copy of the same in English and Persian, under his seal and signature; and the Raja has delivered another copy of the same under his seal and signature, and C.T. Metcalfe engages to procure within the space of two months a copy of the same, duly ratified by the Right Honourable the Governor-General in Council, on the receipt of which by the Raja, the present treaty shall be deemed complete and binding on both parties, and the copy of it now delivered to the Raja shall be returned.

[Ratified by the Governor-General
Lord Minto on 21 May 1809]

The British fully honoured the treaty in the early years despite being irked by the rapid expansion of the Sikh state. They turned down appeals for help against Ranjit Singh from both Sansar Chand of Kangra and the Gurkhas. During the first unsuccessful siege of Multan in 1810 by the Lahore Durbar, the beleaguered city's governor was similarly told that in view of the treaty there was little the British could do to help him.

The British were to adhere to the treaty, to Ranjit Singh's advantage, on other occasions as well. In 1819 Kashmir's Afghan governor Azim Khan pleaded with them to place Kashmir under their protection but was refused. Shah Zaman and Shah Shuja, who also asked for British intervention, were turned down. When an over-zealous British envoy to Afghanistan, Alexander Burnes, tried to persuade Company officials to help the Afghans take back Peshawar from Ranjit Singh, the British governor-general Lord Auckland, after some thought, turned down the suggestion.

How did the British view the treaty when it came to serving their interests? According to Captain Claude Wade, British political agent at Ludhiana: 'Ranjit Singh has hitherto derived nothing but advantage from his alliance with us. While we have been engaged in consolidating our power in Hindustan, he has been extending his conquests throughout the Punjab and across the Indus, and as we are now beginning to prescribe limits to his power, which it cannot be supposed he will regard with complacency, he is now more likely to encourage than to withdraw from an alliance, which may hold out to him a hope of creating a balance of power.'[25]

In the final summing up, did the Sutlej Treaty benefit Ranjit Singh more than it did the British? A consideration of the different mindsets of the two signatories will help to begin to answer this question. The British, of course, were pastmasters in the art of diplomacy; they were able to judge precisely where their self-interest lay and had centuries of experience in wars, battles, victories, defeats, annexations, treaties and much else. Ranjit Singh, by contrast, a school drop-out in his twenties, had no experience of negotiating treaties or dealing with Europeans. Yet, relying entirely on his own unaided perception and evaluation, he arrived at a clear and intelligent assessment of his adversary's strengths. After the eight-month negotiations he got what he wanted from the treaty.

Having witnessed how the British had dealt with the Marathas in 1803 after Jaswant Rao Holkar had seized Delhi and ravaged the East India Company's territories between the Jamuna and the Sutlej, he had a prime example to go by. Holkar had got no help from the Punjab Sardars of that region, and subsequently he had been defeated and forced to come to terms with the British. The conclusion Ranjit Singh drew from this was that he could never build up his Sikh state without accurately assessing his own limitations against his adversary's advantages.

Some of his critics suggest that the treaty showed him in a poor light since he abandoned all the Sikhs living between the Jamuna and the Sutlej, but this is to discount his strategy and his vision for the future. He wanted the Sikh state to extend far beyond the boundaries of the Punjab. He had his eyes on prized Afghan possessions all the way up to Kabul, as also other vast territories in northern India. So the first article of the treaty assured him that the British government would not concern itself with his territorial acquisitions north of the River Sutlej. It was because of his decisive victories against the Afghans that he was able to seal the routes through which invaders had entered India over the centuries. Had he not signed the treaty and secured his southern boundary effectively, he could not have achieved what he did so spectacularly.

Ranjit Singh's success as a statesman with regard to the Sutlej Treaty can only be judged with this consideration in mind. Even Metcalfe, who was often at odds with him and robustly represented British interests in the period preceding the finalization of the treaty, acknowledged his gain. His suave remark to the Maharaja on signing it, 'Your Excellency will reap the fruits of the alliance with the British in a period of twenty years',[26] was to be proved right – in fact in less than twenty years.

❦

With his southern border secured, Ranjit Singh now began to pursue his ambitions of strengthening and extending his kingdom in the north. Zaman Shah would give him little more trouble. On returning home after being ousted from Lahore he had been plunged back into the thick of court intrigues and as a consequence of his execution of a powerful tribal leader had been blinded by his own younger brother Mahmud. His other brother Shah Shuja had fled to India, taking with him, along with his hopes of regaining the Afghan throne, the famous Koh-i-noor diamond.

Shah Shuja sought Ranjit Singh's help to try to regain his kingdom. A cordial but wary Ranjit Singh was not keen on allowing a claimant to the Afghan throne to use Multan, on the south bank of the Ravi. as his base, which in the Sikh ruler's view was an integral part of India. So in a sudden assault on Multan city he invested it himself in February 1810, although Multan Fort under its brave commander Muzaffar Khan held out until it eventually fell to the Sikhs in early 1818.

Shah Shuja returned briefly to Kabul for a brief stint on the throne before being thrown out again. This time he headed for the northerly town of Attock as its governor Jahan Dad Khan's guest. It was an unwise choice because the governor, on learning that Shuja was in touch with Wazir Fateh Khan, the power behind the Afghan throne whom Dad Khan passionately hated, had Shuja manacled and dispatched to his brother, Ata Mohammed, governor of Kashmir. Shuja soon found himself in a dungeon, cut off from his wife Wafa Begum and his blinded brother Zaman Shah. Even though these two, now resident in Rawalpindi, were living on a pension they received from Ranjit Singh, Zaman Shah was busy intriguing with outside powers to regain his throne. Ranjit Singh had both families brought to Lahore where he could keep an eye on them. They were, however, honoured as state guests.

Shuja's wife, Wafa Begum, now entered upon the scene. Desperate over her husband's fate, she begged Ranjit Singh to rescue him from Ata Mohammed's hold in Kashmir before the latter dispatched him, in the style of her fellow Afghans. She offered Ranjit the Koh-i-noor diamond in return for sending a military expedition to Kashmir.[27]

Ranjit Singh, attracted by the idea, now turned his eyes to Kashmir which was a prized possession of the Afghans, who had in turn taken it from the Mughals in 1752. Ranjit Singh was drawn to it for many reasons. He was lured as much by its wondrous lakes, valleys, snow-covered peaks, saffron fields, flora, fauna and flowering trees as by its exquisite crafts – carpets, shawls, walnut woodwork, jewellery, sapphires, beautiful women and much else. In 1812 the excuse he needed for a dramatic entry into Kashmir was, ironically enough, again provided by the Afghans, just as in the case of Attock and Multan.

Wazir Fateh Khan of the Barakzai tribe in Afghanistan, who had caused Zaman Shah to be blinded, wanted to lay hands on Shah Shuja, possessor of the Koh-i-noor and currently the Kashmir governor's captive. But there was no way he could get to

Kashmir with his forces since Ranjit Singh's Sikh army stood in his way at Attock. So he had to ask Ranjit Singh for his help in the invasion of Kashmir. With the modalities carefully worked out to the advantage of the Lahore Darbar, the combined Sikh and Afghan forces headed for Shergarh where Shuja was imprisoned.

The man Ranjit Singh handpicked to command the Sikh army in this joint expedition was Diwan Mohkam Chand, an outstanding commander and wise in the ways of the world. It did not take him long to see through the game the Afghans were planning to play – to outpace Diwan Mohkam Chand, reach Shergarh before him and take custody not only of Shuja but of the treasury as well. The Diwan informed Ranjit Singh of this plan, who told him to outwit Fateh Khan and, if he persisted in his double-crossing, to deal with him accordingly.

Mohkam Chand rose to the occasion by taking a more precipitous but shorter route to Shergarh Fort and mounting an assault on it before the Afghans were anywhere in sight. Completely taken aback by being so easily outwitted, Fateh Khan hastened to join in the assault, and when Shergarh fell he and his men put their energies into looting the treasury while the Sikhs mounted a massive search for Shuja. On finding him they swiftly transferred him to the Sikh camp and from there to Lahore.

With Shah Shuja and Wafa Begum reunited in Lahore, the Koh-i-noor again became a bone of contention, this time between Shuja and Wafa on one side and Ranjit Singh on the other. Having promised the Koh-i-noor to Ranjit Singh when she was fearful for her husband's life, Wafa and her husband were now most reluctant to hand it over to their rescuer. But he had his way and took possession of it on 1 June 1813.

'Take five strong men,' said Shah Shuja to Ranjit Singh on being asked the value of the Koh-i-noor. 'Let the first throw a stone northward, the second eastward, the third southward, the fourth westward, and the fifth upward. Fill all the space thus outlined with gold and you will still not have achieved the value of the Mountain of Light.'[28]

The history of the Koh-i-noor diamond is as fascinating as the stone itself but can be only briefly touched on here. It was seized around 1306 from Rai Mahlak Deo, ruler of Malwa in the Deccan by Ala-ud-din Khilji, Delhi's ruling Sultan. Emperor Ibrahim Lodhi of the Lodhi Dynasty then acquired it for a time, before it was taken over by the Mughals. Babur records in his memoirs that 'every appraiser has estimated its value at two-and-a-half days' food for the whole world. Apparently it weighs eight misqals [approximately 188 carats]. Humayun [his son] offered it to me when I arrived at Agra; I just gave it back to him.'[29] Oval in shape, brilliant, colourless, around one and a quarter inches in length and just under one and a half inches in width, the Koh-i-noor came from the Golconda mines in south India, the source of other famous diamonds such as the great Mughal, the Orlov, the Pigot, Regent, Sancy and Hope. The Golconda diamond mines were situated five miles south of Hyderabad between the rivers Krishna and Godavari. The Koh-i-noor disappeared for a hundred years, then surfaced again in 1656 at the court of the Mughal Shah Jahan, who set it in his peacock throne. It was forcibly taken from the Mughals by the Persian Nadir Shah when he sacked Delhi in 1739 and slaughtered 100,000 Muslims and Hindus in eight hours. Nadir Shah is credited with naming the diamond Koh-i-noor, 'mountain of light' in Persian. When Nadir was hacked to death in a family coup in 1747, Ahmed Shah Abdali removed the Koh-i-noor from his body, and through him it eventually came into the possession of Shah Shuja.

✿

There was still unfinished business for Ranjit Singh to deal with. It concerned Fateh Khan's deceitful moves during the joint expedition to Shergarh. Ranjit Singh did not take kindly to duplicity. He asked his general Mohkam Chand to annex Attock. After the battle that took place at Haidru on 9 July 1813 the Sikh forces walked in without any resistance. Four months later Wazir Fateh Khan, embittered by the loss of a major invasion route which the Afghans had traditionally taken into India, resorted to letter-writing in lieu of armed retaliation. On 25 December 1813 he wrote to Mohkam Chand: 'Still nothing is lost. Give the fort of Attock to me so that the relations of friendship between the two parties may become strong.' Mohkam Chand replied: 'The fort of Attock will never be handed over to you, and the country of Kashmir will soon be conquered by us.'[30] Unable to reconcile himself to the loss of Attock, he died in 1818 still obsessed with getting it back.

While the incursion into Kashmir in 1812 had been a spin-off of the Koh-i-noor's seductive lure, the fall of Multan Fort in 1818 was due to another symbol of Afghan pride – the Zam Zama,[31] the great cannon. Rated as one of the most formidable cannons in the world, it had helped Ahmed Shah Abdali win the Battle of Panipat against the Marathas. If the Koh-i-noor was soon to fall into Ranjit Singh's hands, the legendary Zam Zama was already his, and in a supremely ironic turn of events the cannon Abdali had wanted to decimate his enemies with would now be turned by Ranjit Singh against the Afghans entrenched in Multan Fort. As the cannon tore gaping holes in the massive walls of the fort, the Nihangs, the fearsome Sikh warrior sect, launched their do-or-die attacks through them. The second of the four principal Afghan cities in India, following the annexation of Attock in 1813, was now in Sikh hands. Since Multan, a city of great antiquity from the time of Alexander the Great and a flourishing centre of trade, yielded considerable revenues, Ranjit Singh took care to appoint able governors to administer it. The third, Diwan Sawan Mal, appointed in 1821, was to be the most outstanding of all, holding the post for an unusually long spell of almost a quarter of a century.

The capitulation of Multan Fort, a significant victory at no less than a seventh attempt, was also a blot on the reputation of Ranjit Singh's army, known for its just treatment of vanquished foes. For some reason, never satisfactorily explained, the Sikh troops seemed to have lost their sense of self-restraint when the fort fell. Every house was searched and looted. Ranjit Singh ordered his forces to give up whatever they had taken and proclaimed the death penalty in case of default, but no evidence has survived as to whether the death penalty was ever actually carried out. Only some shawls, utensils, rich apparel, books and carpets worth a few lakhs of rupees were returned but no gold or silver coins or jewellery or precious objects.[32]

It is scarcely possible to list comprehensively all the territories Ranjt Singh annexed to the Sikh state, because in addition to outright annexations many were left under the political and administrative control of their chieftains or rulers while being under his suzerainty and subject to a tribute they paid annually to him until they were eventually taken over. Other such interim arrangements, with many variations, were also entered into. Some idea of how the Sikh empire grew out of this bewildering chequerboard of territorial acquisitions can be had from a glimpse provided over a nine-year period by the Sikh historian J.S. Grewal – the years between the Treaty of Amritsar signed in 1809 and the conquest of Multan in 1818. It was during this period, and the conquest of Kashmir and the north-west in the 1820s and 1830s, that Ranjit Singh's realm emerged into an entity that may truly be termed an empire.

Grewal lists a number of towns which are familiar Sikh place-names:

> The Sikh territories annexed by Ranjit Singh included Hariana, Jalalpur, Manawar, Islamgarh, Bajwat, Gujrat, Chunian, Dipalpur, Satghara, Jethpur, Haveli, Muhiyuddinpur, Jalandhar, Patti, Fatehgarh, Sujanpur, Hajipur, Mukerian, Rawalpindi, Sri Hargobindpur and Miani . . . The Hindu

territories annexed by Ranjit Singh included Kangra, Sayyidgarh, Kotla, Jandiala, Samba, Kathua, Guler, Nurpur and Jaswan. With the exception of Jandiala, all these territories were in the hills close to the plains. In the process, about half a dozen chiefs were subverted, and the most powerful hill principalities of Kangra and Jammu suffered diminution. . . . The Muslim territories annexed by Ranjit Singh included Khushab, Kachh, Sahiwal, Kusk, Attock, Makhad, Jhang, Tulamba and Kot Nau. In the process, some Baloch and Sial chiefs were subverted and the rulers of Bahawalpur, Multan and Kabul lost some of their territories. Thus, before the conquest of Multan, the lower hills and upper and middle portions of all the five doabs fell under the effective control of Maharaja Ranjit Singh.[33]

There was little doubt in anyone's mind that with the Sikhs' conquest of Multan – the richest addition yet to their state – the next in line would be Kashmir, the second richest. And indeed, the very next year, on 3 July 1819, Sikh forces defeated the Afghan army led by its governor, Azim Khan, in a hard-fought battle at Supaiya; once again it was the Nihangs who decided the day, with their do-or-die charge against the Afghan horsemen and infantry. The remnants of the shattered Afghans fled into the hills, and the Sikh forces entered Kashmir's principal city, Srinagar, on 5 July. With the Afghans on the run from most of Punjab, Ranjit Singh's thoughts now turned increasingly to the North-West Frontier, the gateway to Afghanistan and Central Asia, Peshawar being the pivotal town of this wild and unruly region. But before he launched any major moves in this direction the administration of Kashmir had to be placed on a sound footing.

Srinagar was made the capital of the Kashmir Valley, and from it the governors appointed by the Lahore court would administer this vast region. That a great deal had to be done in Kashmir after

years of Afghan misrule is graphically expressed in this quatrain by
Gwasha Lal Kaul:

> *Khwast Haq keh in zamin-e-mina rang,*
> *Chun dil-e-nai shawad ba fughan rang,*
> *Kard bar wai musallat Afghan ra*
> *Bagh-e-Jamshed dad dahqan ra.*
> (God willed that this enchanting land
> Should become stinking like the smoking
>   reed pipe with lamentation;
> Placed it under the control of Afghans,
> Gave away the garden of Eden to the vulgar.)[34]

The first of the governors appointed to improve conditions in the
woefully run and neglected valley, Moti Ram, was the son of
Diwan Mohkam Chand, who had outmanoeuvred Wazir Fateh
Khan in the rescue of Shah Shuja. He gave priority to the restoration of law and order and the administration of even-handed
justice; he was considered an outstanding governor, compassion-
ate, popular and by all accounts incorruptible. Kirpa Ram also had
a reputation for honesty and good governance and did much to
add to Srinagar's appeal by laying out beautiful gardens such as
the Rambagh Garden and another on the west side, Bud Dal (on
Dal Lake) at the village of Badmarg, which is named after him, the
Diwan Kirpa Ram Ka Bagh.

Another outstanding governor of Kashmir under Ranjit Singh
was Hari Singh Nalwa. Like Ranjit Singh he was born in Gujranwala and lost his father at an early age, at seven. His grandfather
and father had fought alongside the Maharaja's father and grandfather, Sukerchakia chiefs Mahan Singh and Charat Singh. He had
distinguished himself as a soldier time and again, at the siege of
Kasur in 1807, Multan in 1810 and 1818 and Kashmir in 1819. He

was a no-nonsense man, a strict disciplinarian and considered at times to be too harsh. Yet he was a spiritualist, a reformer and a man with strong social concerns who constructed gurdwaras at Kathi Darwaza, Srinagar, Matan and Baramula, places that had been visited by Guru Hargobind. He did away with all the restrictions which the Afghans had imposed on Kashmiri pandits regarding worship, dress and various customs, freed Hindus who had been made to convert to Islam to return to their original religion and abolished *bega*, forced unpaid service by villagers to government officials. He encouraged the cultivation of saffron by reducing the government share in its production and enforced correct weights and measures. He accorded priority to the government's humanitarian responsibilities, especially during the famine of 1820–22, when at a time of complete economic, social and political chaos he geared the entire administrative machinery to a rescue operation.

Like Ranjit Singh, Hari Singh Nalwa has attracted adverse judgements from a number of historians. Syad Muhammad Latif, while acknowledging him as a good soldier, calls him a failure as an administrator and a tyrant. According to Henry T. Prinsep, Nalwa was removed from his post as governor because he was 'obnoxious to the inhabitants of Kashmir'. William Moorcroft accuses all Sikhs of looking on Kashmiris as little better than cattle.

What such comments from both contemporaries and later historians show, if not a deep-seated reluctance to give credit to the Sikhs or even a form of anti-Sikhism, is surely this, that it is rare to find accurate accounts of eventful times. The charges against Hari Singh Nalwa have been repeated among the voluminous commentary on Ranjit Singh – failure as an administrator, tyranny and much else, without any factual evidence. Who are we to believe when we are also told by a contemporary how much the Kashmiris benefited under Sikh rule in Kashmir? 'Before Ranjit Singh took possession of the valley, her trade routes were not safe and the costly shawls were often looted *en route* by the robbers. The Maharaja made special arrangements to safeguard the goods of the traders . . . In case of any loss of goods in transit, the traders were compensated. The trade routes were made safe to the extent that highway robberies became a thing of the past . . . The longest trade route was from Lahore to Petersburg via Kashmir.'[35]

Ranjit Singh devoted much attention to the shawl-making industry and helped promote this trade more than did any other foreign power. Shawl-weaving came to account for almost one-third of Kashmir's revenue. Some years later Russian shawl dealers started to visit Kashmir, although shawls intended for export to Russia had hitherto usually been dispatched via Kabul and Herat.

Ranjit Singh's agenda after Kashmir included the trans-Himalayan region of Ladakh, with its borders touching Kashmir, Baltistan and Tibet – a 30,000-square-mile tableland at a height of 14,000 feet, surrounded by mountain ranges 26,000 to 28,000 feet high. Its Buddhist population was of Mongolian descent, while its neighbour Baltistan, with its capital at Iskardu, was ruled by a Muslim prince, Ahmed Shah. Ranjit's governor of Jammu, the Dogra Gulab Singh, also had his eyes on Ladakh. An obsessively ambitious man, he annexed it in 1834 with Ranjit Singh's consent. Since the latter was a ruler few men in their right mind would cross, Gulab Singh stayed subservient to him during his lifetime, but after his death the wily Dogra was to show his true colours.

More importantly, Peshawar, the last major symbol of Afghan rule in northern India, was also very much on Ranjit Singh's agenda; but before that a number of lesser foreign territories throughout the Derajat belt had to be brought under Sikh rule. These included Dera Ghazi Khan, Dera Ismail Khan, Leiah, Mankera and Bannu. While the first two and the last lay west of the River Indus, the remaining two were located east of it. This entire region north-west of the Indus, whether part of Peshawar province or outside it, was of great importance to anyone with designs on the strategically important city of Peshawar located almost next to the Khyber Pass. So a year after annexing Kashmir, in 1820, Ranjit Singh personally led an expedition to Dera Ghazi Khan and invested this dependency of Kabul. It was a valuable acquisition since it brought Sikh forces nearer the route that Central Asians and Afghans had customarily taken into India on their way to its other rich regions and nearer realization of the Sikhs' aim of cutting it off altogether.

In the following year the busy trade centre of Dera Ismail Khan was annexed, and then, when the key fort of Mankera fell, its Afghan governor was made a feudatory of the Sikhs. After the capture of Leiah towards the end of the same year Ranjit Singh had the arid 1,650 square miles of Bannu district in his sights. Its annexation, accomplished in 1825, consolidated the hold of the Sikhs on this area west of the Indus inhabited by the most turbulent people who harboured a fierce hatred of Hindus and Sikhs. It was first made a tributary of the Dera Ismail Khan region before being brought under the direct control of Lahore in 1836. The warlike tribes of this volatile region – the Pathans, Baluchis, Sials, Awans, Saiyads, Qureshis and others – have lived by their own laws and codes of conduct for centuries. In establishing his sway over these formidable people, Ranjit Singh achieved a solution that has eluded the dominant powers of this part of the world in our own time, for whom the lawlessness of the area causes such grave problems.

Before the prized city of Peshawar was brought under Sikh control many more possessions of the Afghans and other regional chieftains were taken over: Kohat, Manzai, Rawalpindi, Bhera, Jhang, Kangra, Kasur, Waziristan – the land of the Waziri Pathans – and a number of others. Finally it was the turn of Peshawar.

Peshawar was perhaps the most strategically vital city in India at that time. It had been used as the gateway into the Indian subcontinent over the centuries by the Lodhis, Mughals, Durranis, Nadir Shah of Persia and many others. The name of this historic city has many variants. The Chinese pilgrim Hieun Tsang referred to it in the seventh century as Po-lu-sha-pu-lo, while the eleventh-century Muslim historian A.D. Alberuni called it Parshawar and sometimes Purshur. The Mughal emperor Babur referred to it as Parashawar, which was the name Akbar, too, preferred, although Akbar's court historian Abul Fazl used the name Peshawar (frontier town) as well. The original name of the city was Posha-pura, among the many other names it was given. It became the seat of Gandharan art and culture around the middle of the first millennium BC and an important fountainhead of the Buddhist faith, despite the alien environment in which it found itself. Several historians hold the view that Peshawar was a part of the Kushan Empire (first to third centuries AD).

In keeping with its critical strategic importance, the conquest of Peshawar demanded all of Ranjit Singh's tenacity and military skills. The first attack on it was launched from Attock in 1818 by his favourite general Hari Singh Nalwa. It was currently in the hands of the Barakzais, the powerful Afghan chiefs who had dispossessed the Durranis of it. The Barakzais, who had found it easy to defeat the Durranis, met their match in the combined Sikh forces which first occupied Peshawar on 20 November 1818. While its governor Yar Mohammad Khan Barakzai fled, the city's citizens raised a tribute of 25,000 rupees and offered it to Ranjit Singh for its pro-tection. He in turn appointed Jahan Dad Khan, former governor of Attock, to administer Peshawar. It was Ranjit Singh's frequent practice as his conquests multiplied to levy a yearly tribute on his fallen foes, instead of a policy of permanent occupation. He broke with this policy only if tribute was not paid on time or if the tributary tried to double-cross him. Since he treated his defeated adversaries fairly, he did not take well to any attempt to disregard agreements arrived at.

This, in fact, is what happened in the case of Peshawar. No sooner had Ranjit Singh left for Lahore after appointing Jahan Dad

Khan as governor when Yar Mohammad Khan returned to expel the latter. Because of his other priorities in the north, it took Ranjit Singh several years to address the situation, which he finally did on 14 March 1823, the opportunity being provided by the Afghans themselves. Muhammad Azim Khan, former governor of Kashmir, was now prime minister in Kabul, and he had no love lost for Ranjit Singh. He decided to assemble a formidable force to put an end to Ranjit Singh's spectacular career and advanced from Kabul towards Peshawar, to be met by the Sikh army at Nowshera.

As the *Gazetteer of the Peshawar District*, based on first-hand data, states: 'The Pathans fought with desperate valour, but could not make head against the superior numbers and discipline of the Sikhs; frequently rallying, however, upon some low hills adjacent, they bore down bravely upon the enemy, who began to waver towards evening, but regained their advantage when Ranjit Singh, seizing a standard, himself led them to victory. The last stand was made at sunset by a party of 200 Yusafzai, who fell gallantly fighting. In this action 10,000 Pathans are said to have been slain.'[35]

After the Battle of Nowshera, a victorious Ranjit Singh once again rode into Peshawar and with his customary liberality made Yar Muhammad Khan his tributary governor of Peshawar. The defeated prime minister of Afghanistan, Azim Khan, a broken man, unable to deal with the humiliation of this defeat, died soon afterwards.

The permanent Sikh occupation of Peshawar, however, was still years away. It was not until 1834 that the Sikhs brought it directly under the control of the Lahore Durbar. In the intervening years the Afghan rulers made repeated attempts to re-establish Kabul's suzerainty over the city, but Ranjit Singh always foiled them. In 1834, feeling it was time to take direct charge of Peshawar, he chose an able and trusted man to annex it, General Hari Singh Nalwa, who has been called 'the Murat of the Khalsa' – after Napoleon's brother-in-law and outstanding marshal of the French army. With a force of 9,000 men, Hari Singh crossed the Indus and took up an unexpected position to the west of Peshawar. His moves unnerved the Barakzai Sardars, who fled and left the city to the Sikhs. In 1835 the Afghans under Dost Mohammad made an unsuccessful attempt to retake Peshawar, but it remained a part of the Sikh kingdom with Hari Singh Nalwa in charge of it with a force of 10,000 men.

Nalwa, like Murat, was known as a general's general, and living up to his reputation he soon initiated a project to build a fort at Jamrud, which dominates the entrance to the Khyber Pass. Within a year of its construction in 1836, the resentful Kabul regime, furious at the audacity of the Sikhs even to think of building a fort in their territory, overlooking the traditional route they had taken into India for centuries, mounted an attack against it with a large force. They opened up with their guns on the walls of the fort and were about to begin an assault when Hari Singh, who had held back until the enemy advanced, suddenly fell upon them with his customary vigour, broke their ranks without much loss and put them to flight.[37]

Soon, however, with the arrival of Afghan reinforcements the ebb and flow of battle resumed with intensity. The outcome was in favour of the Sikhs but at a terrible cost – the death of Hari Singh Nalwa. Badly wounded, this great warrior died the same night. His contribution to upholding the valour of the Khalsa is reflected to this day in the inscription still to be seen on the inner gateway of the Bala Hisar or High Fort of Peshawar:

Victory to Purakh [the Supreme Being]. Through grace of Sri Akal. Under the liberal government of Maharaja Ranjeet Singh Bahadur over the region of Peshawar, in the year [Vikram Samvat] 1891 [AD 1834].[38]

4

Campaigns, Conquests and Consolidation

The truly enlightened ones
Are those who neither incite fear in others
Nor fear anyone themselves.

GURU GRANTH SAHIB, Slok, 16, p. 1427

Many writers have been at pains to give credit for some of Ranjit Singh's dazzling military victories to the European officers serving under him. But in fact, these officers were recruited only from 1822, and much before that many campaigns using forces made up of Sikhs and other citizens of Punjab had been fought, especially against the Afghans, battle-tested and bloodied fighters steeped for generations in a tradition of relentless armed conflict. Ranjit Singh was used to winning victories and calling the shots unaided well before the year 1822 in which Jean-François Allard and Jean-Baptiste Ventura arrived in Lahore.

He was in no doubt over the exceptional fighting qualities of the Sikhs and their courage and commitment on the battlefield, against the British or any other adversaries. But he was also aware of the need for other inputs and that his armies lacked modern weapons which the British and other Western powers had in plenty. He had been well aware since his secret nocturnal visit to General Lake's camp on the Beas during the British campaign against the Marathas in 1803 that his forces' effectiveness could be considerably enhanced with newer and more advanced methods of training and a stronger sense of discipline and order. He hired foreign military instructors from early in his reign, mostly from within the subcontinent, including Anglo-Indians. The end of the Napoleonic Wars in 1815 released a ready supply of European professional soldiers, and a number of these entered the Maharaja's service from the 1820s as officers, those who had served under Napoleon being especially selected. He endlessly grilled those he knew could contribute towards the efficiency of his armies, since he had no problems with learning from others.

He was not to be taken in by smooth and facile statements and reviewed with the utmost care the pedigree of those who sought to enter his service, and even after they had effectively answered his barrage of questions he had them investigated still more thoroughly. When Allard and Ventura appeared before him, he had heard that they had both served in Napoleon's army, but to satisfy himself still further he had them checked out by his own men to eliminate the danger of moles. When he was convinced of their integrity, Allard was given a responsible position with the Sikh cavalry and Ventura with the infantry.

Jean-François Allard, a Frenchman with an impressive background, had fought in Naples, Spain and Portugal before joining Napoleon's Imperial Guard. Starting with the command of a company of a hundred men, Allard rose to be the senior general in Ranjit Singh's cavalry. Jean-Baptiste Ventura, an Italian, had an equally sound record and had served in Napoleon's army under Joachim Murat, Marshal of France. After Waterloo he had served in Turkey and Egypt, and when he met Allard in Tehran they both decided to go to India. A few years younger than Allard, Ventura was a colourful character; married to a Muslim woman, he kept a sizeable harem and had a roving eye. After serving with distinction for seventeen years he died in Peshawar of a heart attack in 1839. Ranjit Singh, who was himself seriously ill at the time, was not told of his death as it was feared it might prove too much for him because of the extent of his affection and regard for Allard. Ventura served on after Ranjit Singh's death and retired in 1843. During his career with the Lahore Darbar he fought against the Afghans in 1823, in Kangra in 1828 and at Peshawar in 1832, also being appointed, successively, governor of Derajat and Lahore.

Two other generals who served Ranjit Singh with distinction were Paolo di Batolomeo Avitabile and Claude-Auguste Court. Both, like Allard and Ventura, had served in Napoleon's army. Avitabile joined the Sikh army in 1826 and Court in 1827. Avitabile, over six feet tall and inclined to stoutness, spoke fluent Persian, Hindustani, French and Italian. Further to his other appointments, he was made governor of Wazirabad in 1829 and of Peshawar in 1837. Court, a short, plump, well-dressed man with a pockmarked face, trained the Gurkhas serving in the Sikh army and provided major impetus to the development of the artillery. Figures vary regarding how many Europeans served in Ranjit Singh's army, although the number of forty-two is generally agreed upon. Of these twelve were Frenchmen, four Italians, four Germans, three Americans, two Spaniards, one Russian, one Scot, three Englishmen, seven Anglo-Indians, and there were five others.

After a period of induction during which they familiarized themselves with all aspects of the Sikh army, Ranjit Singh gave Allard and Ventura sweeping authority to organize new units, advise on the appointment of new officers and introduce French drill and training throughout the regular army. The change to the Fauj-i-ain, using French terminology and words of command, with beat of drum, in place of the existing system modelled on the British, took more than a decade to accomplish. The steady increase in the strength of the Sikh army's infantry and cavalry up to and beyond Ranjit Singh's death can be substantially attributed to the impetus provided by these two. Another change they brought about was a restructuring of the Fauj-i-ain introducing the larger unit of the brigade.

Together with Avitabile, Allard and Ventura created the 'Royal Army', the Fauj-i-khas, which became known as 'the French Legion', containing units of all three main branches of the army. In two years its infantry strength was four battalions and two cavalry regiments, with a smaller artillery corps under a Muslim officer; it eventually attained a total strength approaching 6,000 men.[1] Whereas the effectiveness of Allard's cavalry is a matter of some debate, especially after Allard's death in 1839, the infantry component of the Royal Army went from strength to strength, seasoned by the actions at Naushehra (1823), Peshawar (1837–9), Kulu and Mandi (1841) and reaching a pinnacle of performance in the First Sikh War (1845–6).

Although Court was given the task of developing the regular artillery soon after his entry into the Maharaja's service in 1827, it took four years and Governor-General Bentinck's artillery demonstration at the Ropar meeting of 1831 to bring home the full scale of reform that was needed. Court followed his French compatriots in introducing French gun drill and words of command, at the same time training the artillerymen with a French manual he translated into Persian. He greatly increased the scale of production of guns at the Sikh foundries and taught the ordnance workmen how to cast shells and make fuses. At Ranjit Singh's death in 1839 the regular artillery possessed some 192 field pieces (compared with roughly a hundred in 1826), not counting guns in fortresses and in the hands of the *jagirdars*. By the outbreak of the First Sikh War six years later this figure was to double, although a number of these guns were old pieces taken from fortresses and refurbished.

One authoritative answer to those who insist that Ranjit Singh's military victories were only made possible by European officers is given by J.D. Cunningham, himself a British army officer and assistant to the British political agent at the Sikh frontier in 1837: 'It has been usual to attribute the superiority of the Sikh army to the labours of these two officers [Generals Allard and Ventura] and of their subsequent coadjutors, the Generals Court and Avitabile; but, in truth, the Sikh owes his excellence as a soldier to his own hardihood of character, to that spirit of adaptation which has distinguished every new people and to that feeling of a common interest and destiny implanted in him by his great teachers.'[2]

No one better understood the need for adaptation, commitment and practical wisdom for achieving military goals than Ranjit Singh. He not only displayed these qualities personally, motivating soldiers to battle determined to win or die in the attempt, but he chose generals who themselves became legends in their lifetime. His generals took pride in proving to the enemy that they were no ordinary men, that they belonged to the army of the Khalsa. And to set the example he would very often lead them into battle himself. He proved in more ways than one that a good leader of men must also be a good judge of men. While we have seen him as soldier, statesman, humanist and liberal, it is time to look at another side of him – as a leader who knew how to pick men who would help him achieve his aims in the many armed struggles he knew he would be involved in all his life and also men who would help him administer his expanding empire.

It should be noted at this point that while most of the men Ranjit Singh chose served him well during his lifetime, some betrayed his successors and the Sikh empire after his death, notoriously the two Dogras and two Brahmins Gulab Singh, Dhian Singh, Tej Singh and Lal Singh. For the British historian Lepel Griffin 'there are, perhaps, no characters in Punjab history more repulsive than Rajas Dhian Singh and Gulab Singh', and he writes of their 'atrocious cruelty, their treachery, their avarice, and their unscrupulous ambition'.[3] But, vile as they were, these men served Ranjit Singh well while he lived and showed their true colours only after his death. Their actions are described in the last chapter of this book; they are mentioned here in order to illustrate that while Ranjit Singh had no difficulty in getting the most perfidious men to do his bidding he did not provide for the possibility that some might ill-serve his legacy after his death, and in this lapse he has to share some of the responsibility for the fall of the Sikh empire.

Hari Singh Nalwa, Ranjit's stalwart in Kashmir, is only one of some forty-seven generals acclaimed for 'sealing his victories with their blood'. In stark contrast to the prevalent tendency in India to favour men of one's own faith, caste or class, Ranjit Singh showed no such bias in the choice of these men. He looked for merit and rewarded it with high rank and respect. So it is no surprise that the Hindu, Sikh, Muslim and Christian generals who earned the empire distinction through their military victories also helped strengthen the secular traditions of the Sikh state. Many biographers have been unable or unwilling to acknowledge this quality of Ranjit Singh's.

⤝⤞

Ranjit Singh proceeded in exactly the same way in selecting his cabinet of ministers. There was no discrimination whatsoever, and in fact it was the Sikhs who held the least number of posts in his cabinet.

What stands out in the different stages of Ranjit Singh's life is how he was able to interact with people of different religions and races. He used diplomacy and treaties to deal with the British but bargained and warred with the Afghans. He was at ease with both, just as he was at home either in the saddle riding fifty miles a day or at a grand Durbar held in honour of some dignitary. Military genius, empire-builder, ladies' man – all this would have been of no account had he lacked the ability to consolidate his empire and keep it stable. This he managed to do for forty years through just administration – no mean feat for an uneducated school drop-out. 'Governing', writes Sir Lepel Griffin, 'is an art which may no doubt be brilliantly practised without special training by some men of exceptional genius.'[4]

The young Ranjit Singh as a *misldar* had a small body of people to help him administer his *misl*. Its affairs were looked after by Diwan Lakpat Rai, who was in charge of a treasury-keeper or *toshania*, an accountant or *munim* and a few clerks or *munshis*. Ranjit Singh allocated the portfolios of civil and military affairs, revenue collection and expenditure to himself. After he became Maharaja he built up his administrative department, which at one time consisted of fifteen different offices of state.

Lahore was the headquarters of the Sarkar Khalsa or central government. Maharaja Ranjit Singh's system of governance reflected his own strong personality and secular beliefs. He was the supreme head of the government, and his orders were obeyed implicitly. All matters and decisions were referred to him – military, civil or judicial. Everyone, including the army, diwans, generals, governors, foreign travellers, princes, treasurers, down to messengers, reported directly to him. The power and authority of the Sikh empire rested solely with Ranjit Singh.

The administration, in its developed form, was divided into different *daftars* or offices of state, such as: Daftari-i-Toshakhana, Treasury; Daftari-i-Abwab-ul-Mal, Land Revenue; Daftari-i-Darogha, Excise and Octroi; Daftar-i-Roznamcha, Accounts and Audits; Daftari-i-Mohar Yani, Royal State Seals and Commissions; and so on. The names given to these departments were in Persian, and accounts, documents and records were also kept in Persian. Maharaja Ranjit Singh chose each office-bearer very carefully, focusing only on the man's ability, character and loyalty. Religious beliefs, caste or station in life mattered little.

Ranjit Singh had a tremendous capacity for remembering financial facts and figures but he also appointed key people to look after them. Bhawani Das of Peshawar, who was earlier Diwan to Shah

Shuja, joined Ranjit Singh's administration in 1808. He looked after land revenues, incomes and expenditure and laid down the basis for their systemization. Ganga Ram, a Kashmiri Pandit, arrived at the Lahore Durbar in 1817 and further developed Bhawani Das's system. His grandson Dina Nath had worked in the revenue section from 1811, so when Ganga Ram died in 1826 Dina Nath took over his post and that of the keeper of the Royal Seal. The seal *Akal Sahai* ('With God's help') *Ranjit Singh* was affixed to all documents approved by the Maharaja; without the seal none was valid. For each seal affixed the Keeper of the Seal charged a sum which was deposited in the Treasury. Dina Nath was far-sighted, intelligent and well educated and proved to be hard-working and loyal. He was styled 'the Talleyrand of the Punjab . . . He hated the English with a bitter hatred, for they were stronger than he or his country.'[5]

Dina Nath became finance minister in 1834, following which the department was divided into sections with separate officers dealing with revenue from customs, transit duties, tributes, gifts, forfeitures, registration fees and so on. There was a special cash keeper who looked after government funds. These included the central treasury funds, army funding and building expenses. Another section maintained records on the Durbar's daily purchases, robes of honour, rewards, charity, grants of land (*jagirs*), entertainment and the royal kitchen.

Having gained Ranjit Singh's trust and confidence over the years as his chamberlain, Dhian Singh Dogra was made Wazir or prime minister. In 1828 he was given the title of Raja Kalan (most senior Raja). Osborne describes him in 1838 as 'a noble specimen of the human race' and a 'deserving candidate for the throne of the Punjab on Runjeet's decease'[6] – and yet the extent of the treachery of this man then, who advised Ranjit Singh on all matters of state and through whom all important papers went to the Maharaja, was to be breathtaking.

Jamadar Khushal Singh held the post of royal chamberlain or Deorhiwala from 1811 to roughly 1826. A Brahmin from Meerut, he came to Lahore in 1807 to seek his fortune. Through friends at court he was put on guard duty at the palace. The story goes that Ranjit Singh, out in disguise one night, returned to find himself stopped at the gates and kept in the watch house till the morning. The Maharaja, pleased with Khushal Singh's sense of duty and soldierly bearing, promoted him to his personal attendant. Khushal Singh grew rich and powerful, and in 1831 he was sent to help Kanwar Sher Singh govern Kashmir. In 1833, despite a severe famine, he brought back large sums of money as revenue. Ranjit Singh was not pleased and ordered thousands of sacks of wheat and provisions to be sent to Kashmir for the starving people, to be distributed from mosques and temples, and he had soldiers from four regiments give out flour, blankets and money.

Fakir Aziz-ud-din, the eldest of the Fakir brothers, entered Ranjit Singh's service as early as 1799. Starting off as physician to the young ruler and then serving in the army, he was over time rewarded with *jagirs* by a grateful Maharaja as he went from victory to victory. Ranjit Singh trusted him implicitly, sending him on various important expeditions and campaigns: Gujrat in 1810, Attock in 1831, as envoy to the Bahawalpur Court in 1819, Phillaur in 1826, Peshawar in 1835. A fine-looking, pleasant, well-mannered, good-humoured and unassuming figure, a skilful negotiator and diplomat – he played a major part in the signing of the Sutlej Treaty in 1809 – who spoke Persian beautifully, he became foreign minister. He was personally in charge of all dealings with the Afghans, British and other Europeans, as well as the cis-Sutlej states. In April 1831 he accompanied Sardar Hari Singh Nalwa and Diwan Moti Ram to Simla for a meeting with Governor-General Lord Bentinck. During this mission an English officer asked Fakir Aziz-ud-din in which eye the Maharaja was blind. He replied: 'The splendour of his face is such that I have never been able to look close enough to discover.'[7] No wonder he was a popular figure not only with foreigners but with the Lahore Durbar as well.

The first treasurer was a Brahmin, Basti Ram; when he died in 1816 his grand-nephew Beli Ram, who had been his assistant, succeeded him at the age of nineteen. The treasurer was also a keeper of records; all treaties, royal *firmans* or orders, documents and important correspondence were under his supervision. He was in charge of the royal wardrobe and regalia as well.

The Toshakhana or treasury housed, apart from silver and gold bullion, the rarest of jewels, pearls, gold and silver, carved and chased saddles, howdahs, dishes and plate. All the rarities collected by Ranjit Singh were kept here, including the Koh-i-noor and Guru Gobind Singh's *kalgi*. His personal treasury in Lahore Fort, the Moti Masjid, had three keys to its gate, one of which was held by the treasurer, one by the commander of the fort and one by the *thanedar* or keeper. Captain William Murray, political agent at Ambala, reported in the 1830s that the wealth of Ranjit Singh stored at the Gobind-Gurh Fort Treasury at Amritsar was valued at around 10 crore rupees or £10 million.

Ranjit Singh divided Punjab into eight major provinces, each under its own *nizam* or governor: Lahore, Jalandhar, Kangra, Multan, Jammu, Kashmir, Gujrat and Peshawar. These were subdivided into districts under a *kardar* or district administrator, whose appointment was sanctioned by the *nizam* with Ranjit Singh's approval. The Mughal administrative system had been similar. There were 51 *kardars* in all in Punjab; their duties were to collect revenues, customs and excise duties and taxes and remit them in time. They also administered justice and settled disputes, developed cultivation and generally kept in touch with people and reported back. From 1826 to 1838 Charles Masson, an American, went around Punjab disguised as a beggar; he reported that the state under Ranjit Singh's rule was better run and more prosperous than those parts of India under British administration.

Land revenue was the Lahore Durbar's main source of income. The state took one-tenth to one-half of the produce in kind, not coin. The assessment depended on various factors: the condition of the soil, irrigation and nearness to the market-place. In the case of famines, floods or any other natural disasters, the state gave up its share of the crop. At such times free seed, cattle and money were also distributed to the affected areas.

Estimates of the amount of revenue generated in Punjab under Ranjit Singh vary between 25,000,000 and 32,500,000 rupees yearly. Captain William Murray in 1832 gave the annual revenue figure as 25,809,500 rupees, the break-up being land revenue and tributes 12,403,900 rupees, customs duties 1,900,600 rupees, *jagirs* 10,928,000 rupees and stamp duties and the sealing of papers 577,000 rupees. One report on the annual revenue generated from provinces under individual governors gave Multan under Diwan Sawan Mal 3,898,550 rupees, Kashmir under Colonel Mian Singh 3,675,000 rupees, Jullundur under Missr Rup Lal 1,872,902 rupees and Peshawar under M. Avitabile 1,834,738 rupees. There were eight salt mines in Punjab, which brought in an annual revenue of 463,675 rupees.

Maharaja Ranjit Singh's system of justice worked efficiently and swiftly. The *panchayat* or local village body dealt with crimes, thefts, murders, disputes and in fact all civil or criminal misdemeanours. The victim or accused could appeal to the *kardar* if unsatisfied with the verdict or even file a written appeal to the Maharaja himself. Ranjit Singh would sometimes ask for reports on certain judgements. There was no capital punishment in the land. The criminal was either fined, gaoled or in some hard cases there was a loss of limbs, nose or ears.

Urban development flourished under Ranjit Singh's rule, as did commerce, industry, arts and crafts (see Chapter 6). The major cities were quite well populated for those times. Lahore had a population of 75,000, Amritsar 60,000, Peshawar 55,000 and Multan 45,000. Even with the poor sanitation in these cities, outbreaks of cholera, typhus or plague were rare. Free dispensaries were set up in some towns, and at Lahore free medicine was available under Fakir Nur-ud-din's supervision.

Ranjit Singh received weekly reports from every province of the kingdom. He often went on surprise visits to places where he thought things were not going as they should. Every day he would be available either at Lahore Fort or at his camp to listen to requests or complaints from the public. Through his long rule he managed to give his people a sense of security, prosperity, growth and, more than anything else, a sense of pride.

⁓

Ranjit Singh's true stature becomes apparent in the game which was played out by Bentinck on London's instructions on the banks of the Sutlej at the end of October 1831. While the governor-general's brief was to gauge the extent to which Ranjit Singh would go along with Britain's plans for the Indus, Ranjit Singh was far from ignorant about what they had in mind. His own intelligence network kept him informed through daily reports brought by special messengers about what went on every day in places as far away as Kabul, Sind, Kashmir and the cis-Sutlej territories under British protection. These reports, both of immediate and long-term interest, helped him further understand the significance of Britain's increased activity in the Sind region and on the River Indus.

The first serious strain in Anglo-Sikh relations came more than twenty years after the signing of the Sutlej Treaty; the bone of contention was the vast landscape of Sind. The land derives its name from the River Sinde or Indus which flows through it. This region of nearly 58,000 square miles lies south-east of Baluchistan and south of Punjab. Bordered by the River Indus and the Thar Desert, it also has strategic importance since it overlooks the Arabian sea. The site of the Harappan city of Mohenjo Daro, dating from the

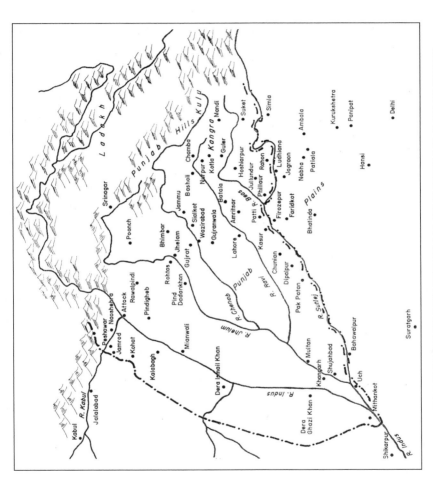

THE TERRITORIES IN THE KINGDOM OF MAHARAJA RANJIT SINGH

third millennium BC, was discovered here about 180 miles north-east of Karachi soon after the First World War. Alexander the Great passed through Sind on his expedition to India in 325 BC. After the Macedonian period the region came under various Buddhist, Brahmin and Muslim kings before becoming part of the Mughal Empire when Emperor Akbar annexed it in 1583. As the Mughal dynasty weakened, Sind's rulers changed, and finally it fell to the Amirs (Muslim chieftains) of Talpur.

The Amirs invited the British to trade in woollen and other goods, and in 1758 the East India Company established a small settlement in Sind. Although trading ceased in 1775 owing to various problems, the Company's efforts to renew the agreement continued and eventually succeeded in 1799, although at first the Amirs would not give permission for the building of a factory and the creation of a settlement. Eventually, however, a factory was set up at Tatta and did well in trade with Multan and Lahore. On 22 August 1808 a formal treaty was signed between the Amirs of Sind and the British and renewed on 19 November 1820; one of its clauses stipulated that no Americans or continental Europeans would be allowed to trade in Sind. With trading rights and other settlements of theirs in the region very much on their minds, the British finally decided to prescribe limits to Ranjit Singh's power.

At the same time Sikh appetites, too, had been whetted, for reasons of revenue and commerce, by the prospects of Sind's conquest. To Ranjit Singh the logic of Sikh control of the region was clear: he had divested the Afghans of all the territories they had conquered in India, and so it was right that whatever tributaries they had left in it, like Sind, should also be under the Lahore Durbar.

The British saw otherwise. They had already sent Alexander Burnes to study the entire lie of the land, as also the potential for commercial navigation on the Indus. In his report *Geographical and Military Memoirs* Burnes, who was considered an ardent expansionist, was compellingly persuasive and is believed to have influenced the alliance between the British and the Amirs. One of the principal aims of this alliance, besides opening up Sind to the British and the Indus to British ships, was to check Sikh moves in the region.

Since the time he had signed the Sutlej Treaty in October 1809, the treaty had worked to Ranjit Singh's advantage on a number of significant occasions, some of them noted in the previous chapter, and even though the British were now itching to prevent the extension of Sikh power along the Indus Ranjit Singh was well ahead of them and still calling the shots.

Between 1820 and 1825 he had taken the first steps towards annexation of Dera Ghazi Khan, Dera Ismail Khan, Bannu, Kohat and Peshawar, all of them located to the right of the Indus, and a whole string of lesser Afghan possessions. At first a tribute was levied on them, but in course of time they were occupied either because they defaulted in their annual tributes or because changed conditions called for their permanent absorption in the Sikh state. Each of Ranjit Singh's conquests left the British either outraged or fretful, and they were especially irked by any inroads into Sind or the adjoining regions west of the Indus because of their own designs on them.

British annoyance at the systematic expansion and consolidation of the Sikh state had been building up since the very signing of the Sutlej Treaty, even though it was signed to secure British interests, just as the Sikhs signed it to secure theirs. The key difference between the two sides was that, while the British wanted to absorb the Sikh state by one means or another in order to complete their hold on the whole of India, Ranjit Singh entertained no such ambitions about bringing all of India under his own sway.

Even in 1809, while negotiating terms of a treaty of peace and friendship with the Sikh kingdom, Metcalfe had been harbouring ideas completely to the contrary. In the words of a modern historian: 'Metcalfe started interfering in [Sikh] internal matters. In

fact, more than Lord Minto, he now advocated a complete exter-
mination of the Sikh empire. So much so he openly talked of a
full-scale British invasion of the Punjab. He incited the Maharaja
against Dewan Mokham Chand and vice versa. He had the audacity to accuse the Dewan of insubordination and told the open
court that the real ruler of the Punjab was Mokham Chand and
not Ranjit Singh. The Maharaja knew the old British game of
divide and rule and refused to be provoked.'[8]

What made Ranjit Singh restrain his generals from precipi-
tating matters was his awareness of British intentions for a
showdown. Despite two Sikh armies poised along the Indus, and
his military commanders urging him 'not to yield to the demands
of the English, for to their understanding it was not clear where
such demands would stop',[9] Ranjit Singh would not be hustled
into a hasty decision. His caustic response to his generals who
urged him to cross the Indus and to annex Sind was to tell them
to jog their memories about the fate of the 200,000 men the
Marathas had fielded against the British not so long before.

His acute sense of realism is again evident in the remark he is said
to have made on seeing a map of India with the areas under British
control in red, telling his top commanders that 'the whole map will
be red one day'. For he recognized Britain's limitless resources, the
range and variety of its weapons, the efficiency of its armed forces
and the degree to which it could quickly augment fivefold whatever
it needed. He also recognized the fact that his ready access to
weapons required to wage a war against the British could never
match his adversary's resources. He knew where to draw the line.

∽∾

The main cause of tensions was the question of who would control the River Indus. With their presence already established in
Sind, the British were in no mood to compromise on this, since it
was the next logical step in their expansionist design on the entire

Sind region and beyond. After all, Sind and the Sikh state were the only two exceptions to Britain's total control of India. But to allay Ranjit Singh's suspicions with regard to their intentions, the British decided to stage a grand and cordial meeting between Governor-General Lord William Bentinck and Maharaja Ranjit Singh.

It was to present some of the East India Company's moves and manoeuvres relating to control of the Indus in an attractive package for the Sikhs that Bentinck offered to meet the Maharaja with the idea of both sides making a spectacular event of it. Ranjit Singh, although clear in his mind about the real purpose of this proposal, responded wholeheartedly to it, as he was keen to see through the smokescreen of fun and games and assess for himself what was being hatched by the British. He had accurately assessed already what lay ahead without being privy to the secret records of British agents. 'Thus was Ranjit Singh gradually feeling his way . . . but the English had, in the meantime, resolved to go far beyond him in diplomacy.'[10] The event was designed to provide a festive screen for two very serious and interrelated British concerns – their ongoing negotiations with the Amirs of Sind and their objective of preventing Sikh armies from advancing to Sind and the strategic town of Shikarpur on the west bank of the Indus. Both concerns were vital to their efforts to extend their hold over India and were never to leave their agenda in the coming years.

The site selected for the meeting, Ropar, a town on the banks of the River Sutlej, was considered an appropriate setting for the extravaganza which took place from 26 October to 1 November 1831. Earlier, in July of that year Alexander Burnes and Captain Claude Wade had gone to Lahore and presented Ranjit Singh, with great ceremony, with a coach and five horses as a gift from their king. It was then agreed when and where the meeting would be held.

The celebrated 'Field of the Cloth of Gold' meeting that had taken place near Calais 300 years earlier, in 1520, between Henry VIII of England and Francis I of France, a continuous display of magnificence, feasting and tournaments in which each ruler tried to outdo the other, was the model for what was intended to be another momentous meeting. For Ranjit Singh certainly knew how to entertain on a grand scale.

A shimmering, double-storeyed silver structure, resembling a villa on wheels, was assembled so that the chief guests would have an unimpeded view of events, the festivities and the parade. The villa was placed in a wide expanse of open fields. A bridge of boats was constructed over the River Sutlej, by which the Maharaja and his entourage, seated on large, magnificently caparisoned elephants, would cross to reach the British side.

On the right bank of the Sutlej, the Maharaja's camp, built on eight acres of land, consisted of various pavilions and tents of scarlet hue, made of fine pashmina materials, beautifully embroidered, and velvet worked with silver and gold thread. Gold and brocade carpets were placed inside as well as outside the tents, in which gold canopied beds and footstools were placed. In one of the tents was a dining hall with gold and silver dishes, plates and utensils sparkling under a large bejewelled canopy. The spaces between the pavilions and tents were filled with beds of fragrant herbs, roses and endless other varieties of scented flowers.

With Maharaja Ranjit Singh came his entourage consisting of his heir Kanwar Kharak Singh and his half-brother Kanwar Sher Singh and son Nau Nihal Singh; Hari Singh Nalwa, the Dogra brothers Raja Dhian Singh, Gulab Singh and Suchet Singh, and the Maharaja's favourite, Dhian Singh's son Hira; also the rulers of Jind, Ladwa and Kaithal, the Ahluwalia, Majithia, Attariwala, Sandhanwalia and Kalianwala Sardars and Generals Allard and Court. In all, the entourage consisted of over a hundred elite members of the Lahore Durbar. The cavalry consisted of 16,000 men of the best, with 6,000 chosen from the infantry.

The British camp was no less impressive, the governor-general arriving with his secretaries, military officers and officials, squadrons of Lancers, two battalions of Native Infantry, two squadrons of Skinner's Irregular Horse, a mounted band and eight guns.

On the morning of 26 October Maharaja Ranjit Singh and his chiefs crossed the bridge to the governor-general's camp with an escort of 3,000 cavalry and 800 infantry. The Maharaja and Sardars were dressed in their favourite saffron yellow colour and striking headgear and many wore exquisitely chased armour and armlets of diamonds, pearls and precious stones the size of small pebbles. Gifts were exchanged, the conversation was lively, and the Maharaja was in great spirits. After the meeting came the singers and dancing girls, with wine flowing freely.

The next day it was the governor-general's turn to return Ranjit Singh's visit. He arrived escorted by his Lancers who were preceded by a mounted band. The entourage was welcomed by a *nazar* (offering) of gold ducats. The governor-general was then escorted to the silver bungalow. The Political Secretary, Henry T. Prinsep, at one point asked if they could see the Maharaja's famous Amazons, and the hosts were only too happy to oblige. This unit of beautiful recruits from Punjab, Kashmir and Persia, magnificently dressed in garments specially made for the occasion, armed with bows and arrows, moving with 'attractive coquetry and blandishments', was a beguiling sight to see. The Maharaja proudly pointed out to the guests their commanding officer and her subordinate officers – *subedar, jamadar* and *chobdar* – and then asked the unit to sing and dance, which they did with an appealing grace which went well with a popular ballad, 'Motian Wala Banna' ('My Pearl-Bedecked Bridegroom'). They were rewarded with a thousand rupees by the British guests.

Different forms of entertainment, parades and festivities were laid on during each day that followed. No evening was complete without a display of illuminations, fireworks or dancing girls. One evening, with the English party – both men and women – thoroughly enjoying themselves, Ranjit Singh threw handfuls of coloured powder made from lac dye on them and on the dancing girls. The English sahibs in turn threw it on the Maharaja and the Sardars, and everyone was soon enveloped in fine misty colours.

Troops were paraded and duly inspected, and cannons fired in countless gun salutes as a part of the drill conducted by British soldiers. Ranjit Singh not only witnessed different types of guns and bullets being used but also examined them minutely afterwards. Targets were set up for the Sardars to show their skills with weapons, and Sardar Hari Singh Nalwa, an especially good shot and a skilled swordsman, was seen at his best. The Maharaja took part in sword play and tent-pegging – hitting the peg with his spear while on horseback. In full gallop he also cut a lemon in half, picked up a banana with the tip of his sword and drew three lines with the point of his sword on the bottom of a jug on the ground.

Gifts were then exchanged. The governor-general presented Ranjit Singh with nine-pounder horse artillery guns complete with horses and equipment, a model of an iron suspension bridge especially made in Calcutta for the presentation, fifty-one robes of honour, various ornaments, two horses with gold saddles and an elephant with velvet and gold trappings. The princes and Sikh chiefs also received robes of honour and jewellery.

The Sikhs, never to be outdone in generosity, far exceeded the British in the gifts they gave. Apart from showering everyone with gold ducats, Ranjit Singh presented the governor-general with bejewelled Afghan swords, Persian guns beautifully wrought and gilded, shields, a gold-wrought bow and quiver, horses with gold saddles, elephants with carved silver seats, a pearl necklace and other fine jewellery; also pashmina articles, shawls, mattresses, bed covers and coverings and robes of honour in worked brocade and silk. While the other ladies in the party were given shawls and ornaments, the governor-general's wife received twenty-six garments, pieces of brocade, handkerchiefs of red silk (red being auspicious), *chunis* (long scarves), an *arsi* (thumb ring) and a pearl necklace, *jugni* (typical Punjab Kundan jewellery), *pohnchis* (bracelets) and pearl earrings.

The meeting at Ropar was a highly successful event, an enjoyable combination of spectacle and conviviality – but a cover for the real agenda of the British, summed up in words quoted by a modern historian: 'The government of India is bound by the strongest considerations of political interest to prevent the extension of Sikh power along the whole course of the Indus.'[11]

No formal discussions took place at Ropar, but on the last evening, at a parting meeting during the entertainment given by Bentinck, Ranjit Singh, who might have got wind of or at least suspected British intentions in Sind, pressed for a written assurance of the continuation of 'eternal relations of friendship' between his kingdom and Britain. The appropriate document was duly prepared and presented to the Maharaja on the spot. Ranjit Singh took the opportunity of inviting the two men who seemed to him most in Bentinck's confidence (one of them was his official secretary) to his tent and opened a conversation about Sind, 'as if desirous to open a negotiation, and concert measures, in relation to that state; or at least to come to an understanding, as to the views of the British Government in respect to it'. The British, however, kept their cards close to the chest, 'for it was conceived, that, if made aware of the intentions of the British Government, [Ranjit Singh] might, with every profession of a desire to forward them, contrive by intrigue and secret working to counteract the negotiation'.[12] In his report back to the British government, Bentinck commented on 'the anxiety shown by His Highness for the introduction of this assurance'.[13] On the very day before the governor-general arrived at Ropar, in fact, he had instructed Henry Pottinger to prepare for a mission to Sind with the object of negotiating a treaty opening up the Indus to trade with Europe and the rest of India.[14]

⤛⤜

145

In the aftermath of the Ropar meeting the British made their designs on Sind plain, and the area would become an increasing bone of contention with the Lahore Durbar. Since the establishment of the first trading station by the East India Company in 1758, the British relationship with the Amirs had been a precarious one at best, with the isolationist Amirs first giving the Company permission to stay and then after a while asking them to leave. By the mid-1820s the British had flexed their muscles at the Amirs to the extent that it left them in no doubt of their intentions.

At the same time the Amirs, fearing Ranjit Singh's growing power and interest in their holdings and territories, had asked the British for their protection, and the British had acted promptly, with Colonel Pottinger's mission to Sind actually coinciding with the meeting at Ropar. The treaty signed in April 1832 was a follow-up to Burnes's visit to Sind the previous year. The British, leaving nothing to chance, sent Captain Wade to negotiate an 'Indus Navigation Treaty' with Ranjit Singh, duly signed in December 1832. The purpose of the treaty was 'to regulate the navigation of the Indus and the collection of duties on merchandise'. The levy of duties on the value and quantity of goods, however, gave rise to misunderstandings, and in November 1834 a supplementary treaty was concluded to substitute a toll, to be levied on all boats 'with whatever merchandise laden'. This was further supplemented in May 1839 by an agreement which provided for the levy of duty on merchandise 'at one place and not on the boats'.[15]

Far-fetched as it may sound, Sind and the Sikh kingdom occupied a pivotal place in Britain's bid for world domination. Britain's problems had been aggravated by the convergence of many momentous events, especially the loss of its American colonies in 1776 and Washington's declaration of the Monroe Doctrine in 1823 that no European power would be allowed to establish itself in North or South America. (In the words of the doctrine, 'the occasion has been judged proper for asserting, as a principle in which the rights and interests of the United States are involved, that the American continents, by the free and independent condition which they have assumed and maintain, are henceforth not to be considered as subjects for future colonization by any European power'.)

The closure of these territories was particularly galling to Britain which, having clearly established a lead over other nations with its Industrial Revolution, now needed endless supplies of a vast range of raw materials for its industries. This need could be met fully by India, one of the world's most mineral-rich nations in iron ore, chromites, manganese ore, bauxite, mica, barites, titanium and a whole variety of gemstones. So clearly, if Britain was to be denied access to other continents with the exception of Africa, its absolute control and dominance of India was a must. India was also of vital importance as a gateway to some of the richest and strategically most important countries in South and South-East Asia and the Far East. The chronology of Britain's expansionist moves in this part of the world was itself revealing, with Burma partially colonized in 1826, China forced into an Opium War in 1839 to make it easier to subjugate and Hong Kong becoming a British colony in 1842.

What stood in the way of Britain's complete control of India was the Sikh empire under its shrewd and powerful ruler. Of course Sind had to be taken over, too, but that would have presented no difficulty to the British had it not been for Ranjit Singh's menacing presence across the Indus. However, even as the British continued to manoeuvre in every possible way through various missions, visits, gifts, flowery communications and deputations vowing eternal friendship, Ranjit Singh, realistic to the end, decided to forgo Sind.

He had the foresight to understand that with the larger goals the British had set their eyes on in Asia, and with their weapons as well as the resources they could draw upon from the entire subcontinent of India which they now controlled, as also from Europe and elsewhere, it would be imprudent of him to fight them over Sind. Especially as they would do everything they possibly could to prevent him from becoming a sea power, which he would if Sind along with the port of Karachi fell into his hands. It must have been a hard decision for him to forgo Sind, and he showed wisdom in taking it.

༺ঞ্চ

It is hard to understand the comments of a historian such as Hari Ram Gupta on the subject of Ranjit Singh's political capabilities and his decision against annexing Sind. Gupta's five-volume *History of the Sikhs* (1984) has been acknowledged as a painstaking chronicle of those turbulent times. He comments: 'in diplomacy Ranjit Singh proved a complete failure'; and 'throughout his reign he behaved as if he were a vassal of the British government'; and 'immediately after the acquisition of Attock in 1813 he should have directed his steps towards Sind'.[16]

But as we have seen, Ranjit Singh's signing of the Sutlej Treaty while still in his twenties showed vision, skill and finesse in negotiating skills that might not have been found together even in a seasoned diplomat. By keeping the British south of the River Sutlej with the help of this treaty, he opened up limitless horizons for carving out a Sikh kingdom in the north.

On Gupta's second point, to Henry T. Prinsep, chief secretary to the governor-general, it was clear that Ranjit Singh was no vassal to anyone. In *Origin of the Sikh Power in the Punjab* (1834) he writes: 'The territorial possessions of Ranjit Singh comprise now the entire fork of the Punjab, as bounded by the Indus and Sutlej, the two extreme rivers. He holds besides Kashmir, and the entire hill country to the snowy range, and even Ladakh beyond the Himalayas: for though many of the rajas of this tract still remain in their possessions, they have been reduced to the character of subjects, paying tribute equal to their utmost means, and contributing men to the armies of Lahore, whenever called upon.'[17] And Prinsep leaves out of account the former Afghan territories beyond Peshawar and the regions around it.

The last of Gupta's comments just quoted – that after the acquisition of Attock in 1813 Ranjit Singh should have turned to Sind – seems to this author equally unrealistic. The year 1813 was an extremely active one for him, seeing the taking of Attock in March, the first expedition to Kashmir and the acquisition of the Koh-i-noor diamond in June, the second expedition to Kashmir and the Battle of Haidru in July and visits to the easterly Kangra region in October and then westwards to Sialkot, Wazirabad and Jehlum. He arrived at Rohtas on the west bank of the Jhelum on 11 November and proceeded to consolidate his newly won territories, check his troops and artillery, fix sites for granaries where wheat for the troops could be stored and select sites for ammunition storage. He and his generals also planned strategy for taking Kashmir the following year. He finally returned home to Lahore towards the end of December 1813.

He would have been well aware that the strength of his forces did not allow him to spread them too far. Any further advances would have endangered the stability of his realm, and to suggest that he should have made such an advance into Sind is to ignore the scale on which he was campaigning at this time. If Ranjit Singh remained unvanquished throughout his lifetime, even as the British conquered some of the Indian rulers and states including the mighty Mughals, it was because of a very clear-headed acceptance of his own limitations and the wisdom not to imperil the nation he had built with such dedication.

❦

Tensions over Sind continued to build up, even after the 'eternal friendship' declaration of 1831. Ranjit Singh questioned the right of the British to hold negotiations with the Amirs of Sind when the Sutlej Treaty of 1809 stipulated that any dealings by the British with countries north of the Sutlej would violate the treaty's conditions. The British response was in character. They contended that while the 1809 treaty put limits on the Lahore Durbar's actions south of the Sutlej it placed no such limits on British moves north and west of the Indus. As to Ranjit Singh's claim on Shikarpur (in Sind) as a dependency of Peshawar which was in Sikh territory, the British government in a flight of fancy said that any territory or dependency of Peshawar equally belonged to the Shah of Persia and the Amir of Afghanistan!

While the above was the public position taken by the British, the governor-general Lord Auckland, in a confidential letter to the president of the East India Company's Board of Control dated 7 October 1836, wrote:

> Runjeet Singh . . . has some cause of complaint of us for interfering with him on this side of the Indus. Our treaty with him fixed the Sutlege as the boundary to his ambition on our side ... As long as it suited our purpose, we maintained that the treaty made the Sutlege, when it became merged in the Indus, the bar to Runjeet Singh's power on this side. On that account when he took the territories of the Nawab of Bahawalpur on the other side of the river, we did not allow him to touch on this side, although we had no treaty with Bahawalpur, and that state was not in contemplation when the treaty with Runjeet Singh for the protection of the Sikhs on this side of the Sutlege was made. Are we at liberty to put one construction of treaty at one time, and another at another when it suits our convenience? If not, we can hardly say that we have any right to interfere between Runjeet Singh and Sind.[18]

Auckland's final question sums it all up: *Are we at liberty to put one construction of treaty at one time, and another at another when it suits our convenience?*

The following excerpt from the East India Company's Ludhiana Agency Records for 1812–14 gives another indication of how it handled its side of the relationship – ostensibly based on peace and friendship – with the Lahore Durbar. Lieutenant-Colonel D. Ochterlony, the agent in Ludhiana, after a visit to the Maharaja in February 1812, wrote to the governor-general Lord Minto:

> It may not be deemed improper to offer such observations as occurred to me during my late intercourse with Runjeet to the notice and consideration of the Right Hon'ble the Governor-General in Council, in which I shall endeavour to divest my mind from any bias it may have received from his great attention and from oft-repeated expressions of personal respect. Runjeet's ambition is as unbounded as his rapacity . . . If Runjeet's opinions are decisively formed on any one subject they are on his utter inability to contend with the British arms; but the more firm this belief the more he is inclined to doubt the pacific intentions of the British Government, whose forbearance is to him incomprehensible . . . At this moment when our European enemy has been expelled from every possession in the East, when we are not aware of any reverse of fortune in Europe, and when there is no expectation of any invasion of our Asiatic dominions from the north-west, I would wish to propose to Runjeet the junction of a large British army with his own troops to repel . . . invaders . . . It cannot be difficult to find arguments to prove to Runjeet that his own interests are deeply connected with ours should such an event occur, and I feel confident not only of his acquiescence, but that such a proposition, by showing him clearly how our interests were united, would of itself serve to dispel his suspicions.[19]

To what extent the reports periodically sent to the governor-general by Company officials such as Ochterlony reflected a reasonable understanding of Ranjit Singh's intentions and strategies is open to doubt, since many such officials will have been influenced by their own personal agendas and ambitions. But there seems little doubt that the proposals put to Ranjit Singh were more often than not meant to dispel his suspicions rather than strengthen ties of friendship.

In the end, no matter how hard the British tried, Ranjit Singh was not taken in. His policies remained focused on the interests of the Sikh state and not on the fanciful proposals put to him by his less than dependable co-signatories of treaties.

5

The Unabashed Sensualist

> On the borderline between Ranjit Singh's harem and
> his court, between his private and his public life, there
> was a no man's land, a land of wine and song and
> dance. It was here that he used to spend his hours of
> relaxation – an evening once or twice a week.
>
> FAKIR SYED WAHEEDUDDIN[1]

No less impressive than Ranjit Singh's achievements as an empire builder were his amatory exploits. The joys of dalliance with seductive and striking-looking women seemed to give Ranjit Singh the same pleasure as his conquests on the battlefield did. He exulted in their company, viewing them as cherished trophies won in more intimate encounters. If a temptress caught his fancy he was perfectly willing to be tempted. He savoured the joys of sex with those who appealed to him and made clear to courtiers, visitors and his populace that he regarded the delight he got out of his beautiful consorts as his personal right.

Since he always insisted on upholding the rights of others, Ranjit Singh saw no reason to compromise in exercising his own. Or to be furtive about it. Inevitably, in this, too, along with other spheres of life in which commentators seem to have been over-taken by feelings of envy or inadequacy, he has had more than his share of detractors. Henry Prinsep, in a sudden about-face, ser-monized about what he termed as Ranjit Singh's 'dissolute life' and wrote that 'his debaucheries, particularly during Hoolee [Holi] and Dussera, were shameless, and the scenes exhibited on such occasions openly before the Court, and even in the streets of Lahore, were the conversation of Hindoostan, and rival the worst that is reported in history of the profligacies of ancient Rome'.[2] Here Prinsep seems to have gone completely overboard. As if people had nothing better to do than gossip about 'excesses' committed at various festivals all over 'Hindoostan' – and as if India's communication network in those times was good enough to enable them to do so!

On the subject of Holi, during which people gaily spray each other with coloured water, another prudish observer felt that 'the dirtiest part of the entertainment consists in the sprinkling with coloured waters . . . Spirits are drunk, and the amusements are then carried far beyond our European ideas of propriety, but the Hindu thinks no harm of them.'[3] Although these two writers ask to be taken as if they had been close to events, they seem rather to be retailing gossip, their comfortable sense of public propriety apparently blotting out any awareness of the history of some of their own monarchs' far more shocking behaviour. Even a contemporary writer who did get hold of at least part of the truth contrived to put a lurid slant on it. 'The character of this great man is darkened by his dissolute life, especially the vice of drunkenness, which at last increased to such a degree that, in his latter years, he could not exist without the strongest spirituous liquors.'[4]

A more balanced and accurate view is provided, as so often, by Joseph Cunningham: 'It would be idle to regard Ranjit Singh as an habitual drunkard or as one greatly devoted to sensual pleasures; and it would be equally unreasonable to believe the mass of the Sikh people as wholly lost to shame, and as revellers in every vice which disgraces humanity . . . those who vilify the Sikhs . . . [should] reflect that what common-sense and the better feelings of our nature have always condemned, can never be the ordinary practice of a nation.'[5] And he adds the sobering point: 'Europeans carry their potations and the pleasures of the table to an excess unknown to the Turk and Persian, and which greatly scandalize the frugal Hindu.'[6]

No matter what others thought of him, Ranjit Singh lived his life in just the way he wanted to. He compromised neither in his drinking nor in his sexual appetites. He indulged in them to the fullest – but never at the cost of his commitment to the nation he had founded. He did not permit his driving passion and goal, to create a strong Sikh state, to be compromised by anything in his personal life, and any judgement of him needs to take this into account.

On the subject of Ranjit Singh's personal life, Faqir Syed Waheeduddin has this to say:

> He was susceptible to feminine influence, but as a man and not as a ruler ... there was little of debauchery in the way he used to spend his time in the company of his singing and dancing girls. He loved singing and dancing for their own sake and took a connoisseur's interest in them. The performances, therefore, used to be displays of art and not the orgies of dissipation which some people have imagined them to be ... Being fond of repartee and badinage, he would now and again engage in a wordy duel with some particularly vivacious girl; and usually such a one served as cup-bearer. There was, however, never any coarseness or vulgarity in the process. The singing and dancing soirées thus used to be quite sober and dignified affairs.[7]

Unabashed sensualist, however, that he undoubtedly was, Ranjit Singh was not one to force anyone to grant him favours and went out of his way to make those who did happy; his generosity and civilized conduct towards them were well known. There is a particularly appealing case of a courtesan he was so deeply in love with that he not only married her and had a mosque named after her in Lahore and also a village in Amritsar district but had a coin struck in her name – the only woman to be so honoured.

She was Moran, a Kashmiri dancing girl from Amritsar, who completely captivated Ranjit Singh when he first set eyes on her. He was twenty-two then and Moran twelve or thirteen. Her glowing face, large eyes, beautiful black hair, melodious voice and quickness of mind completely won him over. She danced with grace and dignity. Lean and wiry himself, Ranjit Singh, short of stature, with one eye and smallpox scars, was still a striking-looking man with an attractive face, penetrating right eye, a long slightly upturned nose, firm mouth, excellent teeth, broad shoulders and a beard which cascaded down his chest. He had a presence and personality all his own.

Although this girl was a courtesan and he the ruler of Punjab, Ranjit Singh was gentlemanly enough in 1802 to ask her father for his daughter's hand. There is a charming account of the father's reaction. He was terrified at the idea of marrying his daughter outside his class and tried to frighten the royal suitor away by making a condition, one that was in fact a tradition – that the bridegroom should build and 'blow ablaze with his own breath' a fire in his father-in-law's house. Ranjit Singh had the fire roaring in no time.[8]

This story alone provides more than one point of insight into the character of this unusual man: that he should even think of asking for the hand of a dancing girl from her father, when all he had to do was have her brought to him; his willingness to agree to the condition laid down; and although his bride was a Muslim he never once asked her to convert, respecting her right to abide by her own faith. The degree to which Ranjit Singh acknowledged the supremacy of his own faith is revealed by his response to the directives of Sikhism's highest authority in Amritsar concerning this affair.

The Maharaja's deep involvement with Moran had upset the conservative religious establishment of the Golden Temple. While its members resented his devotion to her, he made no effort to hide it. What particularly incensed them was that whenever he had the time he would take her for an outing on his elephant, either about the streets of Lahore or from the fort to the Shalimar Gardens. This was his way of enjoying his leisure, and there would be a drink or two served during the ride. Unwilling to take any more of this the Akalis, the strict sect who were keepers of the Golden Temple, summoned him to Amritsar to appear at the Akal Takht, the seat of temporal authority, and answer the charges against him.

When he appeared before the five chosen ones – in addition to whom a large congregation had also assembled for the occasion – he was charged with conduct unworthy of a Sikh and with belittling the faith. He was sentenced to a hundred lashes on the back in public, along with a fine. Ranjit Singh accepted this writ with folded hands. But on reconsideration the decision was made to drop the sentence of flogging, and the announcement was joyfully acclaimed. Some accounts suggest that the ruler was symbolically struck once on the back, but others dispute it. The fine of 125,000 rupees was, however, dutifully paid.

Yet another story of Ranjit Singh's love for Moran is revealing. After his meeting with Lord and Lady Bentick at Ropar in 1831, an observer of the scene wrote of the deep impression one particular moment had made on him: 'As soon as the Begum Sahiba crossed the river by a boat, the Nawab Sahib personally went forward to receive her and, taking her by the hand, made her sit in a chair in such a way that it indicated his heartfelt affection and deep love between [the two]. The Maharaja said that at that moment he was put in mind of his connection with Bibi Moran, for he said that he had exactly the same kind of love and unity with her and could not prepare his mind to accept separation from her even for a moment and every moment they remained fully aware of each other's doings.'[9] Thus the seigneur, in this case a monarch, whom the social system of the time allowed as many wives as he pleased was at one with those who lived and loved under quite a different social system.

Given Ranjit Singh's limitless capacity for love, it was not long before Moran's sister Mamola also caught his fancy, and he married her as well. She was a dancer, too. Later in life Ranjit Singh became infatuated with yet another Kashmiri girl, 'a demi-mondaine of Amritsar, Gul Badam, and married her with pomp and splendour' in 1833.[10] The bridegroom, wearing a garland of flowers, was decked out in a pearl necklace and was lightly sprinkled with saffron water by no less than Mamola. The newly-wed ruler, wanting to show off his new bride Gul (later called Gul Begum) to his subjects, would often put her before him on his favourite horse and ride through the streets of Lahore. Badami Bagh, the park near Lahore Fort, was named after her, and she was buried there in 1863. It should be mentioned that Ranjit Singh kept all his wives happy by giving them handsome *jagirs* and maintenance allowances so that they wouldn't feel either rejected or overlooked.

༼༽

Coping with his women must have been no less daunting a task for Ranjit Singh than dealing with the many adversaries he faced during his eventful reign. They numbered literally hundreds if the count includes all his wives, concubines and the regiment of Amazons he had created with an eye on both their physical fitness and striking looks. And then there were the ladies, mostly widows, who came under the category of *chadar dalna* (under his protection). Historians disagree on the numbers in each category.

Ranjit Singh's detachment of Amazons seems, not surprisingly, to have been a draw for most of the British officers. In conversation with W.G. Osborne on military discipline, Ranjit Singh once said that there was one regiment he could not manage and which gave him more trouble than his entire army put together –

Maharaja Ranjit Singh Listening to the Guru Granth Sahib at the Golden Temple by August Theodor Schoefft, c. 1850

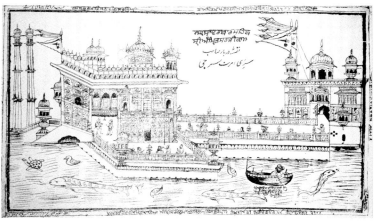

Woodcuts depicting the Gurus (above) and (below) the Harmandir Sahib (Golden Temple), both dating from *c.* 1870

An early watercolour showing traditional Sikh warriors

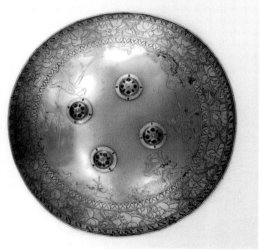

Top left: A study of Sikh arms and armour by W.G. Osborne, 1838; published in his book *The Court and Camp of Runjeet Sing*, 1840

Top right: A late-eighteenth-century steel and gold Sikh helmet

Bottom: Mid-nineteenth-century jewelled Sikh shield with hunting scenes

Top: Ranjit Singh on horseback with his army; sketch by W.G. Osborne, 1838; published in *The Court and Camp of Runjeet Sing*

Above: Ranjit Singh's sword. Mounts are of solid gold with an emblem of a lion on guard on the sword hilt. The blade is made of watered steel.

Top: The two Dogra brothers: Gulab Singh by C.S. Hardinge, 1846 (left) and Dhian Singh

Bottom: Raja Lal Singh (left) and Raj Tej Singh; both watercolour on ivory

Top: Ranjit Singh in 1838, drawn by Emily Eden

Right: Fakir Azizuddin, Ranjit Singh's confidant, by W.O. Osborne, 1838, published in *The Court and Camp of Runjeet Sing*

Bottom: Diwan Mulraj of Multan; watercolour on ivory

Oil portrait of General Hari Singh Nalwa, an outstanding officer of Ranjit Singh's army and governor of Kashmir; by an unknown artist. He was an excellent shot and an accomplished swordsman.

Top: Maharaja Ranjit Singh's heir, Kanwar Kharak Singh; watercolour

Above: *The Court of Lahore*; oil painting by August Theodor Schoefft, *c.* 1850–5

Right: Maharaja Ranjit Singh's second son, Kanwar Sher Singh; sketch by W.G. Osborne, 1838, published in *The Court and Camp of Runjeet Sing*

Below: Emily Eden's drawing of the Maharaja's adored horse Leila

Top: Dancing girls; drawing by W.G. Osborne, 1838, published in *The Court and Camp of Runjeet Sing*

Above: Mirror and gold-trimmed work in the Harmandir Sahib

Above: A woodcut of 1870 depicting Maharaja Ranjit Singh on horseback against the city of Lahore (detail)

Right: The Koh-i-noor, set between two smaller diamonds, worn by Maharaja Ranjit Singh as an armlet

Maharaja Ranjit Singh on horseback, by Alfred de Dreux (1810–60); oil painting commissioned by General Ventura and gifted by him to King Louis-Philippe of France in 1838

The famous Zam Zama gun, captured by Ranjit Singh in his campaign against the Bhangi chiefs at Amritsar. It was used in various campaigns including the Battle of Multan.

Below: The Shalimar Gardens, laid out in 1667 and well loved by the Maharaja; drawing by W.G. Osborne, 1838, published in *The Court and Camp of Runjeet Sing*

Opposite: Three Sikh Akalis, drawn by Emily Eden

Engraving of Maharaja Ranjit Singh by George J. Stodart after a drawing by an unknown Indian artist, 1860

Previous page: Maharaja Ranjit Singh in Durbar; oil painting in the Central Sikh Museum, Darbar Sahib, Amritsar

Left: Posthumous oil portrait of Maharaja Ranjit Singh, *c.* 1850

Right: An important Sikh chieftain, Sham Singh Attariwala; watercolour

Rani Jindan, mother of Maharaja Dalip Singh and a powerful woman in the Punjab in the final years of the Sikh state; oil painting by George Richmond, 1863 (detail)

Left: *Bridging the River Chenab*; oil painting by Charles Hardinge

Below: *Governor-General Viscount Hardinge, His Two Sons and Colonel Wood on the Battlefield of Ferozeshahr*; oil painting by Sir Francis Grant

Maharaja Dalip Singh, last in the line of Maharaja Ranjit Singh. As the British hold tightened on the Punjab, he was banished from his homeland and exiled to Europe in 1854. Engraving from the *Illustrated London News* after a photograph by O.G. Rajlander

Top: The first coin the *misls* minted at Lahore was a silver rupee bearing the Gobindshahi couplet in Persian; on the reverse (second from top) the coin carries the date VS 1822 (AD 1765.)

Second from bottom: Silver rupee struck in Lahore in 1801, the year Ranjit Singh was proclaimed ruler of Punjab; the coin carries the Nanakshahi couplet, with the date VS 1858 on the reverse (bottom).

Top: A Morashahi rupee, minted at Amritsar, is adorned with branches and berries, symbolizing Ranjit Singh's passion for Moran, his Kashmiri love.

Second from top: General Hari Singh Nalwa, governor of Kashmir, minted this coin in 1822. The letters *Har* on it in Gurmukhi are the first letters of Nalwa's name but also stand for the Almighty, underlining Nalwa's firm faith.

Second from bottom: The words *Sahai Sat Guru* ('Help from the true Lord') were stamped on this unique golden rupee used by Mulraj, Diwan of Multan, to pay his troops during the siege of Multan in 1848.

Bottom: Possibly the only coin of its kind in existence, this Nanakshahi was minted at Amritsar in 1849. It lasted only a short time because the British annexed Punjab in March of the same year.

Right: The emerald seal of Ranjit Singh mounted on his ring and inscribed *Akal Sahai Ranjit Singh 1809* ('With the help of the eternal one Ranjit Singh 1809')

Left: The Harmandir Sahib today

Right: Detail of inlay work in marble inside the Harmandir Sahib

the beautiful recruits from Kashmir, Persia and the Punjab: the Amazons. He also added jestingly: would the British be able to manage such a formation better?

At first there were around a hundred and fifty warriors in this regiment, but the numbers varied. Osborne describes how once when he and his party visited Lahore, 'a considerable degree of excitement prevailed among the fairer portion of the Sikh army' owing to rumours that, following the East India Company's example, the Maharaja also intended to take back all grants for which no formal title deeds could be produced. 'I believe', writes Osborne, 'Runjeet would sooner face Dost Mahommed and his Afghans than a single individual of his Amazonian body-guard.'[11] Fortunately for everyone, the rumours proved to be inaccurate. These beautiful, enticingly dressed, voluptuous women armed with bows and arrows were mounted on horseback *en cavalier* – a position that greatly appealed to the Maharaja. They also entertained guests in the evenings with music and dance, often against a backdrop of fireworks.

One Amazon of colourful character and exquisite beauty was called Lotus. She was sent as a tribute from Kashmir to Ranjit Singh in the mid-1830s. He was totally captivated by her and assumed she was madly in love with him. One day, while Lotus was dancing before them, he remarked to General Ventura that the dancer was so taken with him that she would not entertain offers from any other man. The Italian general's face showed disbelief. Ranjit Singh, irked at the doubt cast on his own powers of attraction, challenged Ventura to seduce her. He added that he would put no pressure on her and she would be kept secluded in his *zenana*. After much hesitation on Ventura's part on the desirability of vying for the affections of his sovereign's favourite, he accepted the challenge. Within forty-eight hours it was known throughout the court that the lovely Lotus was now no more in her royal lover's garden but in the Italian general's. Ranjit Singh did not seem to mind her desertion very much, but Lotus did and soon left her lover to return to the Lahore court and Ranjit Singh.

It was far from Ranjit Singh's nature and temperament to confine himself to just one of his loves; another Amazon he was irresistibly drawn to was the celebrated Bashiran. Because she had gorgeous cat-like eyes he would call her Billo, which in Punjabi is slang for 'cat'. With a beautiful voice and an exceptional singing talent, she would keep the Maharaja entranced. Ranjit Singh made her rich with his gifts of land and jewels.

Billo was not only a singer but commanded a company of Amazons, consisting of thirty or forty singing and dancing girls, hand-picked for their beauty, playfulness and agility. Their uniform has been described as follows: 'a lemon-yellow *banarsi* turban with a bejewelled crest; a dark green jumper over a blue satin gown, fastened with a gold belt; deep crimson skin-tight pyjamas of *gulbadan* silk; and a pair of pointed golden shoes. As for jewellery, they wore a pair of gold earrings set with stones, a diamond nose-stud, a pair of gold bracelets and a ruby ring on the middle finger. Their accoutrement was completed by bows and arrows; but their arrows were less deadly than the glances of their eyes.'[12]

The Amazons received a daily allowance, and some were given *jagirs*, from which they got good rent. Lotus was gifted seven prosperous villages by Ranjit Singh as tokens of his affection. She was devoted to him until the end and committed *sati* when he died.

In addition to the exquisite Amazons, there were others of equal versatility to entertain and enchant Ranjit Singh with their repertoire of dances. W.G. Osborne, military secretary to the Earl of Auckland, invited to dinner by the Maharaja, describes a memorable dance by four recently arrived Kashmiri girls, whose large, luminous eyes and expressive countenances might have entitled them to be considered 'beautiful anywhere in the world': 'They were richly and gracefully dressed in scarlet and gold embroidered shawl dresses, with large and enormously loose petticoats of handsomely worked silk. Their head ornaments were singular and very becoming; their glossy black hair hanging down the back in a number of long plaits, with gold coins and small bunches of pearls suspended to the ends.'[13]

Ranjit Singh was prepared to extend his range beyond Persian, Afghan and Kashmiri women, as one young English officer with whom he had a conversation discovered. 'When Ranjit Singh asked him: "Why don't you marry?" [his reply was] "I can't afford it." [When asked] "Why not? Are English wives very expensive?" [he was told:] "Yes; very." [To which Ranjit Singh replied:] "I wanted one myself some time ago, and wrote to the government about it, but they did not send me one." [The officer said:] "It would be difficult to find one in this country that would suit your highness." [Ranjit then queried:] "Are there any in England?" [and was told:] "Plenty." [Ranjit Singh's response was] "Ah! I often wish for one." '[14]

Although he didn't quite 'wish for' Queen Victoria, an endearing story is told by Fane in his Indian memoir. When the Maharaja was presented with an oil painting of the Queen sent to him by the governor-general, he is said to have remarked that 'Her Majesty [would] make a very decent Nautch girl.'[15]

᠙᠙

The number of Ranjit Singh's wives is generally placed at around twenty, which includes those in the *chadar dalna* category. While the latter did not fully qualify as wives of the first order, they were close seconds because they, too, had to go through a religious ceremony. Three Hindu, Muslim and British historians vary slightly in their calculations of the number of Ranjit Singh's wives. While Gupta settles for twenty,[16] Waheeduddin's figure is eighteen, with nine in each of the two classifications.[17] Griffin's total comes to sixteen, of whom nine were wives and seven *chadar dalna*.[18] As to the number of concubines, it is anybody's guess.

Ranjit Singh's childless marriage with Mehtab Kaur proved of far less consequence than his alliance with the Kanhayias, her father's *misl*, thanks to the inputs of the energetic and enterprising Sada Kaur, who helped her son-in-law realize not only some of his goals but some of her own as well in the process. Although his marriage with her daughter did not last long, Sada Kaur, while no doubt disappointed, was a pragmatic and clear-headed woman. She was as determined as ever to exploit the opportunities the alliance with the Sukerchakias had opened up for her. Her eventual goal was to dominate the whole of Punjab.

In 1798 Ranjit Singh married again, and in 1802 his second wife, Raj Kaur of the Nakkai *misl*, presented him with his first son, Kharak Singh, earning her the title of First Rani. As Ranjit Singh's heir, Kharak Singh was to prove disastrous.

Sada Kaur, knowing well that the only way of increasing her power with her son-in-law was through her daughter and aware of the growing importance of others in Ranjit Singh's life after the birth of Kharak Singh, insisted that her daughter, too, should have a child by him, even though she now lived in Batala where he visited her rather infrequently. In 1807 Mehtab Kaur duly produced two boys, Sher Singh and Tara Singh. Her plan was to procure the children by any means and pass them off as the Maharaja's. Ranjit Singh was not fooled but, wishing to avoid a breach with Sada Kaur, treated Sher Singh as a son and gave him the title of prince.[19]

But the friendliness between Ranjit Singh and Sada Kaur was not destined to last long, because as the energetic lady began to expand her role in the affairs of his kingdom Ranjit Singh's resentment at her presumptuousness grew. While the two boys were growing up, the ever-ambitious Sada Kaur's strategy was to get Ranjit Singh to settle handsome *jagirs* on them. She wished to induce her son-in-law to settle an estate on Sher Singh independently of her own, her aim being to establish a solid claim on Ranjit Singh's territories through Sher Singh in the years to come.[20] But the Maharaja, no novice in this game of wile and guile, insisted that Sada Kaur present the prince with a *jagir* appropriate to his status out of the extensive Kanhayia territories which were now hers. With the steady souring of their relationship over the years Ranjit Singh had his own eyes on the Kanhayia possessions, and Sher Singh, ironically enough, was now pivotal to the game plan of each.

By October 1820 matters came to a head. Ranjit Singh ordered Sada Kaur to set aside half of her own estates for the maintenance of the two princes, Sher Singh and Tara Singh. Sada Kaur was unwilling to obey the order, threatening to cross the Sutlej and place her estate of Wadhni under British protection.[21] With this ill-advised threat she overreached herself and sealed her fate. It was now clear to Ranjit Singh that if his mother-in-law was prepared to resort to the ultimate treachery of turning for help to the British, an enemy-in-waiting, she had to be debarred from any future role not only in his affairs but even in those of her own *misl*. After a few more moves and counter-moves, including an unsuccessful attempt by Sada Kaur to cross over to the British, she was confined to the Lahore Fort, from which she managed to escape, but a force was sent to apprehend her, returning with a good deal of Kanhayia wealth from their stronghold of Batala. The Kanhayia *misl* now became Ranjit Singh's property, and Sada Kaur remained confined in a fort for the rest of her life, first in Lahore and then in Amritsar, where she died in 1832 at the age of seventy.

છ્ક્ત

In 1821 Kharak Singh had a son, Nau Nihal Singh, whose mother, Chand Kaur, was to play a significant part in future political events. It is important at this point, even though it will mean getting ahead of the narrative somewhat, to turn to her son, since a major milestone in his life provides a backdrop to the grim succession of events that unfolded soon after Ranjit Singh's death.

Nau Nihal Singh grew up to be the Maharaja's favourite grandson. Unlike his father, he was intelligent and well mannered. He was not handsome; it is said that he resembled his grandfather in deportment and habits, and his face, too, was pock-marked. Since he was in line for the throne of the Sikh empire after his father Kharak Singh's death, Ranjit Singh, Lion of Punjab and a doting grandfather, wanted his wedding – which was celebrated when the bridegroom was sixteen years of age – to be symbolic of a kingdom that had come to stay and the third generation of which was already coming into its own. His bride Nanki was the daughter of an important Sikh chieftain, Sardar Sham Singh Attariwala. The wedding and attendant events and festivities, held in and near Amritsar in March 1837, lasted just over three weeks, and more than three million rupees were spent on it.

The guest list read like an Indian who's who. The rajas of Patiala, Jind, Nabha and Faridkot, the Nawab Maler Kotla and the Chiefs of Suket, Mandi, Chamba and Nurpur were all invited. On the British side those on the invitation list included the governor-general Lord Auckland, Sir Charles Metcalfe, now governor of Agra, and Sir Henry Fane, commander-in-chief of the British Army in India. The latter was among those who attended and left a fascinating eyewitness account of the wedding in his memoir *Five Years in India*.

Fane was received on the River Sutlej on 5 March by Kanwar Sher Singh and then, near Amritsar, by Prince Kharak Singh, Prime Minister Dhian Singh and a deputation of 3,000 splendidly dressed horsemen. He was welcomed with a gift of 5,000 rupees. Kharak Singh was dressed in gold and silver but is said not to have been half as handsome as his brother Sher Singh, who is described as a tall, black-bearded man, majestic in a magnificent *sarpech* (ornamental headpiece) of large diamonds, rubies and emeralds. The emerald belt he wore on this occasion is now at the Victoria and Albert Museum in London. Ranjit Singh's powerful prime minister Dhian Singh was a striking figure. He was above average height, with aquiline features and a high forehead; his attire was bedecked with jewels, the hilts of his sword and dagger were encrusted with gems, and his cuirass of polished steel – a present from King Louis-Philippe of France – was embossed with gold. He sat proud on a large Persian horse, the saddle and bridle of which were embroidered with gold.

Everyone was housed in tents of scarlet material, crowned with gold balls. Floors were covered with rich carpets, and chairs were of carved silver. On his arrival at the camp Fane was greeted by the Maharaja's envoy with 2,100 gold ducats and 500 trays of Indian sweets and fruit.

On the following day a meeting between Ranjit Singh and Fane took place in the garden of Amritsar's Rambagh Palace under a canopy of colourful shawls held up by silver poles. Chairs of gold and silver were placed for the guests. The Maharaja and his entourage came on elephants gorgeously caparisoned. Ranjit Singh, who struck eyewitnesses as beginning to look elderly, although without any diminution in his mental alertness, was plainly dressed in green, but what stood out was a single string of huge pearls around his neck and two diamond armbands. Raja Dhian Singh's eighteen-year-old son Hira Singh, another favourite of Ranjit Singh's, stood out in the crowd. Very handsome although rather effeminate, he was covered from head to toe in a profusion of jewels. It is said that he was one of the few allowed to be seated in the Maharaja's presence. As usual, Ranjit Singh questioned his interlocutor closely and continuously about all aspects of his army.

The Maharaja showered the people with gold and silver coins as he rode through the streets. At the Bhangi Fort the *watna* ceremony (applying oil to the hair) took place, with Ranjit Singh the first to apply oil on his grandson after first throwing hundreds of gold ducats into the vessel full of oil. The others followed suit. Prince Kharak Singh and his mother Raj Kaur made a *sarwarna* or blessing of 125 rupees each over the bridegroom. The latter's sister then performed the traditional custom of rubbing oil into Ranjit Singh's beard. The pleased Maharaja gave her 500 rupees, but she returned the money and asked for a *jagir* instead, which was instantly granted. This ceremony was followed by an evening of feasting. Gifts of money and gold then arrived for the bridegroom from the bride's home in Attari.

In the morning of the third day, 7 March, the ceremony of investiture of the bridegroom with the bridal chaplet or wreath took place at the Golden Temple. Ranjit Singh personally covered the bridegroom's face with a *sehra* or veil of uncut diamonds and pearls, and monetary offerings were placed before the holy book, the Guru Granth Sahib, and at the Akal Takht. In the afternoon the procession left for Attari, headquarters of the Attariwalas. It is estimated that not less than 600,000 people lined the roads on either side.

On reaching the baronial-looking castle of Sardar Sham Singh Attariwala, a stout and easy-going man, the Maharaja was presented with 101 gold mohurs and five richly caparisoned horses, Kharak Singh with 51 gold mohurs[22] and a horse, and all the other Sardars received commensurate gifts. The marriage ceremony took place in the evening at what was considered an auspicious hour. Under a large canopy attached to the roof of the main building, before a large assembly of guests and spectators, the bridegroom was seen for the first time, his face covered by the *sehra*. The ceremony ended at nine o'clock. The Maharaja was moved to say to his wife Raj Kaur, grandmother of the bridegroom: 'This is the most auspicious and fortunate day which it has been vouchsafed me by God to see. I must thank the Almighty, for such a day was not vouchsafed even to my forefathers.'[23]

Immediately after the ceremony there was a fireworks display and feasting followed by dancing which carried on all night. On this occasion Ranjit Singh, seated on his chair of state, wore the Koh-i-noor diamond on his arm along with his famous pearls.

Even a sip of his favourite fiery liquor brought tears to the eyes of his English guests, but the Maharaja drank several glasses of it with no visible effect.

The next day the bride's dowry was displayed to the people in an enormous enclosure five miles in circumference. It consisted of 101 horses with gold and silver trappings, hundreds of cows, buffaloes, camels and elephants, shawls from Kashmir, silks from Multan, gold and red brocade from Benares, beautifully carved silver and gold plate and dishes and precious stones. The clothes alone are said to have covered an acre. Sir Henry Fane gave the bridegroom 11,000 rupees and Raja Dhian Singh 125,000 rupees, while the other chiefs gave what was appropriate to their rank and position. Money was also distributed to the poor in the same enclosure; it is said that over a million people were given one rupee each.

The wedding festivities continued at Lahore where on the evening of 12 March the British and other guests were entertained at the Shalimar Gardens, which had a fairyland atmosphere, with decorations and illuminations from countless oil lamps in different colours hanging from trees, roofs and walls and along the walks, all reflected in the cascading waterfalls. The English ladies were enchanted, and after they left the dancing gathered tempo and liquor flowed.

A few days later, with so much military presence on both sides, it was time for reviews. On 16 March a grand review of the Sikh army was held; it is recorded that 18,000 men assembled in Lahore, well clothed and armed in the European fashion. On the following day Fane's escort of cavalry, horse artillery and infantry units held their review. Ranjit Singh's overtly expressed admiration for what he saw was immense, as an eyewitness describes: 'The extreme delight of the old man at the discipline of the men and the explanation the General gave him of the movements, and how they would act with a large body, surpasses belief. He rode through and looked at every gun, examined the appointments of the men, counted the number in each square, and quite gained all our hearts by the interest he took and the acuteness which he showed by his questions.'[24] He was so delighted to see a six-pounder of the Horse Artillery dismounted from its carriage, taken to pieces and put together again inside five minutes that he afterwards sent a gift of 11,000 rupees to be divided among the soldiers. And he responded similarly at a British artillery demonstration on the following day.

On 22 March the Holi (spring) festival was celebrated with traditional vigour. The British commander-in-chief was present, and the Maharaja poured red powder and yellow saffron over his head while the prime minister rubbed him all over with gold and silver leaf mixed with red powder. The Sardars, seated on chairs with baskets of red powder beside them, pelted each other with balls filled with saffron. The Afghan ambassador, just arrived from Kandahar, a devout Muslim, was covered in coloured dust from head to foot and, not having any idea what was happening, took flight amid roars of laughter – 'etiquette for the nonce was thrown to the winds'.[25]

Twenty-two days after General Fane had been received, on 27 March, he took his leave of the Maharaja in a farewell visit to him in his garden house, seated on a carpet with tame pigeons feeding around him, attended by his court.

Ironically enough, since it was Ranjit Singh who openly asked the questions and soaked up information, it was the British who had seriously set about gaining military intelligence on this occasion. The commander-in-chief's party had used the opportunity to make a detailed appraisal of the Sikhs' military power, which was reckoned to consist of 67 infantry regiments, 700 pieces of artillery and innumerable cavalry. Fane's confidential report to the governor-general contained estimates of the British army's ability to destroy Ranjit Singh's military might, which had now reached formidable proportions.[26] In his *History of the Sikhs*

(1849) Joseph Cunningham called this use of what was supposed to be a social occasion to form an estimate of the force which would be required for the complete subjugation of the Punjab 'a base and graceless act'.[27]

❧

Returning to the question of Ranjit Singh's principal wives, if we place the total number at nine, the preceding account leaves seven others. The two who deserve mention here, both of whom he married in 1828, are Mahtab Devi and Raj Banso, daughters of Raja Sansar Chand of Kangra: the first because of her deep devotion to him and the second because she committed suicide when Ranjit Singh compared her exceptionally beautiful looks to those of a dancing girl – coming from a ruling family of Rajputs, Raj Banso took this slight to heart and overdosed on opium. Since there is nothing on record of interest about the remaining five wives they are left out of this account, but since those in the *chadar dalna* category bore Ranjit sons, they come into the story.

In 1810 Ranjit Singh had decided it was time to annex the territories of the Bhangi *misl* in Gujrat, but its chief Sahib Singh, realizing the futility of resisting the ruler's superior forces, had withdrawn to his Deva Butala fort without a fight, leaving the *misl*'s possessions to the victor. Moved by the pleading of the Bhangi chief's mother Mai Lachhmi, he gifted her son a holding worth 100,000 rupees. Sahib Singh did not live long enough to enjoy this largesse as he died a year later, whereupon his two widows, Daya Kaur and Ratan Kaur, became a part of Ranjit Singh's household through *chadar dalna*. It was not long before the two ranis, seeing how Mehtab Kaur had had her two sons accepted by Ranjit Singh, decided to follow the precedent she and Sada Kaur had so successfully set.

Daya Kaur, taking the lead, produced two sons, Kashmira Singh in 1819 and Peshoura Singh in 1821, named after Ranjit Singh's victories, and Ratan Kaur produced Multana Singh, named in the same vein, in 1819. Although the paternity of these three was in doubt, Ranjit Singh accepted them as his own sons and allotted *jagirs* to them befitting their princely status.

The number of daughters fathered by Ranjit Singh has remained a mystery to this day in the absence of any conclusive evidence. The closest the authors of this book have come to finding an answer was the discovery of a page in a handwritten diary kept by the Maharaja's youngest son, Dalip Singh. In this diary, which we chanced upon in Britain, Dalip Singh had entered the names of three women (whether wives or concubines was unclear) who had borne the Maharaja four daughters. Only the mothers are named, as Jagdeo (one daughter), Hurdsir (two) and Aso Sircar (one).

The last woman of significance in Ranjit Singh's life, although it seems they were never married, was Rani Jindan. Born in 1817, when he was thirty-seven, she was the daughter of a kennel-keeper who eventually became a chamberlain at court. Attracted to her when she was eleven years old, Ranjit Singh took charge of her education and maintenance by arranging for her to be brought up by a family in Amritsar. She arrived at the Lahore court when she was sixteen and completely captivated the ageing but still vigorous Maharaja. In 1838 she presented him with his seventh son, Dalip Singh. He was ecstatic at this welcome new addition to his family.

Described by one historian as 'one of the most misunderstood characters of nineteenth-century India', Rani Jindan was to rule the Sikh state for most of the last few years of its existence, from 1843 to 1848. She attracted British admiration, a British resident calling her 'the only effective enemy of British policy in the whole of India'. During this time she 'removed the veil, addressed the military Panchayats, inspected the troops, held court'.[28] Never easily impressed by his adversaries or one to give them any credit even when clearly due, Governor-General Lord Dalhousie had this to say about her: 'Rely upon it, she is worth more than all the soldiers of the state put together', and for good measure referred to her as 'the only person having manly understanding in Punjab'.[29]

A woman of great spirit and a high sense of self-esteem, Jindan, although faced with overwhelming odds, was not one to keep quiet or cringe before the occupying power. In the first of three letters she wrote to Henry Lawrence, the British resident at Lahore, she said on 7 August 1847: 'Why do you take over the kingdom by underhand means? Why don't you do it openly? On the one hand you protest friendship and on the other you put us in prison. At the bidding of three or four traitors you are putting the whole Punjab to sword.'[30] In her second letter of 20 August she wrote: 'You have snatched my son from me. For nine months I kept him in my womb. Then I brought him up with great difficulty. In the name of God you worship and in the name of the King whose salt you eat, restore my son to me. I cannot bear the pain of separation.'[31] And in her third of 30 August: 'Well, has the friendship between the two kingdoms repaid? I have lost my honour and you your word.'[32]

Whatever the astrologers of the time may have forecast for the prince, the destructive forces that would come out of the woodwork to put an end to the empire Ranjit Singh had constructed with such energy, enthusiasm and skill would emerge when Dalip Singh was not yet out of infancy. The plots, intrigues and betrayals inside the Durbar, combined with the ambitions of the British across the Sutlej scheming to annex the subcontinent's last great stronghold, would make Dalip Singh the setting 'son' on a failing empire.

Patron of the Arts and Minter Extraordinary

Creation is my obsession. Whatever is not giving
birth is for me dead.

HENRY MILLER

Although much has been written about his conquests and
military genius, little is known about Ranjit Singh's other contributions towards making Punjab one of India's most progressive
states. Whether it was in developing Punjab's crafts and their
exports, patronage to the arts, creating a unique coinage, sustain-
ing Punjab's environment or giving its citizens a sense of security
and ensuring the safety of travellers on its highways, nothing
escaped his attention.

Ranjit Singh's court attracted many talented artists from the
Punjab hills, Jammu, Kangra and Kulu. Under Rajput rulers these
artists had developed a distinctive style of painting in miniature
form. These miniatures were smaller than those of Mughal and
Rajasthani artists and concentrated more on stylization, on detail,
line and colour. Although the Kangra school was most highly
developed, there were many other important centres in the region
– Guler, Basholi, Mandi and Bilaspur. After Ranjit Singh's
conquest of Kangra, where miniature painting had flourished
under Raja Sansar Chand, it received a fresh impetus on making
its appearance at the Lahore Durbar. The years 1810 to 1830 saw

increasing interest in hill paintings on the part of Sikh patrons.

A charming example of Ranjit Singh's personal patronage of the hill artists is provided by W.G. Archer in *Paintings of the Sikhs*: 'Besides the Gurus, other Sikh characters were portrayed, and among them, a local person famous for his Sikh affiliations. Amar Singh "Darhiwala", a connection of the Kotla family, had so impressed Ranjit Singh with his stupendously long beard, that he was given a monthly stipend with which to cultivate it.'

Archer also pays handsome tribute to the courtesy and considerateness with which Desa Singh Majithia – appointed governor of Kangra after the region was taken over by the Sikhs – treated the people of Kangra, Guler, Nurpur and other centres of hill paintings.

> Tactful, affable and generous by nature, he had become warmly attached to the Kangra Hills. When not residing at the Kangra Fort or visiting other states, he lived in Guler and mingled with the local people. He also expressed his love for the area by marrying a hill woman who bore him a son, Ranjodh Singh. His gentle courtesy may well have mollified the embittered [raja] Bhup Singh and, perhaps as a result, Guler artists began to shed their reliance on Rajput subjects and experiment with paintings for the Sikhs.
>
> For Sikhs . . . Kangra painters devised a new kind of picture . . . the leading Kangra style had been passionate and poetic, interpreting the moods of ideal lovers, the romance of Radha and Krishna and the courtly conventions of Rajput feudal life. So long as these subjects were Rajput, their pictures had little appeal to Sikhs. Yet their basic themes – the charms of courtly love, the need of graceful women for handsome lovers – touched the Sikh imagination . . . Kangra pictures flattered their pride and by portraying Sikhs as aristocrats and lovers testified to their success.[1]

The ties with Kangra were also strengthened in 1838 when Ranjit Singh married two of the hill raja Sansar Chand's daughters.

He was painted on horseback, with his right side showing and an umbrella over his head – a sign of royalty. Sometimes his head was depicted with a halo around it. Ranjit Singh's portraits by Guler and Kangra painters show three stages. 'In the first they painted the likeness of Maharaja Ranjit Singh, with due deference to his blind eye. In the second stage after 1840 they took the liberty of depicting him in one or two paintings from the front. But in the third stage the cycle of their work comes full circle, as the myth of Maharaja Ranjit Singh finds its articulation in a decked-up horse, golden canopy, and the radiant halo.'[2]

The popular theme in this form of miniature art was Ranjit Singh holding court, with his sons, ministers, courtiers and foreign dignitaries. The hill artists preferred painting the grandeur of the court in all its glory to realistic portrayal. Among the Durbar figures depicted were the Fakir Brothers, Jamadar Kushal Singh, Hari Singh Nalwa, Diwan Mulraj and Dina Nath.

It was natural that portraits of the Gurus should be in demand in Punjab, but few such early paintings seem to have survived. Those that do are from the early eighteenth century. The miniaturists and other painters had to rely on their own imagery. Guru Nanak was depicted seated under a tree, with his two followers Bala and Mardana, with other holy men or surrounded by nine other Gurus. Guru Gobind Singh was mostly depicted riding his horse with a falcon in his hand. The other Gurus were invariably seated, with an audience around them and an attendant with a fly whisk. A series of miniatures was done in a late Mughal style – some beautifully painted, with an eye for detail and in brilliant colours, often gilded in pure gold. Scenes from Hindu mythology and gods and goddesses were also in great demand. Pahari artists from the Rajol school came to the Lahore court and flourished under the patronage of Maharaja Ranjit Singh and his family.

Among the well-known artists were Nikka, Gokal, Harkhu, Chhajju and Damodar.

The art of wall painting which can be seen through the centuries in many parts of India was practised in a more popular form in Punjab. Maharaja Ranjit Singh commissioned a Kangra artist to paint a mural with Guru Gobind Singh inside the Harmandir Sahib. He is depicted in strong and vibrant colours on horseback with his attendants. Since he was known for his love of falconry, two of them are shown holding his falcons. This fresco is the only one of its kind inside the Harmandir. Gurdwaras had portions of their walls, panels, arches and roofs painted to immortalize the Gurus, and the stories of their lives were told in bold, living colour and life-size. Parts of the walls were decorated as acts of dedication by the faithful, who donated money for the murals.

Ranjit Singh himself had religious themes painted in his palaces. According to Baron Hugel, the walls at Wazirabad Palace built by him had life-size paintings of all the Gurus, even though this goes against the Sikh ethic, as is discussed later in this chapter. Lieutenant William Barr describes frescoes in the Royal Palace at Lahore: 'The Maharaja in the presence of Baba Nanak, the founder of the Sikh sect: the holy father being most splendidly robed in a suit of embroidered gold, and sitting; whilst his disciple [Ranjit Singh], who has done so much to extend the domains of his followers, is dressed in bright green silk, and standing, with his hands joined in a supplicatory manner.'[3]

Ranjit Singh's interview with the governor-general at Ropar was also depicted, with both parties on opposite sides inside a large tent with the key figures, the Lion of Punjab and Lord William Bentinck, in the middle and Lady Bentinck seated behind her husband. According to Barr, such paintings, done in oils, were of a 'very extravagant description'.

Murals in the houses of Generals Allard and Ventura represented the Maharaja's court. Over a thousand figures were depicted, includ-

ing many detailed studies of courtiers. Many portraits, some from life
and others based on imagination, mostly depicting nineteenth-
century Sikh royalty and aristocracy, are to be seen among the extant
wall paintings throughout the Punjab. In addition, in written records
there are references to portraits which no longer survive.[4]

Ranjit Singh also had the Durbar Sahib, the holiest of Sikh
shrines, encased in gold and marble. After taking Amritsar in 1802,
he wanted the Harmandir Sahib and the Akal Takht, which had been
so badly desecrated by the Durranis, to be once again a magnetic
draw for the Sikhs, befitting their revered place in all Sikh hearts.
Master craftsmen were commissioned to lay carefully chosen slabs
of marble not only around the Harmandir but on the walls as well.

One of the present writers has published the following description of this work:

> Once the choice of marble and gold as the principal materials
> for the Harmandir had been made, work was begun to face
> its lower storeys with marble panels. These were inlaid with a
> wide range of exuberant and often whimsical designs and mo-
> tifs – from geometrics and abstracts to arabesques, flowers,
> foliage, fish, animals and a few human figures. Onyx, mother-
> of-pearl, lapis lazuli, red carnelian and other semi-precious
> and coloured stones were used for the inlays. The most elo-
> quent testimonial to the quality of this pietra dura work, and
> the skills of the craftsmen who executed it, is the way in which
> these mosaics on the outside walls of the Harmandir have sur-
> vived for almost 150 years. Their colours, clarity and visual
> appeal remain undiminished. This technique of inlaying
> coloured stones in marble is known as *jaratkari* in India.[5]

While the walls of the Harmandir were encased in marble,
copper panels covered in gold, exquisitely embossed, adorned the
upper stories. Above the entrance, in bas relief and blessing all

those who enter, are the figures of Guru Nanak, seated with Bala and Mardana, and Guru Gobind Singh on horseback. Over the main door is a panel inscribed with written testimony of the help given by Ranjit Singh to the Golden Temple.

Despite the patronage extended to artists, miniaturists, wall painters and others, it must be emphasized that artistic depiction of the Gurus is against the Sikh ethic, and here Sikh art has eroded a fundamental principle of Sikhism, which rejects idol worship and emphasizes the enduring importance of respecting the life-given form of fellow humans; the collective wisdom and philosophical vigour of the Gurus is what must be looked up to by all Sikhs, not their mythical or idolized forms. The life-supporting sense of direction can come only through the Sikh scriptures, the Granth Sahib, not through idolatory.

✑

Ranjit Singh disliked sitting for portraits. Conscious of his scarred face and blind left eye, he constantly put off the British traveller G.T. Vigne who was keen to paint him. Finally, according to an eyewitness account, 'Vigne Sahib . . . showed to the Maharaja his portrait, which he said he would take to his own country as a gift and a souvenir. The Maharaja was pleased to have a look at it. Then the said Sahib presented a map of the country of the Punjab which the Maharaja studied very closely.'[6]

Although he was ill at the time, he let Lord Auckland's sister, Emily Eden, do a sketch of him at Lahore in December 1838. The focus in this sketch is on the left profile. The surviving images of the Lion of Punjab in his later years usually show his right profile. The Durbar scene and its glamour and pomp fascinated Emily, but even more so she was fascinated by Ranjit Singh. 'He retained a perfect simplicity or rather plainness of appearance, while his chiefs and courtiers around him wore the most brilliant draperies and a rich profusion of jewels. His manners were always quiet . . .

He had a curious and constant trick, while sitting and engaged in conversation, of raising one of his legs under him on the chair . . . he had the use only of one eye, which age and a hard life of exposure and excesses had dimmed at the period now spoken of, but it still retained the traces of the vigour and penetration for which he was remarkable.[7] Emily Eden also sketched several members of Ranjit Singh's family – and his court – including his son Sher Singh, grandson Partap Singh and Hira Singh Dogra.

Another European artist, the Hungarian August Schoefft, arrived in Lahore in 1841, during Sher Singh's reign, and was very impressed with the pomp and splendour of the court. Although remembered for his magnificent oil painting of Maharaja Sher Singh, he did two paintings in which Ranjit Singh is also portrayed: *The Court of Lahore* and *Ranjit Singh Listening to the Guru Granth Sahib at the Golden Temple*. These were large canvases with Ranjit Singh's likeness reproduced with the help of other paintings or through how people remembered him. Schoefft also painted Rani Jindan, the mother of Ranjit Singh's youngest son Dalip Singh, reclining on a bolster and also young Prince Dalip Singh. 'Of all the numerous enduring images of the peacock splendour of the Sikh Durbar,' one art historian has written, 'none – not even the contemporary miniature paintings of that period, nor the pen-portraits left behind by gifted writers such as William Osborne or his aunt, Miss Emily Eden, or G.T. Vigne or Dr Martin Honigberger – can match the sweeping flourish with which the painter August Theodor Schoefft (1809–88) brought to life on a single canvas [*The Court of Lahore*] the hierarchy which was responsible for the establishment of the Sikh State in the Punjab, and also for its ultimate disintegration.'[8]

❧

Ranjit Singh liked to see colour, jewellery and rich fabrics about him, as evidenced in the interior decoration he commissioned, notably in the hall of the Lahore Durbar and on great ceremonial occasions such as the meeting with Lord Bentinck at Ropar and the wedding of his grandson Nau Nihal Singh. The shawl industry in particular, developed in Mughal times, flourished during his reign, and shawls were part of the annual tribute paid to the Durbar by the governors of Kashmir. The main trade centres were Srinagar, Amritsar and Lahore.

Patterns and colours of shawls worn in the Punjab changed during the Afghan occupations of the eighteenth century. Yellow was a popular colour and the paisley became more elongated. The 'moon' shawl or *chand dar* – so named from the round pattern woven at its centre in a different colour – was much in demand between 1815 and 1830. Finely woven shawls which could be passed through a ring were known as ring shawls and were highly valued. Shawls were not only gifted to courtiers to be worn as sashes and turbans but were also made into tents.

A Kashmiri embroidered pashmina wool shawl has always been the vogue in Europe. General Allard, shortly before his death, ordered a richly embroidered piece at a cost of 3,000 rupees as a gift for the Queen of France. General Ventura's shawl, especially made for him, cost him over 6,000 rupees. Generally the price of a pashmina shawl was upward of 500 rupees. European ladies turned them into dresses and scarves and draped furniture with them. The famine that ravaged Kashmir in 1820–22 slowed down production but did not destroy it. Small carpets made from pashmina were thin, uniform in colour and with a border, and some had silk embroidery worked on them. These carpets were delicate and not very durable; they were mostly used in the *zenanas* (harems), where the women usually went about barefoot.

When travelling Ranjit Singh used a fine scarlet and gold embroidered tent made of pashmina. Even when at rest at night his sword and shield were always at his side, and his favourite horse was saddled and kept ready for him to ride at a moment's notice. His horses were adorned with velvet trappings encrusted with pearls and rubies and draped with embroidered pashmina shawls. He mostly travelled in a sedan chair made of glass and gold gilt. Sometimes he used a procession of carriages. His state carriage was very large, drawn by six horses and with a platform around it which could accommodate up to twenty courtiers.

Silk, a fabric mainly worn by courtiers, was considered a great gift for visiting dignitaries. *Kinkhab*, a brocade made of silk and gold thread woven in intricate designs, was especially favoured. Raw silk was imported either from Bokhara or China, as Kashmir could not supply the demand, but it was woven in many parts of Punjab, for example, Multan, Ludhiana and Shahpur. Multan was also famous for its fine woodwork and carving, especially on screens and doors. There were other centres for furniture and decorative woodwork in Kashmir, Peshawar, Gujrat, Lahore and Hoshiarpur. Examples of this splendid workmanship can be seen today in old traditional homes and museums.

Before Ranjit Singh, trade in and out of Punjab was almost non-existent owing to chaotic conditions created by centuries of wars and invasions. The main route into the Punjab, the Grand Trunk Road, was closed. Most of the other roads were infested with robbers and very unsafe for travellers. During Ranjit Singh's time it was decreed that wrongdoers would be severely dealt with, but although chastisement at times could be harsh there was no capital punishment. People in Punjab under Ranjit Singh felt more secure, and his kingdom had a better safety record than most other parts of India. When asked why he did not improve the roads, he replied that should he do so it would make it easier for the enemy to advance on him.

❦

Despite all he had to deal with, Ranjit Singh was an environmentalist far ahead of his time, who realized that wood and forests had to be preserved for the ultimate survival of humankind and not cut down indiscriminately. Lieutenant William Barr, writing around 1844 of his experiences in Punjab during Ranjit Singh's reign, reported: 'Wood, strange to say, is not to be bought, nor could I ever get sufficient for a small frame; which appeared so extraordinary that I concluded my servant was either misinforming me, or had not made sufficient inquiries; however, on asking the Maharajah's officers about it, they told me it was true, and that Ranjeet Singh will not allow a tree to be felled until it is actually required for use.'[9]

Ranjit Singh was fond of planting gardens and trees, notable testimony of this being the park at Amritsar, the Ram Bagh, completed in 1831. And during his brief reign his son Kharak Singh continued the tradition; he ordered trees to be planted along either side of the fifteen-mile stretch of road from Amritsar to the Tarn Taran, a tank of healing waters around a gurdwara built by Ranjit Singh.[10]

❧

The Maharaja was a superb horseman, and horses were his passion. He would often spend a whole day in the saddle without tiring. A connoisseur, he had over 1,200 horses in his stables out of which he kept a thousand for his private use. The king of England presented him with horses from Scotland, and Arabian thoroughbreds were gifted to him by the Nizam of Hyderabad. The extent to which horses affected him comes through movingly in this description dating from his later years: 'as soon as he mounts his horse with his black shield at his back, [it] puts him on his mettle – his whole form seems animated by the spirit within, and assumes a certain grace, of which nobody could believe it susceptible. In spite of the paralysis affecting one side, he manages his horse with the greatest ease.'[11]

If Ranjit Singh heard of a horse of particular beauty or grace, he had to have it – no matter what the cost. He would willingly spend the equivalent of £30,000 or more for one that caught his fancy. In the 1820s he was captivated by stories of a horse called Leila. But her owner, Yar Mohammad Khan Barakzai, governor of Peshawar, flatly refused to part with it. Not prepared to take no for an answer, Ranjit Singh ordered a detachment of his army to Peshawar to bring him the mare. It took two expeditions against the Afghans, but in the end Ranjit Singh had his Leila. A rare beauty, dark grey with black legs, Leila was joyously celebrated on her arrival at Lahore by her adoring new owner, who thought her to be 'the most perfect animal he had ever seen'.

The saddles and bridles of Ranjit's horses were exquisitely tooled in silver and gold, a rich mixture called *ganga jamni*. This is described as follows by a contemporary: 'Runjeet's own horse-equipments are very gorgeous, the holster pipes being covered with gold tinsel, and studded with precious stones, particularly emeralds and topazes; while the bridle reins are formed of pieces of gold or silver, connected together over the leather which is thus concealed.'[12]

Baron Charles Hugel, who was taken to have a closer look at the horses by Ranjit Singh, noted: 'a pommel of one of the saddles struck me as particularly worthy of remark, having a ruby two inches square, bearing on it the name of Jehanghir. Dow, in his *History of Hindosthan*, tells us, that when Jehanghir had his name engraved on this beautiful stone the celebrated Empress Nur Jehan told him that she thought it a pity; to which he answered, "This jewel will more assuredly hand down my name to posterity than any written history. The House of Timur may fall, but as long as there is a king, this jewel will have its price." Many other names are now engraved on it, the best known being Ahmed Shah's.'[13] This 352.5-carat stone originally belonged to Timur who carved his name on it. Although known as the 'Timur Ruby', the stone is actually a spinel. It was a gift from the East India Company, along with other incomparable treasures including the Koh-i-noor, to Queen Victoria in 1851 after the annexation of Punjab.

Ranjit Singh much enjoyed hunting as a sport. He and his guests participated enthusiastically in tiger, wild hog, black partridge and hare shoots while riding on elephant-back. Fields of sugarcane and grain were especially cultivated for game. Since elephants played an important role in his hunting expeditions, he owned about 700 of them; his favourite, Sundargaj ('beautiful elephant'), the most imposing of them all, was a gift from the king of Nepal. Hugel describes him as being of immense size and 'ornamented with a splendid gilt howdah and crimson velvet cushions. Red velvet housings fell as low as his knees, trimmed with a gold border and fringe. The long tusks were cut at the end, as is the case with all tame elephants; but this deficiency was supplied by tops of silver gilt, united by a golden chain. Round his ankles were curiously wrought heavy gold bangles such as the Hindus wear. The price of this elephant's ornaments, according to the Maharaja's account, was 130,000 florins [£13,000].'[14]

Ranjit Singh had his elephants serve another enjoyable purpose in his life. These stately creatures, uniquely attired and outfitted under his specific instructions, had beautifully carved lanterns fixed to their upturned tusks, so that when the Maharaja took a favourite like Moran or Gul Begum through the streets of Lahore at night his path was romantically lit by them. It is said that Sundargaj looked like a well-lit jeweller's shop as he made his way through Lahore in all his finery and lanterns.

Little has been written on the distinctive coinage of the Sikhs. Yet it is an integral part of the Sikh heritage. Apart from C.J. Rodgers, who wrote on Sikh coins in 1881, it has taken numismatists over a century to study them. They are original in a way that sets them apart from any other currency of the time, exhibiting a theme of divinity and valour which the Sikhs see as their hallmark. So coins are a part and parcel of the struggle and sacrifices of the Gurus,

Banda Bahadur, the *misls* and of Ranjit Singh himself – all of whom carried a vision of a Sikh nation to which each in his own way gave specific form and substance. They testify to a nation in which its people were at last free to practise their religion and live in peace and harmony; a land in which the tenets of the Gurus and other religions could coexist – a truly secular land. It is impossible to describe the coinage of Maharaja Ranjit Singh's period without touching on earlier history.

The first Sikh coin was minted at a time of upheaval. Baba Banda Singh Bahadur – appointed leader of the Sikhs by Guru Gobind Singh in 1708, intent on avenging the brutal killing of the Guru's two sons by the Mughals, hounded though he was by the Mughal army and fighting one battle after another with them, unfazed nevertheless – struck the first Sikh coin in 1710 after he had consolidated the Sikh seat of power at Lohgarh. The coin was historically unique. It broke away from the accepted numismatic practice of bearing the ruler's name, title or portrait. The Sikh rupee carried none of these and was dedicated instead to the glory of the Sikh faith and its Gurus. In those troubled times this helped reinforce the Sikhs' resolve and self-assurance and gave them added strength in their fight for their rights and beliefs. They believed that *fateh* or victory and power could not be gained without the help, blessings and guidance of the Sachcha Padshah, the True Lord. The coins were minted with the following couplets in Persian. On the obverse:

Sikka Zad Bar Har Do Alam Fazl Sachcha
Sahib Ast Fath-I-Gur Gobind Singh
Shah-I-Shahan Tegh-I-Nanak Wahib Ast
('Coin struck in the two worlds [spiritual and secular] by the grace of the true Lord, Nanak, the provider of the sword [power] by which Guru Gobind Singh, King of Kings, is victorious.')

On the reverse:

> *Zarb Khalsa Mubarak Bakht*
> *Ba-Aman Ud-Dahr*
> *Zinat At-Takht*
> *Mashwarat Shahr*
> *Sanah – 2*

('Struck at the Refuge [presumably Lohgarh] of the world, the Council City, the Ornament of the Throne, of the Blessed Fortune of the Khalsa, year 2 or 3.')

Banda Bahadur's victory at Sirhind on 14 May 1710 inaugurated a new calendar starting with the year 1, and the regnal years 2 and 3 pertain to this new era. There is no mint name, but from the honorific names assigned to cities at the time Lohgarh seems to be the most probable location. The verse on the obverse would later come to be known as the Nanakshahi couplet.

The Sikh coins were minted in the names of Guru Nanak and Guru Gobind Singh to further emphasize the message of Sikhism. They also served as symbols of defiance against the religious persecution which the Mughals relentlessly carried out against the Sikhs in their ongoing efforts to force them to convert to Islam. Thousands of Sikhs were killed because they refused to renounce their faith. So the first Sikh coins were struck to send a clear message to their Mughal oppressors that the Sikhs, with the help and blessings of their Gurus, would never succumb or be vanquished. After Banda's execution in 1716 these coins were accorded great reverence by the Sikhs. This was anathema to the Mughals, who confiscated them and put to death anyone caught possessing them.

Some Mughal coins from Lahore also dated 1710, in the name of Emperor Shah Alam Bahadur (1707–12), have a *khanda*, emblem of the Khalsa, on them. The *khanda* symbol was perhaps put on a few of the coins quietly, unbeknown to the Mughals, by a few daring Sikhs, an act which elated all Sikhs, who were thrilled at seeing a Mughal coin with a Sikh symbol circulating in Punjab. By late October 1710 the Sikhs had taken most of Punjab east of Lahore, and Banda had even reached the outskirts of Lahore.

When the *misls*, leaderless after Banda's death and banded together to achieve their common goal of annexing the cities in Punjab which were under Afghan and Mughal rule, emerged victorious after taking Lahore in 1765 they minted coins as a mark of their sovereignty. The couplet used on these coins was taken from the official seal of Banda Bahadur, which he used on *hukamnamas* and *farmans* – edicts and orders – and patterned after Guru Gobind Singh's seal. The legend on these coins, too, was in Persian. On the obverse:

> *Deg Teg O Fateh Nusrat Be-dirang*
> *Yaft Az Nanak Guru Gobind Singh*

('Abundance, the sword, victory and help without delay Guru Gobind Singh obtained from Nanak.')

The Kanahiya and Bhangi *misls* kept a steady flow of coinage through the years after 1765 even while having to defend Lahore against the Afghans. In 1772, after taking Multan, the Sikhs issued silver rupees from there until 1779 when the city was taken back by the Afghans. In 1775 coins were issued for the first time from the sacred city of Amritsar. Once they had achieved paramountcy in Punjab the Sikhs kept the mints at Amritsar, Lahore and Multan fully employed in striking coins in praise of the Gurus. The legend used was taken from Banda Bahadur's coins. In addition it had on the reverse:

> *Sri Ambratsarjio zarb [VS ... year]*
> *Maimanat Julus Bakht Akal Takht*

('Struck at the blessed Amritsar [VS ... year] during the tranquil reign of the Akal Takht.')

The history of the major *misls* can be traced through their coins. Although the coinage from Amritsar, Lahore and Multan is attributed to the Bhangi *misl*, there is enough evidence to believe that other *misls*, too, minted coins in these cities, especially Amritsar. Because the couplets were in praise of the Gurus, the coins came to be known as Gobindshahis and Nanakshahis. The *misls* played a significant role in propagating the Sikh faith and continued to mint coins till the ascendancy of Ranjit Singh. Starting with the messages on the coins, they rallied Sikhs from far and wide to join together to throw the Afghans out of their cities, reclaim their lands and to look forward to a period of consolidation and growth.

It was accepted practice for a monarch on attaining power to mint coins in his own name, so that with their circulation throughout the realm not only his subjects but neighbouring kingdoms and other countries would come to know who was the current ruler of the kingdom. Coinage was considered an important part of governance, as necessary then as it is now, and has been for millennia. India and Greece, in fact, were the first two civilizations to mint their own coins. What is rare about Ranjit Singh is that when he became monarch of Punjab at the age of twenty the coins he struck on Baisakhi Day in 1801 were in the name of the Gurus, not his own. Even though a monarch, he believed that he was but a servant of the Gurus and hence the coinage should bear their names, not his. Even his official seals reflect his deep humility and the reverence in which he held the Gurus and his faith.

Brilliant administrator that he was, Ranjit Singh knew the importance of a monetary system. His contemporaries, the Marathas, Durranis, Mughals and others, all had their own to collect revenues, pay soldiers' salaries and for barter and trade, all of which took place in the currency of the reigning monarch. Now for the first time among the Sikhs Ranjit Singh developed a complete and comprehensive currency system which consisted of the gold mohur, silver rupee, half and quarter rupees and two, one and half paisas in copper, a system which remains the basis of India's currency today. The gold mohur was not used as currency but on special occasions as *nazaranas* (gifts and tributes). The gold coins in circulation were the Dutch and Venetian ducats, which were called *buttkis*. The copper paisas introduced by Ranjit Singh were minted at Amritsar, in Gurmukhi script, and had the legend 'Akal Sahai Guru Nanakji' – 'Help from God and Guru Nanak'.

Since Ranjit Singh was a secularist all his life – in his choice of ministers, generals and administrators, in matters of religion and of wives – his coinage reflected his secularism. The script was in Persian, the legend was of the Sikh faith, the dates followed the Hindu calendar established by King Vikramaditya, the Vikramditya Samvat, in which VS year 57 corresponds to AD 1 and New Year is defined by the vernal equinox. The rupee (10.7–11.1 g) had the highest purity of silver and was much in demand for its intrinsic value, as opposed to the other currencies in circulation – Mughal, Durrani and East India Company. It was in Ranjit Singh's reign that the rupee coins of the Sikhs came to be known as Nanakshahi rupees.

With his eye for detail, Ranjit Singh took a keen interest in his coinage, especially as he associated it with the Gurus. While the *misl* coins were rather crude in material and style, Ranjit Singh's currency exhibits a refinement in terms of both artistry and workmanship. Embellished with *chand* and *sitara* – moon and stars – little flowers, beads and chevron and dotted borders, their calligraphy was of superb quality, especially those minted in Peshawar. A variety of symbols appear from time to time. In 1802 a hand (*punja*) is seen on the coins of Amritsar – the year Ranjit Singh took it over. A royal umbrella, fish, *kartar* (dagger), and the Hindu god Ram can be seen in different years. Significantly, all Ranjit Singh's coins have one symbol in common: a leaf; because of its stylistic variations it is difficult to trace its botanical origins. It has been speculated that it could be a *pipal, ber* or lotus leaf, but whatever its origin it is always very prominent and easily recognizable. The intention was most probably that the people of Punjab should be able to identify their own coins easily, and so the mints wisely continued to put the leaf on all coins.

As his dominions increased, Ranjit Singh set up mints in Multan (1818), Kashmir (1819), Derajat (1821) and Peshawar (1834), with Lahore (1801) and Amritsar (1802) remaining the Durbar's main mints. Between 1801 and 1849 it was estimated that the amount of rupees struck from Lahore and Amritsar alone was in the region of 65 million. Amritsar's annual output was over one million rupees, and there between 1830 and 1840 one Nanakshahi rupee could buy 82.5 lb of wheat, 17 lb of rice, just over 8 lb of cotton, two rupees a sheep, 40–50 rupees a cow and 100 rupees a milk buffalo.

Eleven successive governors held office in Kashmir during Ranjit Singh's time, and only coins from this province carry an initial or symbol of each individual governor. Bhim Singh (1830–31) had *Bha* in Gurmukhi, Sher Singh (1831–34) a small tiger. Hari Singh Nalwa (1820–21) had *Har* in both Gurmukhi and Nagri scripts on the coins issued during his governorship. So deep was the impression left by his rule that the Nanakshahis of Kashmir came to be known as Hari Singhjis, and the term continued long after Punjab's annexation in 1849.

Ranjit Singh also put coinage to a more personal use. Bibi Moran, as we have seen, was the love of Ranjit Singh's life, and at the beginning of their relationship he could deny her nothing. Moran, a romantic, had heard stories of how Emperor Jahangir loved his legendary wife Nur Jahan so much that he had coins minted in her name; Moran, too, wanted her name engraved on the coins of the realm and even laid a wager to this effect. Not wanting to give offence to his subjects, yet wanting to indulge his favourite, Ranjit Singh found a way out.

Although *moran* generally means 'peacock' in Punjabi, it also has a secondary meaning, 'a long dry branch with twigs'.[15] So Ranjit Singh gave orders that the rupees issued from Amritsar between 1804 and 1806 should have highly stylized branches and berries, replacing the leaf on the reverse side. These charming rupees were called Morashahis and were kept as curiosities after the fall of the Sikh empire.[16] The 1805–6 Arsiwalashahis – mirror rings worn by brides and dancing girls – were also associated with Bibi Moran. A century later, these coins and rings were still known as Morashahis and Arsiwalashahis, immortalizing Moran and Ranjit Singh's love for her.

Although Ranjit Singh's successors continued the monetary system he had established, the turmoil that followed his death was reflected in the coinage of that period. With the Dogras in the thick of the battle for power and intrigues and chaos in and around the Durbar, it is no wonder that different types of symbols began appearing on the Nanakshahis. During the turbulent rule of Kharak Singh (1839–40) Rani Chand Kaur had an *om*, a Hindu chant, put on the obverse side of the coin where the couplet to the Gurus had been imprinted earlier. During Sher Singh's reign (1841–3) a *trishul* or trident and a *chhatra* or royal umbrella appeared on the coinage, signifying strife and a fight to keep the throne. There are some disturbing designs on the rupees of the minor Dalip Singh (1843–9) in which religious and martial marks or symbols tell their tale of the changing times: *chhatras*, flags, the word *sat* or truth in Gurmukhi, Shiva the Hindu God of destruction in Nagri and so on.

The most intriguing Nanakshahi of this period belongs to Multan, the setting for the rebellion in 1848 which brought on the Second Sikh War. Mulraj, the Diwan of Multan, had a war forced on him by the British who wished to annex it. During the first siege of Multan on 15 and 16 September 1848 Mulraj possessed no silver to pay his troops but had a quantity of gold rupees. A letter of 24 May 1864 from the financial commissioner in Punjab, D.F. McLeod, to the finance minister in India, Sir Charles Trevelyan, throws light on this: 'I send you one of Mulraj's gold rupees, which you particularly wished for. It was some time before I succeeded in getting it, as they are now very rare. He had in Multan some 40 lakhs (4 million) of rupees hoarded in gold, and, being short of cash wherewith to pay his troops, he is said to have coined the whole into these pieces, which passed for one rupee. On one side, the legend is *Sat-Gur-Sahai* [Sahai Sat Guru] and on the other an emblem which I suppose is intended for a spearhead [it is a leaf], with the Sumbut year 1905 [AD 1848] above it, and a legend below, which reads like *Sundar Kal* [Mandar Ka].'[17] Mulraj, a Hindu Khatri, desperate for help, inscribed *Sahai Sat Guru* – 'Help from the True Lord' – on one side and *Mandar Ka* – 'Belonging to the Temple' – on the other. This was an invocation to inspire and provide his troops with hope.

These little gold rupees weighing 0.65 g are a fascinating rarity, since an Indian rupee coin is usually made of silver. The British certainly thought so. In a letter to the editor of the *Numismatic Circular* dated 18 December 1895 Oliver Codrington of Clapham wrote: 'My old friend Major Benett, formerly of the Bombay Fusiliers, who gained his commission from Sergeant at the siege of Multan for gallantly leading the storming party and placing the British Colours on the walls, told me that they found sacks full of these little coins in the treasury of the citadel when they took it, and that he remembered soldiers looting them and bringing them out off guard stowed away in their boots.'

On 22 September 1848 a Sikh document fell into the hands of a Major Edwards, who sent it from his camp to the resident at Lahore with a covering note: 'This letter is one out of the many incendiary proclamations, with which Raja Shere Singh Attareewala and his accomplices, ever since their own desertion to the enemy, have been endeavouring to seduce those troops in my camp, which are still faithful to the real interests of Maharajah Duleep Sing.'[18] The following is a literal translation of the proclamation, which expresses the sentiments of the Sikh Sardars and soldiers who were fighting to retain the homeland their forefathers had so desperately fought for.

PROCLAMATION:

To all the officers of the Sepoys, and Sikhs, and Mussulmans, and regiments, and others that eat the salt of the Sovereign of the Khalsa, Maharajah Duleep Sing Bahadoor . . . A religious war being now on foot, it becomes every public servant, whether he be Sikh or Moslem, at sight of this document, to march, without delay, and join the camp of the Khalsa, along with Raja Shere Sing Bahadoor and Dewan Moolraj, in the work of eradicating the Feringees [Europeans] from this country of the Punjab.

1st. For their own religion's sake.

2nd. For the salt they have eaten.

3rd. For the sake of fair fame in this world.

Sealed by Raja Shere Sing, Dewan Moolraj, Sirdar Khooshal Sing, Morareea and others.[19]

❦

Punjab was annexed by the British on 29 March 1849. Barely a month later the Nanakshahi mints of Amritsar, Lahore, Derajat, Multan, Pind Dadan Khan, Peshawar and Rawalpindi were abolished and the Sikh currency was withdrawn. The Nanakshahis now fell into a category classified as 'uncurrent' and were systematically replaced with British Company currency. All Nanakshahis were recalled from the treasuries at Moti Mundar, Lahore, Amritsar, Peshawar, Multan and from circulation within Punjab. All transactions, revenues and soldiers' pay were now paid using Company money.

What happened to the Nanakshahis of the Gurus? And to Ranjit Singh's currency? 'The "dead coinages" [as the British now chose to call the Sikh currency] were called in and sent to Bombay and Calcutta to be melted down, and their equivalent was remitted to the Punjab, stamped with the mark, not of the Great Guru … but of the English Queen. The coinage of the country was thus made to harmonise with accomplished facts, and within three years, three-fourths of the whole revenue paid into the British treasury was found to be in British coin.'[20] On 5 May 1851 a statement of cash held in the treasuries of the Punjab was sent from the Punjab Secretariat to the central government of India showing 6 million rupees in Punjabi coin, and it was suggested that two steamers should come up the Sutlej or Ravi in August to take the packages of coinage from Lahore to Bombay.[21]

With annexation the Sikhs lost their territories, treasuries, heritage, currency and their empire. The first partition of Punjab was in 1849, not in 1947 as is generally believed. In 1849 Punjab was split up into separate districts and separated into trans- and cis-Sutlej states, Jammu and Kashmir having already been made over to Gulab Singh in 1846 for 7,500,000 rupees (£1 million). The first thing Gulab Singh did in 1846 was to mint his own coinage, called Gulabi, of a baser metal content and lighter in weight than the Nanakshahi, and it was in this coinage, in small instalments, that he paid the British for a substantial piece of territory that did not belong to them.

One does wonder: what if Jammu and Kashmir had not been a separate state but still a part of Punjab in 1947? Would the Sikhs, who have repeatedly shed their blood since then to defend not only Kashmir but the whole of India as well, have allowed it to become a bone of contention?

7

Flouting the Republican Tradition

Sikhs owe their spirit of compassion to the Khalsa.
The inspiration for my learning came from the Khalsa.
Our enemies were vanquished by the steadfastness of the Khalsa.

GURU GOBIND SINGH's *Dasam Granth*

Is it possible that at some point an inner voice might have warned Ranjit Singh that the end of his wondrous life was near? If it did, it seems to have had no effect on him. Seeing the pace he kept until the very end, it is unlikely he would have paid attention to any premonitions. He had already seen off afflictions that might have felled the hardiest. His brush with death from smallpox at the age of six, leaving him scarred and blind in one eye, had not affected his dynamism. He was stricken once more in 1806 by an undiagnosed illness and again in 1826 with a far more serious one which involved a paralytic stroke. But in less than five years of the latter, his excesses notwithstanding, he was fit enough at fifty to participate, during the ceremonial occasion with Lord Bentinck at Ropar in 1831, in strenuous events such as horsemanship and tent-pegging.

In 1834, at the age of fifty-four, he had another stroke even more serious than the earlier one. But he would not be deterred – perhaps because the most momentous years of his life always seemed to lie ahead of him. Of these, the year 1837 was one of the more significant because of several events that took place – some good and some bad. The first highpoint of that year was the wedding of his favourite grandson Nau Nihal Singh, son of his heir Kanwar Kharak Singh, in March at Amritsar, the celebration of which has already been described. Shortly after this event came a second highpoint, the repulse of a determined Afghan effort to take back Jamrud Fort from the Sikhs – even though the Sikh forces were outnumbered – thanks to the brilliant leadership of Hari Singh Nalwa. But this triumph, by which Jamrud looked to be well fortified against future aggressors, also brought a cruel blow for Ranjit, with the loss of his dear childhood friend Nalwa on the battlefield. Not only had the two known each other all their lives, they had fought against great odds, side by side, in countless battles. The Maharaja ranked Nalwa as one of his most dependable generals, and when news of his death reached him he first sent a contingent which included Prince Kharak Singh and other notables but unable to stay behind rode out himself – a gruelling ride of several hundred miles – to be present at the site of his friend's death.

Six months after Hari Singh's death in April 1837 Ranjit Singh's other great friend Fateh Singh, Sardar of Ahluwalia, died of high fever at Kapurthala. He and Ranjit Singh had formed a formal alliance in 1802 to underscore their friendship and mutual regard for each other. They had exchanged turbans, a practice confined to very special relationships among Sikhs. Fateh Singh had been with Ranjit Singh on his cis-Sutlej expeditions in 1806 and 1807 and had also taken part in the Bhimbar, Bahawalpur, Multan and Mankera campaigns.

Ups and downs between the two had ended in a cemented relationship. In 1825, told that Fateh Singh was building a fort at Kapurthala, Ranjit Singh had summoned him to Lahore for an explanation. Fateh Singh, innocent of the charge but fearing his lands might be confiscated, had fled to the British for help and

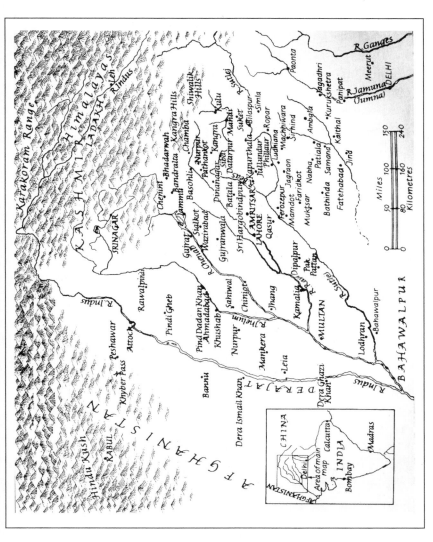

THE SIKH EMPIRE IN 1839, WITH CIS-SUTLEJ TOWNS

protection, and on hearing this the Maharaja had sent Faqir Aziz-ud-din to annex the Ahluwalia territories. However, through British intervention matters were settled between the two, and while lands in the Jullundar Doab remained with Fateh Singh those west of the Beas were acquired by the Lahore Durbar. Ranjit Singh then invited Fateh Singh to return, and the mistrust was put aside. Fateh Singh's bravery and diligence in a number of their joint ventures was publicly acknowledged, and Ranjit Singh was fond of telling his officers that there was no difference between him and the Ahluwalia chief and that the latter's orders should be obeyed along with his own.[1] Fateh Singh's death hit Ranjit Singh as hard as his other friend's had done a few months earlier.

Ranjit Singh experienced a third stroke in 1838 during Governor-General Lord Auckland's visit to Lahore. It was attributed to his robust drinking during the occasion, which came on top of the toll taken by the quantity and strength of his favourite liquor imbibed over the years.

$$\sim$$

All indications are that Ranjit Singh's inner voice finally appeared to have convinced him around 20 June 1839 that the end was near. He confided his concern to his foreign minister Fakir Aziz-ud-din, to whom he also conveyed his wish that Kharak Singh should succeed him, with the Dogra Dhian Singh as his prime minister. On 21 June he ordered all his superior officers, European and Indian, to be assembled in his presence and take the oath of allegiance to the heir apparent, his son Kanwar Kharak Singh; this ensured that, contrary to general expectation, he succeeded smoothly and without opposition to his father's throne.[2] The following day Ranjit Singh became unconscious but rallied and went for a short outing in his litter, always available for such occasions. A British medic, Dr Steele, came from Ludhiana to treat him, but nothing much could be done. On 23 June he again went out early in the morning to the Baradari Gardens, but after giving detailed instructions about the dispensing of charities he again became unconscious – after four hours or so to be his usual self again.

His condition became increasingly serious over the next two days, and on 26 June, sensing that his time had finally come, he had passages from the Granth Sahib recited to him as he bowed deeply before the holy book. He then asked that the Koh-i-noor diamond be donated to the Hindu temple of Jagannathpuri in Orissa on the Bay of Bengal. Surprisingly, the Dogra Dhian Singh who was not in favour of the wish told Ranjit Singh that Prince Kharak Singh should be put in charge of doing this. The Koh-i-noor was sent for, but after a lot of excuses the dying ruler was told that it was in the Amritsar treasury. Dhian Singh's view was supported by the Sardars, to whom possession of the diamond signified the independence of the Sikh kingdom; it was after all a favourite saying of the Maharaja's that whoever owned it would be the ruler of the Punjab.³ If this last wish of Ranjit Singh's had been carried out the Koh-i-noor would still be in India and not a possession of the British crown. During the last few days of his life Ranjit Singh gave away large amounts of cash and sundry items to a number of charities. His gifts ranged from richly caparisoned elephants, horses and cows to jewellery, gems, gold vessels and his personal weapons.

There is a moving account of Ranjit Singh's last hours by C.H. Payne. Although he had managed to recover from yet another stroke, he had lost the power of speech, 'and a curious and inter-esting sight it was now to behold the fast dying monarch, his mind still alive; still by signs giving his orders; still receiving reports; and, assisted by the faithful Fakeer Azeezoodin, almost as usual attend-ing to affairs of state. By a slight turn of his hand to the south, he would inquire the news from the British secretary; by a similar turn to the west, he would demand tidings from the invading army; and most anxious was he for intelligence from the Afghan quarter.'⁴ Clearly, the Lion was still the supreme arbiter of his natural habitat.

∘⨯⌀

The end came on 27 June at five in the afternoon. As the cortège made its way through the capital to the cremation ground, the grief and lamentations of the crowds left no one in any doubt as to what Ranjit Singh had meant to them. He was the personification of a ruler who had earned the respect and love of many of his subjects, not through intimidation or the arrogance of power but by earning their goodwill through his unending concern for them, in which he never faltered. Prayers were said for him by all communities; his subjects knew that at no other time had people of all religious faiths had the liberty to live their lives according to their beliefs, and their grief was truly heartfelt.

The culmination of this day of great emotional upheavals came when four of Ranjit Singh's wives and seven maids burnt themselves on the funeral pyre. His wife Rani Guddan, daughter of Raja Sansar Chand of Kangra, placed his head in her lap as the flame was applied to the sandalwood bier. *Sati* was not the custom among Sikh women, and the only previous exception known had occurred in 1805, in the town of Booreeah, on the death of the chief Rae Singh, when his widow had rejected a handsome provision in land, preferring a voluntary sacrifice of herself.⁵ On 30 June the ashes of the Lion of the Punjab were placed in jewelled urns and taken in a state procession via Amritsar to Hardwar, where some were immersed in the River Ganges and then the rest were taken to Lahore to be placed in a *samadhi* or mausoleum to this great ruler which was built next to the fort – a place he had loved and the seat of his power.

His final resting place is very near to the *samadhi* of Guru Arjan Dev, which Ranjit Singh had built with deep veneration for the fifth Guru. As was customary, the architectural form of his own *samadhi* was influenced by the Hindu and Islamic forms prevalent in those times. The material used was red sandstone in the main structure, with very little marble. Under the central vault and beneath a carved canopy of marble is the symbolic urn also in marble beneath which Ranjit Singh's ashes lie. There are several stone and marble memorials beneath this vault to commemorate his wives and maids who immolated themselves on his pyre. In the increasing chaos which overtook the realm, the Durbar's functionaries found little time to assemble the most sensitive designers and craftsmen to design a truly memorable memorial for one of the most exceptional men of the age.

Ten years later Joseph Cunningham was to sum up what he had stood for from the age of ten onwards. 'Ranjit Singh found the Punjab a waning confederacy, a prey to the factions of its chiefs, pressed by the Afghans and the Marathas, and ready to submit to English supremacy. He consolidated the numerous petty states into a kingdom, he wrested from Kabul the fairest of its provinces, and he gave the potent English no cause for interference. He found the military array of his country a mass of horsemen, brave indeed, but ignorant of war as an art, and he left it mustering fifty thousand disciplined soldiers, fifty thousand well-armed yeomanry and militia, and more than three hundred pieces of cannon for the field.'[6]

❧

Ranjit Singh attributed his own achievements to the grace of the Sikh scriptures. This acknowledgement of the wisdom of the Gurus and his unquestioning acceptance of the authority of the Granth Sahib were in many ways a radical departure from the prevailing practice of his time – and indeed long before it. In other countries, particularly Western, in any conflict between the monarch and the church, even senior members of the clergy were often overruled in favour of the monarchical view. In marked contrast to this, the absolute ruler of the Sikh state had once accepted a sentence of public lashing pronounced by the Golden Temple's clergy for a transgression it had viewed with disfavour even if the sentence was never carried out.

It is all the more surprising, therefore, that given the extent of his reverence for the tenets of Sikhism Ranjit Singh openly flouted one of them by setting himself up as a monarch with absolute authority over the affairs of the state and over all Sikhs resident in it. He thereby ignored the republican tradition which Guru Gobind Singh had established.

The tenth Guru had left no room for any ambiguity regarding the republican underpinnings of the Sikh religion. 'Wherever there are five Sikhs assembled who abide by the Guru's teachings,' he had told his followers, 'know that I am in the midst of them . . . Read the history of your Gurus from the time of Guru Nanak. Henceforth the Guru shall be the Khalsa and the Khalsa the Guru. I have infused my mental and bodily spirit into the Granth Sahib and the Khalsa.'[7] Another verse by him conveys this message:

> The Khalsa is a reflection of my form,
> The Khalsa is my body and soul,
> The Khalsa is my very life.
>
> *Dasam Granth*

Ranjit Singh made the grievous mistake of ignoring the essential meaning of these words, which unequivocally spell out the purpose of the Khalsa and that its goals should be reached through the collective will of its constituents. For each member of the Khalsa to survive and fulfil the aim of his life, he had to view his fellow religionists as representing the Gurus – and in particular the tenth Guru, Gobind Singh, who had founded the Khalsa – as his 'form', as his 'body and soul', as his 'very life'. To try to dominate the Khalsa was tantamount to trying to dominate the Guru.

Decisions had to be arrived at by members of the Sikh faith, collectively and by mutual consent, not by diktat.

Monarchs, since they are by definition sole and absolute rulers, are anathema to the ideals of a faith – like the Sikh – which requires equal representation in all major decisions. For such decisions a large gathering of the Sikhs – a Sarbat Khalsa – would pass a *gurmatta* or a collective resolution on the course to be taken. This is what was done in 1760 and 1765 when the Khalsa assembled at the Durbar Sahib to decide on annexing Lahore from the Afghans. The *panj piyare*, the five chosen ones, could also take decisions on behalf of the *panth*, the Sikh community.

Even though he held these guiding principles of Sikh beliefs in high regard, Ranjit Singh failed to foresee the disastrous consequences his monarchy would have on the Sikh state. He had, obviously, hoped that his successors would be as skilful as he in warfare, statesmanship and general qualities of leadership and would ensure the continuity and growth of the Sikh empire he had built with such confidence and skill. This was not to be. But he also ignored the fact that 'it is the self-respect, the awareness of his own ultimate significance in the creation of God, which imparts to a Sikh of Guru Gobind that Olympian air and independence which fits ill with a totalitarian or autocratic monarchical system of organization of power'.[8]

In his well-researched book *Parasaraprasna*, the Sikh scholar Kapur Singh, in a chapter 'How a "Sikh" Is Knighted a "Singh"', graphically recreates the momentous events which took place at Anandpur Sahib on 30 March 1699, when Guru Gobind Singh created the Khalsa and provided a new dynamic for a fledgeling faith. One of the cardinal conditions underscored for observance by all new entrants into the Khalsa was that its members must henceforth clear their minds of all previous traits, beliefs, superstitions, loyalties and such and believe solely and exclusively in one formless and unchanging god who dwells in each human being.

'Your previous race, name, genealogy, country, religion, customs and beliefs, your subconscious memories and pre-natal endowments, *samskaras*, and your personality-traits have today been burnt up and annihilated. Believe it to be so, without a doubt and with the whole of your heart. You have become the Khalsa, a sovereign man today, owing allegiance to no earthly person, or power. One God Almighty, the Timeless, is the only sovereign to whom you owe allegiance.'[9]

How deeply this idea is ingrained in the minds of Sikhs can be judged by the degree to which they have always asserted themselves in whatever task they have undertaken, whether on the battlefield, in occupations requiring a tough physique such as agriculture or, more recently in industry, transport and much else. So it is not difficult to understand why the monarchical idea thrust on them did not succeed after Ranjit Singh's death and why, when the monarchy collapsed, it brought down with it everything he had built with such flair and faith in his own sense of destiny.

The Gurus had underscored the importance of giving practical form and substance to an idea, not leaving it as an idea in the abstract. That is how Sikhism became a live and vibrant reality. They wanted every Sikh to have a practical bent. In this context Ranjit Singh's contribution was the specific form he gave to a commonwealth of the Sikhs. Before him the *misls* and other groups of Sikhs had more often than not been in conflict with each other. He forged them all together and gave them a sense of pride and power because of the inspiration they received from their religious beliefs.

The resilience and ruggedness of the Sikh faith and its followers, and their resolve and spirit of independence, were and are continuously nurtured by the Guru Granth Sahib and its evocative, balanced, rational and realistic view of life. It has sustained the Sikhs in the past and will continue to do so in the future. Not long after Ranjit Singh's death even the British acknowledged the quality of principled self-confidence he saw in them. In a letter to

Ellenborough, Henry Hardinge, his successor as governor-general, wrote: 'The Sikh soldiers are the finest men I have seen in Asia, bold and daring republicans.' His letter is dated 19 March 1846 – less than three years before the end came for the Sikh empire.

⚬❧⚬

Ranjit Singh achieved his goals because of his uncanny understanding of how to handle the Khalsa's sense of pride and independence and how to motivate each individual to strive for his goals whatever the odds. His iron will inspired his men, held them together and brought out the best in them. He needed men of talent and experience in his government, and because Sikhs accounted for a very small percentage of Punjab's population he had no hesitation in bringing in anyone of merit, whatever his background or faith, to serve the state. He was confident that in the final count he could control them. In the execution of this policy, however, he allowed a split to open up between the phenomenal achievements of his lifetime and his inability to ensure continuity after his death.

After extending Punjab's borders into far-away lands, breaking the Afghan stranglehold on India and knitting together the many culturally diverse religious, ethnic and linguistic groups in his realm, Ranjit Singh diluted the sustainability of what he had created. Had the hill Dogras Dhian Singh and Gulab Singh – whom he raised 'almost from the gutter', as Kapur Singh puts it, to the highest positions in his realm – been the only ones of their ilk, Ranjit Singh's legacy might conceivably have survived. But there were others whose true capacities for bringing down the edifice their sovereign had built were revealed only after his death, and among these the two that stand out are Tej Singh, an 'insignificant Brahmin of the Gangetic-Doab', in Kapur Singh's words, and another Brahmin, Lal Singh; after Ranjit Singh's death the last two were promoted to the top commands of the Sikh army.

To suggest that Ranjit Singh was not a good judge of men is unfair to him. He made sure that the men he chose from different faiths, beliefs and persuasions served him well. His personality and iron will ensured that his writ would prevail throughout his empire, no matter how far the territories of the Sikh state extended, and seldom in his lifetime did anyone have the courage to cross his path.

Although the terms 'kingdom' and 'empire' have been used freely throughout this book they jar with the republican ideal of the Sikh faith. Guru Gobind Singh, foreseeing the pull that India's feudal traditions, nurtured further by its caste system, would exert on Indian minds conditioned to accept hierarchies, emphasized his idea of an 'aristocracy'. It could not be by right of birth. 'Such an aristocracy [had to be] dedicated and consciously trained . . . an aristocracy . . . grounded in virtue, in talent and in the self-imposed code of service and sacrifice, an aristocracy of such men should group themselves into the Order of the Khalsa.'[10] The translator of Guru Gobind Singh's concept of 'an aristocracy' appears to have used this word unwittingly, whereas meritocracy is what Guru Gobind Singh always emphasized as the ideal of the Khalsa. The same ideal was to prove central to secularism, too.

Ranjit Singh did in fact follow the injunction of Guru Gobind Singh by creating a meritocracy based on virtue and talent and dedication. However, the distinction between an aristocracy defined not by 'right of birth' but by its 'self-imposed code of service and sacrifice' is soon lost when upstarts with unearned titles of princes and such usurp the rights of those who have virtue and talent but are humble by birth. This is precisely what happened after Ranjit Singh's death, and it is not surprising that the Khalsa started to revolt:

> The Khalsa is never a satellite to another power,
> they are either fully sovereign or

in a state of war and rebellion.
A subservient coexistence they never accept.
To be fully sovereign and autonomous is
their first and last demand.[11]

The truth of this became evident within months of Ranjit Singh's death. When his sons and their wives, nephews and senior functionaries of the Durbar vengefully turned against each other, the army, too, was inevitably, and irresponsibly, drawn into political decision-making. 'Such a right is not inherent in the concept of the Khalsa,' as one of the present authors has written elsewhere. 'Furthermore, whilst Ranjit Singh's leadership qualities had kept the army in line, its restiveness against his weak successors was now evident and when it spilt over, a major shift occurred from the political system created by the Gurus, in which rights had been invested in the entire Khalsa community, and not just the army. The manner of the army's assertiveness, though not directed at the state, damaged the state's cohesiveness since it lacked the discipline with which the Khalsa had closed its ranks against all adversaries in the past. This time it was divided both against itself and against others; an antithesis to the concept of a united Khalsa.'[12]

The qualities of spirituality, self-discipline and unlimited self-confidence which the Khalsa had introduced into the Indian mosaic were fatally subverted at this time, a process aided and abetted by the elites of India's older religious faiths, led by Hinduism and Islam, which had always at heart resented the vigorous self-assertiveness of the Sikhs. The end result was the weakening of the great legacy of the Khalsa's founding principles, of a magnificent and unprecedented state. This was the ultimate price paid for Ranjit Singh's error of judgement in departing from a key founding principle of his religion and creating a monarchy, even though he never behaved like most despotic monarchs have done through the ages.

Monarchical rule had been habitual during the most significant periods in Indian history, whether Buddhist, Jain, Hindu, Mughal or British. The fountainhead of power was the sovereign, not the people. If the people were restless, the rulers knew how to repress them. Those who were benign and ruled justly did so out of inner convictions, not because they were compelled to by the tenets of their faith. The emergence of the Sikh faith, committed to the republican democratic tradition, was a rare event in an environment in which authority was exercised arbitrarily and decisions in statecraft were whimsical more often than wise.

Another point to note is that whilst all great religions have waged wars against each other in attempts to establish their primacy, the Sikhs never fought wars to establish the supremacy of their faith. Their wars were fought to restore the sovereignty of their country, not the right of their religion to dominate people of other denominations. Ranjit Singh's critics, who rightfully criticize his monarchical bent, give him little or no credit for the even-handedness with which he applied the secular principle to the Sikh state. This quality of the man stood out in barbaric times. If the Sikh faith still has vitality and vigour, despite the setbacks it suffered as a consequence of his mis-step in establishing a monarchy, it is because the Gurus, unlike Ranjit Singh's critics, took into account human foibles and frailties.

8

The Decadent and Deceitful

Many of them, so as to curry favour with tyrants,
for a fistful of coins, or through bribery or corruption,
are shedding the blood of their brothers.

EMILIANO ZAPATA

Within days and months of Ranjit Singh's death his empire began to flounder – something that would have been unlikely to happen had the republican character of the Sikh state remained unchanged. Ranjit Singh's successors were unable to carry their fellow Sikhs with them because the Durbar's intrigues left many of them utterly disenchanted at the spectacle of all major decisions being taken by a few courtiers who lacked any integrity and moral vision. Such men no longer enjoyed the confidence or respect of the fearless and resolute Sikh troops on whom the power of the Sikh state had always rested. That power was now being destroyed from within.

The poet George Herbert writes that 'storms make oaks take deeper root'. Just the opposite happened when Ranjit Singh died. Prince Kharak Singh, who succeeded him as the Maharaja, was no oak, and the storms that began blowing after his father's death destroyed whatever roots he had. He was weak and ineffectual, with neither the charisma nor the qualifications to hold together the extraordinary legacy with which he had been left. He was incapable of dealing with external or internal threats, and it was the latter that put an end both to his rule and to his life. Some contemporaneous historians have their own agendas for holding that he was not as much of a weakling as he has been made out to be and that Dhian Singh ran him down to his father. 'It will readily be acknowledged by all who knew anything of Kurruck Sing', writes one such English historian, 'that in the early part of his life he gave the promise of, or in reality possessed, all the abilities requisite for a sovereign of the Punjaub; with perhaps one exception, viz. that while not so crafty as the minister, Dhian Singh, he was more religiously and peacefully inclined, and far less ambitious. Yet though peaceful, he proved when roused to energy that he possessed no small share of personal bravery, activity, and determination.'[1] It has at least to be admitted that in the immediate aftermath of Ranjit Singh's death and during the brief period in which he was still active Kharak Singh did score victories with the occupation of the hill states of Mandi, Saket and Kulu in 1840 – the same year in which he died, on 5 November.

His son, Nau Nihal Singh, was of a different mettle altogether. To begin with, because he was bright, alert and immensely proud of the legacy of which he was a part, Ranjit Singh saw him as a person who had the necessary energy and enthusiasm to continue the tradition of strengthening the foundations of the Sikh nation he had founded. But that promise remained unfulfilled, in part because of his early end and also because he lacked the humane instincts and wisdom that had set his grandfather apart. He had certainly started out in his footsteps, joining family tradition in being barely thirteen in May 1834 when he fought in the battle in which the Sikhs annexed Peshawar: both his grandfather and great-grandfather had gone out to battle before they were ten. So both at Peshawar and then among the Sikh soldiers who quelled a revolt at Dera Ismail Khan and Tonk, Nau Nihal Singh proved that the blood of his forefathers coursed richly through his veins.

What he completely lacked were scruples of any kind. He was

incapable of distinguishing between good and evil, which was in all likelihood responsible for his early end. While, for example, on the one hand he loathed Dhian Singh – and with considerable justification – he connived with him in crudely removing his father from power and exercising all the ruler's powers himself. On 8 October 1839 he also connived with Dhian Singh in the killing of Chet Singh, his father's closest adviser. It was a chilling and brutal murder, carried out in the presence of a very sick Kharak Singh. Nau Nihal Singh himself, it has been written, was present. According to some accounts Dhian Singh stabbed Chet Singh 'twice through the stomach with a long knife'.[2]

Kharak Singh declined rapidly, both in body and mind, after witnessing the brutal end of his friend and the callous disregard for his own dignity and sensitivity. The eighteen-year-old Nau Nihal Singh viewed his father's sad state as an opportunity to take over as virtual Maharaja of Punjab – a position to which he failed to bring any of his grandfather's qualities of statesmanship and leadership. 'His virtual assumption of power in the name of the titular monarch in December 1839', writes a modern historian, 'was characterized with unwise political steps . . . he prevented the British political agent Wade from meeting the Maharaja in December 1839, and made an attempt that Sir John Keane, the British general, should not have an interview with the Maharaja. He was also responsible for the recall of Wade from Ludhiana for the latter's alleged overbearing and obnoxious conduct towards him and the minister Dhian Singh.'[3]

Not content with these patently unwise moves against the British – in contrast to Ranjit Singh who had always made it a point to curb his own feelings about them – Nau Nihal Singh showed no such finesse. But he certainly stood up to them when the British made various provocative moves, some of which were noted down by the governor-general in his minute dated 20 August 1839. Among other things, he 'proposed the establishment of a permanent British mission at Peshawar and a magazine at Rawalpindi in the territories of the Durbar though they were not stipulated in the Tripartite Treaty [signed on 26 June 1838 by Ranjit Singh with Shah Shuja and the East India Company agreeing on a joint invasion of Afghanistan to put Shah Shuja on the Kabul throne]'.[4]

Nau Nihal Singh was perversely and provocatively rude to his father during the last few weeks of his life. Kharak Singh died on 5 November 1840 at just thirty-eight years of age. Ironically, Nau Nihal Singh's own life also ended the next day with the fall of an archway on him as he and some others were passing under it on their way back from his father's funeral. There are a number of versions of his death, one being that he did not die in the accident but was killed on the orders of Dhian Singh a day or two later, during which time no one was allowed to see him on the plea that he was being treated for his injuries.

Accounts of Nau Nihal Singh's end by writers of the period leave little doubt of Dhian Singh's role in it. 'None of the female inmates [of Lahore Fort], not even his wives, were suffered to see him. Everything was kept locked up for a while . . . and the minister [Dhian Singh] with but two of his followers and chief hill men remained with the prince.'[5] An eyewitness account by Captain Alexander Gardener, an American serving in the Lahore Durbar's artillery, noted that it was some of his own men who put the injured prince into a litter to take him to the fort. 'One of the *palkee* [palanquin] bearers afterwards affirmed, that when the prince was put into the *palkee*, and when he was assisting to place him there, he saw that above the right ear there was a wound which bled so slightly as only to cause a blotch of blood of about the size of a rupee . . . the blood neither flowed nor trickled in any quantity, before his being taken out. Now, it is a curious fact, that when the room was opened, in which his corpse was first exposed . . . blood in great quantity, both in fluid and coagulated pools, was found around the head on the cloth on which the body lay.'[6]

Whatever caused Nau Nihal Singh's death, the consensus of accounts is that the lives of two men whom Ranjit Singh had hoped would ensure the continuity of his legacy came to an end within two days of each other. Although there are other suspects, most fingers point not only at Dhian Singh but also at his brothers Gulab Singh and Suchet Singh (although the last name of each was Singh, they were not Sikhs); they had sworn allegiance to Ranjit Singh, who knew how to retain their loyalty during his lifetime. An added edge to Dhian Singh's intrigues was provided by his obsessive desire to see his son Hira Singh ultimately ascend Ranjit Singh's throne. The conspiracies he hatched after the Maharaja's death involved hatred, mistrust and other violent deaths to clear his son's way to the throne. As prime minister he was in a position to arrange the bloodbaths necessary to attain his ends.

Aside from these Kashmiri Dogras and the Brahmins Tej Singh and Lal Singh, members of Ranjit Singh's own family were equally involved in their own intrigues to capture power, indifferent to the fact that the British were waiting on the sidelines to exercise their skills in manipulation and subversion which inexorably led to domination and subjugation of the Sikh nation. The more active of these participants in the struggle for power were Chand Kaur, Kharak Singh's widow and mother of Nau Nihal Singh, and Sher Singh, Ranjit Singh's second son.

ᴄᴇ⁓

Chand Kaur was at the centre of the struggle that now began in the Lahore Durbar. Although she ascended to power by assuming 'the functions of regent or ruler',[7] she held the reins for all too brief a time, but during this period she conducted herself with extraordinary self-assurance. As she put it, if 'England is ruled by a queen, why should it be a disgrace to the Punjab to be governed by a Rani?'

Which was more easily said than done, considering the nature of those who surrounded her.

It was accepted that Sher Singh, Ranjit Singh's second son, born of Ranjit Singh's first wife Mehtab Kaur, was illegitimate, and even the Maharaja, who had given him the title of prince, had not been entirely comfortable with him, although honouring him in various ways. The young man had an impressive presence, but his dissipated ways and lack of serious convictions earned him no respect, and, as usual, time-servers and others crowded around him for their own ends. Despite coming close to the throne after Ranjit Singh's death, he lost out because of his lack of leaderly qualities, legitimacy and political wisdom.

Sher Singh was out of the capital when his half-brother Kharak Singh and Nau Nihal Singh died, although this news was deliberately sent late to him. He returned to Lahore as soon as he heard it, but by this time Chand Kaur – despite Dhian Singh's attempted moves to delay him – had managed to get herself installed as ruler of the Punjab. The main card she played was that her daughter-in-law, Nau Nihal Singh's widow, was pregnant and she would hold power as Regent until the child was born. If the new-born was a girl instead of a boy, she would be perfectly agreeable to adopting Dhian Singh's son Hira Singh as the heir to the empire – which is what Dhian Singh's plan had been all along. Even the devious Dhian Singh seemed satisfied with Chand Kaur's offer, which Sher Singh was not, wanting to remove her by force of arms. Dissuaded by Dhian Singh from doing anything rash at this stage, Sher Singh was advised to wait for the appropriate moment, which he was assured would not take long. Sher Singh, the 'good-natured voluptuary', was happy to go back to his dissipated ways.

Chand Kaur was doubtless aware that her pacification of Dhian Singh was a lull in the storm he was bound to create. He was much too involved in devious ways to be wholly convinced that Chand Kaur's assurance regarding Hira Singh was etched in stone. Nor was he unmindful of the many other influences that might prevail on her, or of her own intelligence and ambitions. She could also draw on some powerful figures for help. To begin with, she was the daughter of Jaimal Singh, Sardar of the Kanhayia *misl*. She was also close to Attar Singh, the Sandhanwalia chief, as well as to Sardar Lehna Singh Majithia, an influential nobleman although not a *misl* chief. There were several other Sardars she could call upon, too. To consolidate her position further she appointed Attar Singh Sandhanwalia as her prime minister.

A man of Dhian Singh's acuity was wholly aware of the support Chand Kaur was mobilizing to consolidate her position. Aside from his other subterranean moves, the two main cards he chose to play, in order to defend his own interest and that of his Maharaja-in-waiting son Hira Singh, was to edge his brother Gulab Singh into Chand Kaur's circle of close advisers, while at the same time placing his bets on Sher Singh. It was a shrewd move of Dhian Singh's. While his brother could subvert the state from within the Durbar, Sher Singh could be made to mount a frontal attack on it, given his own claim to the throne. This would place both the Dogra brothers in a win–win situation; if things worked out in their favour, they would be rid of both Chand Kaur and Sher Singh.

With the time considered ripe for a march on Lahore, as a late-nineteenth-century historian describes, 'Sher Singh, according to previous arrangements with Dhian Singh, marched from Mukerian, at the head of about 300 followers, and posted himself at the Shalimar gardens. To his great disappointment, however, he was informed that Dhian Singh, instead of joining him at the gardens as previously arranged, had not, up to that moment, even left his hill territory in Jammu. This afforded an opportunity to Jawala Singh, an ambitious Sardar, and one of Sher Singh's principal councillors, who aspired to the wazirship, to instil into the mind of the credulous prince the idea that Dhian Singh cared little for his interests, and that his real sympathies were with his brother, Gulab Singh, who had openly espoused the cause of the Maharani.'[8] Inexorably, the stage was now being set for a showdown, with subversion of the two camps by the Dogra brothers assured.

'For about thirty days,' in the words of an earlier British historian, 'Dhian Singh remained at Jammu, during which time the emissaries he had left at Lahore secretly to ply the Sikh soldiery, had so well played their part as to have received promises from the different corps that as soon as the minister and Sher Singh should present themselves at Lahore, they would place the latter upon the throne. These promises were given on consideration that the army should receive an increase of pay, together with large presents – terms which only were afterwards partially fulfilled.'[9]

All this would soon prove fatal for Sher Singh, who lacked the intelligence to foresee that by making the Sikh army take sides in palace intrigues he was undermining the basic structure on which the supposedly indestructible power of the Lahore Durbar rested. By foolishly drawing the army into the political decision-making process, he gave it the right to assert itself in decisions affecting the state – which was a right invested by the Gurus in the entire Khalsa community and not just the army. What aggravated conditions within the army still further were the feelers Sher Singh sent to the British, seeking their help in capturing Lahore. This angered the army – already ill-disposed towards the British – still further.

Dhian Singh with his men arrived at Shahdara, not far from Lahore, to join Sher Singh on the fifth of the week-long siege of Lahore. Before his arrival the Sikh soldiery had rallied around Sher Singh in numbers that are said to have been close to 70,000 infantrymen. The detachments stationed in the Lahore Fort were also mobilized to the fullest. The battle between the besiegers and the besieged was bloody. As for the Dogra brothers, while Gulab Singh oversaw operations within the fort, according to plan Dhian Singh arrived outside it as an ally of Sher Singh. Sher Singh, on learning of Dhian Singh's arrival, offered to end hostilities and negotiate with Gulab Singh – who refused to accept any overtures except through the mediation of his brother Dhian.[10] What better outcome could the Dogras ask for?

The siege ended on the evening of 17 January 1841 with the capitulation of Chand Kaur's forces. The terms of the peace agreed between Chand Kaur and Sher Singh were as follows: 'The Maharani Chand Kaur to surrender the fort of Lahore to Sher Singh, and to give up all her claims to the throne of Lahore. In return for this Sher Singh was to give the ex-queen a *jagir* of nine lakhs [900,000] of rupees, adjoining the Jammu hills, which should be managed by Gulab Singh, as her regent or *mukhtar*. Secondly, that Sher Singh was to refrain from his wish to marry the Maharani by the ceremony *chadar-dalna*. Thirdly, that the Dogra troops should be permitted to leave the fort and capital unmolested. And fourthly, that security should be furnished for the due fulfilment of the treaty.'[11]

※

It is time now to take a closer look at Gulab Singh. What distinguished him from his brother was not the degree of his capacity for treachery, since here there was very little to choose between the two. It was Gulab Singh's cupidity that set him apart. He regularly helped himself without compunction to what belonged to others. He not only surreptitiously removed an enormous amount of the Lahore Durbar's wealth after Chand Kaur's surrender but had been periodically helping himself to state property even before that and during the time of Maharaja Kharak Singh.

Here is what the newsletters published by the court at this time under the title of *Punjab Akhbar* had to say about this: 'It was reported . . . that "Raja Gulab Singh is removing from the fort of Minawar and from other forts in the Minawar district, lakhs of property and money to Jammu." This amounted to theft of the

State property, and the Maharaja [Kharak Singh] was naturally enraged to hear this and exclaimed: "Who are these Rajas that they should carry away property and coin from the fort of Minawar?" On hearing these remarks Dhian Singh sent word to the Maharaja saying, "It is at the Maharaja's option to sequester all his property, but why abuse and degrade him?"'[12]

More outrageous still was the brazenness with which Gulab Singh helped himself to Chand Kaur's wealth, which she had rightfully inherited from her husband Maharaja Kharak Singh. After her surrender at Lahore Fort, Gulab Singh 'carried off the accumulated treasures of Ranjit Singh ... sixteen carts were filled with rupees and other silver coins, while 500 horsemen were each entrusted with a bag of gold mohurs, and his orderlies were also entrusted with jewellery and other valuable articles. The costly pashminas, and rich wardrobes, and the best horses in Ranjit Singh's stables, were all purloined by Gulab Singh on the occasion of his evacuating Lahore, an event which took place on the night following the cessation of hostilities.'[13]

But this was not all. Adept as he was at the game of stealing on the grand scale, he had over time misappropriated the revenues of twenty-two districts which had been put for just administration under his charge. He had also regularly diverted to his coffers some of the tribute sent to the Lahore Durbar by the hill rajas. Aside from all that the generous Ranjit Singh had gifted him, he owned large tracts of land in Jammu and from 1830 onwards had a monopoly of the salt mines in the Pind Dadan Khan Salt Range which were also a gift from the Maharaja. In addition to all this, the latter had made him Raja as well and granted him Jammu as a *jagir* in 1820.

When Sher Singh arrived outside Lahore in January 1841 in preparation for his assault on the fort, Gulab Singh, who was then Chand Kaur's confidant and factotum, went to see him. After professing his unswerving loyalty to Sher Singh, he pulled the Kohi-i-noor diamond out of his bag and offered it to him as a humble gift. Sher Singh had no problem in accepting it. Having thus put him in a mellow mood, the wily Dogra then proceeded to pledge his abiding loyalty to Sher Singh just as he had, he said, been loyal to his lord and master Ranjit Singh. He explained that it was because of his profound regard for the old Lion that he had stayed by the side of Chand Kaur in these difficult times, so that he could protect and help her in every possible way. Having built his bridges with Sher Singh, he returned to work against him from within the fort. Theoretically Chand Kaur's trusted adviser, he had no qualms about walking off with her wealth the day the Lahore Fort fell.

And what of Chand Kaur? For a spirited lady who had tried to stand up to the menacing intrigues that swirled all around her, her end was particularly tragic. After the capitulation of Lahore Fort she was confined to an apartment there for more than a year. She tried to rally some of the Sikh chiefs around her from there, as also many of the Khalsa regiments. She made overtures to the British as well. But the odds were stacked against her. Both Sher Singh and Dhian Singh sensed danger from her intrigues and the staunch support being given to the Rani by the Sandhanwalias. Gulab Singh feared the disclosure of his looting of the Lahore treasury. All three seem to have agreed to get rid of her, and the execution of their plan was entrusted to Dhian Singh. The Rani's trusted maidservants were won over, and on 9 June 1842 she was administered arsenic poison in a drink. After she had remained in a coma for three days her skull was smashed with a grindstone.[14]

Chand Kaur was the only woman who ruled the Sikh empire. Had she had even a little more time on the throne, without so many malignant presences around her, she might have handled her responsibilities with much greater confidence and success and thereby honoured the injunction of the Sikh Gurus, who had clearly given a call for equal rights to all women in every walk of life.

The spotlight now shifted on to Sher Singh, who had ascended the throne on 18 January 1841 after the removal of Chand Kaur from the throne. In what was surely the most naïve and senseless act of his life, he appointed Dhian Singh as his prime minister. But he had learnt no lessons from the sinister role of Dhian Singh in the Lahore Durbar's affairs after Ranjit Singh's death. As was to be expected, Dhian Singh soon brought back to court his brother Gulab Singh and his own son Hira Singh. Sher Singh compounded his error by being persuaded to make Hira Singh commander-in-chief of the Punjab forces. An indolent profligate, he was only too glad to shift the responsibilities of government on to the shoulders of the willing Dhian, who lost no time in filling all the most important posts in the state service with 'friends of the family'. The Jammu brothers were now at the height of their power.[15]

The inevitable consequence of Sher Singh's unwise moves was his growing alienation from the Sikh forces as also from the Sardar chiefs, who viewed the disintegration of the Durbar's authority under the two Dogra upstarts with anger and dismay. The same Durbar that in Ranjit Singh's time had enjoyed high esteem and affection was now vilified, its writ openly flouted. It was impossible for Sher Singh's Rajput prime minister to make any impact on the chaotic conditions throughout the Punjab; he was able to restore some measure of order within the capital, but without its walls his authority was treated with contempt by an army getting more and more out of hand. In Lahore itself insubordination was rife enough, but in the provinces things were much worse. In Peshawar and Multan, in Kashmir and the newly conquered state of Mandi, the troops rose in open rebellion, and the drastic measures taken by the governors to quell these and other uprisings served only to intensify the general mood of mutiny.[16]

The inconceivable was now happening in Ranjit Singh's redoubtable realm. There are several explanations for the rebellious mood of the soldiers, but the one that stands out is divided loyalties, divided between those in Lahore Fort loyal to Chand Kaur and those outside loyal to Sher Singh. The *esprit de corps* that had held the Sikh army together through some of the great battles they had fought under Ranjit Singh and his generals had begun to erode. To fight with each other was not on the soldiers' agenda, and without charismatic leaders to lead them their discipline, dedication and loyalty came under severe strain. In Multan, Peshawar, Mandi and Kashmir mutinous forces unleashed a reign of terror.

The Sikh soldiers resented the influence and intrigues of the Dogra brothers. This led to the increasing assertiveness of their republican spirit, which was now increasingly manifesting itself. They would never have questioned Ranjit Singh's charismatic leadership but were now thoroughly angered at decisions of great importance being taken – without consultation with them – by ineffectual and conspiratorial men. To top it all were Sher Singh's foolish moves to get the army to take sides in palace intrigues.

No less ill-advised was his constant hankering for British support. He had long tried to woo the British and within five days of his father's death had already conveyed to the British political agent at Ludhiana, George Russel Clerk, his own eminent suitability for the Sikh throne, asking him to convey this to the governor-general, Lord Auckland. Emily Eden, Auckland's sister, visiting Lahore in 1838, had grown quite fond of Sher Singh and at one point observed: 'It is just possible his dear fat head will he chopped off, unless he crosses to our side of the river.'[17] On the death of Chand Kaur the Sandhanwalia Sardars, key supporters of hers, fearing Sher Singh's anger, had fled across the Sutlej to seek British protection, and two of the four Sandhanwalia brothers even went over to the British. In due course, however, all four were persuaded to return to Lahore. George Russel Clerk did his utmost to plead and champion their cause with Sher Singh. The Maharaja had no reason to trust the Sandhanwalias but was swayed by

Clerk's persuasive arguments. He pardoned and allowed them to return to Lahore and made the mistake of befriending them.

It was only a matter of time before they started plotting the downfall of both Sher Singh and Dhian Singh. One day while Sher Singh was in his cups they got him to sign a document ordering the death of Dhian Singh. Next they went to Dhian Singh and showed him his death warrant duly signed by the Maharaja. Dhian Singh, whose loyalties were like the ebbing and flowing tide, hatched a plan with the Sandhanwalias to murder Sher Singh.

Quite apart from his own defects of mind and character, court intrigues, the stigma of illegitimacy and a constant threat to his life made Sher Singh a thoroughly helpless figure, caught between antagonistic political factions and a resurgent republican army, when he was supposed to be a successor to the great Maharaja. He aligned with all and sundry but trusted none. In desperation he was even willing to surrender part of his kingdom to the British in return for their help towards restoring his authority as a sovereign. On 15 September 1843 the predictable end came: both he and Prime Minister Dhian Singh were murdered by the Sandhanwalia chiefs.[18] Shortly after these murders Prince Partap Singh, Sher Singh's son and heir apparent to the throne of Punjab, was stabbed to death.

The odds had been so strongly stacked in favour of an imminent and violent change of power that Clerk and the British would have had to be blind not to know what was likely to happen if the Sandhanwalias went back to Lahore. Were the British guilty of being accomplices or accessories to these treasonous murders? As *The British Friend of India*, published in London, wrote in December 1843 of these murders: 'We have no proof that the Company instigated all the King-Killing in the Punjab since Ranjit Singh died . . . We must say we smell a rat.'[19]

In any objective assessment of the extent of Sher Singh's responsibility for his own murder, the only conclusion possible is that he was responsible. By actively participating in plots to assassinate political rivals he completely reversed Ranjit Singh's policy of tolerance and non-violence even towards his vanquished foes. It was inevitable that he should pay with his life for the folly of failing to understand that, once encouraged, political murders become a way of life. The British knew how to take full advantage of their adversaries' weaknesses, but in the ultimate analysis far more serious was the effect of these palace intrigues on the army. Here again Sher Singh gravely misjudged the dangerous implications of casting the army in the role of king-maker, which he had done by winning over sections of it to help him attack Chand Kaur in Lahore on 14 January 1841.

Bikrama Jit Hasrat pinpoints the situation: 'Sher Singh's accession was unattended by any acts of violence; the army which had enthroned him, had also become his master. It began to wreak vengeance on those whom it considered traitors to the Khalsa. It plundered the houses of several chiefs, dismissed foreigners from state service, and declared its determination to punish those who sought foreign interference.'[20] Sher Singh's contacts with the British stirred up further discontent within the army, which was utterly disapproving of the British.

When, inevitably, the army seriously split down the middle, the very fundamentals of the Khalsa's founding principles were affected, since it was the privilege of the entire Khalsa community to take decisions of profound importance to the faith. Even then, despite the serious schisms in its ranks, the army, while divided against itself and some of the key political players, was not against the Durbar, which even the seasoned British failed to understand. Their assumption that the restlessness of the Sikh forces was directed against the Durbar could not have been more wrong; their resentment was directed at the British who were trying to impose their will on the Khalsa, which would have none of it. This misreading of the army's temper and the mood of the resurgent

Khalsa would take a heavy toll not only of British lives on the battlefield but also of their pride and myth of invulnerability. Sher Singh had been quite incapable of grasping the complexities of the unfolding situation.

∽

The only aspirant left to the throne of Ranjit Singh after Sher Singh's death was five-year-old Dalip Singh, Ranjit Singh's acknowledged son by Rani Jindan. Born on 4 September 1838, he will for ever remain a tragic figure of history. He was ten months old when his father died. His mother Jindan Kaur, although not born into a privileged family, was a remarkably intelligent and attractive woman with a 'ready wit and lack of sexual inhibitions, [which] made her well qualified to organize the more outlandish entertainments of the court'.[21] Dalip may not have been Ranjit Singh's legitimate son but was very much an heir to his father's throne when the time came for him to claim his rights. He continued to live in the palace at Lahore with his mother through the reigns of Kharak Singh and Sher Singh, but she made sure he kept a low profile which would help him stay out of harm's way. In those unsettled times anyone who was seen as a claimant to what others coveted was in mortal danger. As a British historian has noted: 'Probably no one believed that Dalip was the son of Ranjit Singh; but, on the other hand, no one could prove that he was not; and that alone was sufficient to render him a dangerous weapon in the hands of such a master of intrigue as Ghulab Singh.'[22]

The shrewd Rani Jindan Kaur, seeing all the signs of trouble at court, had taken her son Dalip Singh to stay with Gulab Singh at Jammu after Ranjit Singh's death. But she knew that Lahore was where she had to be to get her son on the throne. So despite the relentless struggle for power which had become routine at the Lahore Durbar it was not long before Jindan returned to it with her son. Her remarkable self-confidence and tenacity of purpose enabled her to weather the many ruthless plots and subplots which were being hatched all the time by the aspirants to power.

She not only managed to survive all of them but also became regent to keep the way to the throne open for her son. He was crowned on 18 September 1843 and at the age of six became the Maharaja of Punjab and its vast territories. He would never have made it without the astonishing skill with which his mother dealt with the devious ways of the Lahore Durbar and its key players. But even this forceful woman was to meet her match soon. Not in the form of her own countrymen, whose ways were familiar to her, but of those from a distant land who were waiting on the sidelines to acquire the territories, treasures, natural resources and rare antiquities of her country by whatever means they could. They had not sailed thousands of miles to acquire wealth by signing treaties and such. Treaties were fine as long as they served their purpose; the Sutlej Treaty of 1809 was no longer relevant, with the East India Company's acquisition of Sind and navigation rights on the Indus along with many other advances. The 1809 treaty with Ranjit Singh had already been sidestepped through deft manoeuvres and weasel words.

If they had managed to get away with such tactics even in the time of Ranjit Singh – who was fully a match for them – the strife-torn self-centred men who succeeded him were no match for the seasoned British, who now perceived that the time had come for them to annex Punjab, the most strategic state in India with its rivers and mountains, which was crucial for them to control if the security of the subcontinent they had conquered was to be assured.

9

Twilight of an Empire

There is nothing so bad or so good that you will not find
Englishmen doing it; but you will never find an Englishman
in the wrong. He does everything on principle. He fights you
on patriotic principles; he robs you on business principles;
he enslaves you on imperial principles; he bullies you on
manly principles; he supports his king on loyal principles
and cuts off his king's head on republican principles.

GEORGE BERNARD SHAW

He who knows how to flatter also knows how to slander.

NAPOLEON BONAPARTE

If the Dogras were responsible for the twilight of the Sikh empire,
the British ensured its descent into the darkness of night. They
came to the Punjab in the early nineteenth century as a trading
company – the Honourable East India Company – with the object
of amassing wealth for their shareholders – a goal that was made
clear to all the Company's employees from the governor-general to
the lowliest clerk. 'Money-making being the object, the Directors
. . . impressed upon successive Governors-General the paramount
importance of remembering they were traders, not empire-
builders, and exacted a promise from each that peace and
retrenchment should be the aim of his administration, and each
in turn bound himself to observe his instructions – if he could.'[1]
Most of them, as it happened, couldn't!

The officers of the East India Company were principally experienced in destroying whatever stood in the way of their enduring passion for exploitation and acquisition of an adversary's wealth. After the death of Ranjit Singh, the wealth of the Sikhs, their erstwhile allies, was now viewed as worthy of acquisition. Under Ranjit Singh the Sikhs had kept at bay the Durranis of Afghanistan and had stood rocklike in the way of the Russians, French, Persians and others who had – much to the concern of the British – clearly indicated their interest in India. But since the Sikhs were no longer the strong bulwark they had been under the bold and unbeatable Ranjit Singh, the British now saw no reason to stand by them. Especially as all the difficult peoples of the northern regions – the Afghans, Pathans, tribal chiefs and others – had been subdued and brought under control. From the British point of view it was obviously time to take over what clearly belonged to the Sikhs because they were no longer united enough to defend it.

The strategies devised to subvert the Sikh state ranged from actively encouraging dissensions within the Durbar to a military showdown, with Sikh forces now weakened by their infighting. The British did everything possible to make Punjab's annexation appear a noble undertaking, even though it took many unworthy moves to achieve it.

To start with, in a General Proclamation of 20 August 1847, the governor-general, Lord Henry Hardinge, announced that he felt 'the interest of a father in the education and guardianship of the young Prince [Dalip Singh]' and that 'he had at heart the peace and security of this country [the Punjab], the firm establishment of the State, and the honour of the Maharaja and his ministers'. In order 'to maintain the administration of the Lahore State during the minority of the Maharajah' the governor-general was armed with supreme and plenary power, and was 'at liberty to occupy with British soldiers such possessions as he may think fit, for the security of the capital, for the protection of the Maharajah, and the preservation of the peace of the country'. The British resident was placed at the head of the administration with 'full authority to direct and control all matters in every department of the State'.[2]

This excerpt from the secret papers maintained by the British places in perspective the many devious means by which the British created their Indian empire. The possession of Punjab is justified because of the governor-general's fatherly interest in the 'education and guardianship of the young Prince', to ensure which it will be necessary to bring peace and security to the state and country. Peace and security, of course, will require the presence of British soldiers, who will after all be for 'the protection of the Maharaja'. To quote the American historian Barbara Tuchman on this particular English talent: 'Official histories record every move in monumental and infinite detail but the details serve to obscure . . . other nations attempt but never quite achieve the same self-esteem. It was not by might but by the power of her self-image that Britain in her century dominated the world.'[3]

In planning moves towards the annexation of Punjab after Ranjit Singh's death, no limits were set to encouraging betrayals in the Sikh ranks, nor entering into squalid deals of any kind. Even some British writers, although very few, have shown qualms at their compatriots' use of traitors among their adversaries in the pursuit of military and political ends. 'The Sikh Army fought valiantly and stubbornly,' writes one British military historian, 'in spite of poor generalship from commanders who, for political reasons, did not want to win the war and were constantly in touch with the British commanders to ensure them of that fact.'[4]

When Ranjit Singh died in 1839 the British governor-general at the time was Lord Auckland (March 1836–February 1842) who was succeeded by the Earl of Ellenborough (February 1842–June 1844) and then by Lord Hardinge (July 1844–January 1848) who distinguished himself in the Battle of Waterloo, after which he was awarded Napoleon's sword by the Duke of Wellington, the trophy the duke himself had won at Waterloo. 'Many years afterwards,' we are told by a later member of the family, 'he [Hardinge] wore Napoleon's sword in the battles of the Sutlej; and when matters appeared desperate during the eventful night of the 21st December, 1845, he sent his surgeon with it to a place of safety, lest it should fall into the hands of the Sikhs.'[5]

Lord Ellenborough, a relative of Lord Hardinge by marriage, was recalled in 1844. He was quite elated because he felt that at the end of his term he had left India in a 'state of profound peace'. But would this peace last? And for how long? In June 1844, at a farewell dinner in England for Lord Hardinge who was on his way to India as the next governor-general, the chairman of the Company's court of directors observed in his speech that 'By our latest intelligence we are induced to hope that peace will be preserved in India . . . we feel confident that, while ever ready to maintain unimpaired the honour of the country and the supremacy of our arms, your policy will be essentially pacific. It has always been the desire of the Court that the government of the East India Company should be eminently just, moderate, and conciliatory; but the supremacy of our power must be maintained when necessary by the force of our arms.'[6]

A former financial commissioner of Punjab reminisces in 1883: 'To our officers the prospect of a big fight was cheering: they believed the hordes of wild horsemen, dashing against their disciplined infantry, would break like waves beating against rocks. And the men? Well, the white soldiers had faith in themselves and the sepoys in the sahibs and their guns.'[7]

So much for an 'eminently just, moderate, and conciliatory approach'. These two statements point up the difference between what was professed and what was actually practised by the rulers of nineteenth-century India. The two wars between the British and the Sikhs were a matter of touch and go for the British, and had they not resorted to every dubious tactic in the book the out-come would have been entirely different for them.

Yet when the history of those times is read in the accounts of British historians the verbal nobility so beloved of their nation comes through at every turn, referring to actions of men of influ-ence in the British administration that were questionable to say the least. While some British writers had the integrity to point to the misdeeds of their countrymen when battle was finally joined between the two armies, few indeed wrote of how betrayals in the enemy's forces were encouraged to turn the tide of war in Britain's favour. The one outstanding example of a member of the British establishment of the time who exposed British moves for what they were was Captain J.D. Cunningham, dismissed from service for his pains and sent back to his regiment in disgrace for daring to expose the misdeeds of his countrymen. This former additional aide-de-camp to the governor-general during the Sabraon battle died within two years of being removed from office – of a broken heart, it is said – at the age of thirty-nine.

What were the misdeeds of his countrymen that Cunningham exposed and that earned him the severe displeasure of his country-men? In the Battle of Sabraon, the fourth and last battle of the First Anglo-Sikh War, fought on 10 February 1846, the British used secret deals and every conceivable form of deceit to help them to emerge victorious over the Sikh forces. The methods they used led Cunningham to record them in disgust in his *History of the Sikhs* (1849). What this young officer found utterly distasteful was the understanding Governor-General Hardinge had reached with Gulab Singh whereby the latter would ensure the defeat of his own side and facilitate the victory of the British. Cunningham found it indecent 'that the Sikh army should be attacked by the English, and that when beaten it should be openly abandoned by its own government; and further that the passage of the Sutlej should be unopposed and the road to the capital laid open to the visitors.

Under such circumstances of discreet policy and shameless treason was the Battle of Sabraon fought.'[8]

This can hardly be the line of action enjoined upon the Company's various governor-generals selected to serve in India or the
advice that the chairman of the Company's court of directors gave
to Lord Hardinge at his farewell dinner before he left for India. Yet
it was the same Hardinge who entered into the infamous understanding with Gulab Singh before the Battle of Sabraon. Even after
Sabraon, which opened the road to Lahore, there was no change
in the unbecoming conduct of the English. Unequivocal evidence
exists, which includes the army chief Sir Hugh Gough's dispatches,
showing how Gulab Singh was persuaded by the British to betray
the Sikh government – of which he was the prime minister – in
return for many British favours, the sale of Kashmir to him and his
investiture as Maharaja being the most notorious.

British plans to dismember the Sikh state were initiated with infinite attention to detail soon after the Old Lion's death. The first
and foremost step taken – which had been honed to perfection
over the centuries – was not only to identify and win over, by
whatever means possible, those in the Lahore Durbar who were
susceptible to treasonous offers but to create further rivalries and
rifts which were already beginning to weaken the Lahore Durbar,
the once formidable centre of Sikh power.

The one man with ideal qualifications for the British was Gulab
Singh. To begin with, he was a great survivor. While his brothers
Dhian Singh and Suchet Singh, no less wily than Gulab Singh, had
not survived the many purges that had been rife after Ranjit
Singh's death, Gulab Singh had survived them all. He had also
amassedan immense fortune during these turbulent times, in
addition to lands and estates in Jammu. At the zenith of their
power the Dogras of Jammu held *jagirs* worth an annual revenue

of 1,897,379 rupees – Gulab Singh 737,287 rupees, Hira Singh 462,115 rupees, Suchet Singh 306,865 rupees and Dhian Singh 291,112 rupees. Of the approximate total national revenue of 32,475,000 rupees at Ranjit Singh's death in 1839, the Jammu brothers contributed about one-third from farms, tributes and monopolies.[9] Gulab Singh was aptly described as a man 'whose aspirations left no room for pangs of conscience or purity of ideals'. It did not take the British long to identify him as their most likely instrument of policy so far as annexation of the Punjab was concerned, even though they were mistrustful of his ambitions. Wedded to their old adage of there being no permanent friends or enemies but only permanent interests, however, they were quite prepared to continue to deal with him. He was to prove the ideal ally to help them dismantle the state his mentor had so single-mindedly built.

Two other men who now occupied centre stage but had not held any significant office during Ranjit Singh's time were the two Brahmins, Lal Singh and Tej Singh. While Tej Singh was from the Gangetic Plain, Lal Singh came from the Gandhara Valley; both had risen in the Lahore Durbar through devious means. Yet in November 1845, in a supremely ironic twist of fate, Lal Singh was chosen as prime minister and Tej Singh as commander-in-chief of the Sikh army. Both would grievously betray the Sikh state. There were a number of others whom the British had cannily lined up to help them subvert and put an end to the Sikh empire, but the roles of these three traitors were crucial to the realization of British goals.

It is axiomatic of life's mysterious ways that seldom do events of any momentous significance occur without triggering off equally noteworthy incidents in response. Ranjit Singh's death, and the self-destructive moves and betrayals of his successors, not only put paid to his dream of a strong, secular and impregnable Sikh state but made a mockery of a supremely confident and proud people inspired by ideals of their faith. Unheeding of those who were pressing on Punjab's borders eager to lay hands on its riches, the Sikhs, already vulnerable because of their infighting, were made even more so by the traitors in their midst. The real tragedy for them was the lack of character shown by Ranjit Singh's own kin, as seen in the previous chapter.

❧

Long before these events the wily George Clerk had been busily at work on Britain's long-term interests, and he most likely had a hand in the death of Chet Singh, Kharak Singh's right-hand man. Chet Singh, according to British intelligence, was opposed to the East India Company's demand for the passage of its troops through Punjab, so Clerk's advice to his moles in the Lahore court had been to get rid of him. 'I proved to them that they may effectively remove him,' wrote Clerk in a revealing confidential dispatch to Lord Auckland. Clerk gave encouragement to rival parties against each other.[10] The classic British ploy of divide and rule.

This matter of passage of troops had to do with a tripartite agreement that Ranjit Singh had signed with the East India Company and Shah Shuja on 26 June 1838, agreeing on an Anglo-Sikh double invasion of Afghanistan with the idea of putting Shah Shuja on the throne of Kabul, the British having persuasively used the familiar argument of a 'looming Russian threat' to Afghanistan and northern India. One arm of the planned invasion was to be led by Shah Shuja with British support and the other was to be a thrust by Sikh troops via Peshawar. Lord Auckland did succeed in restoring Shah Shuja to Kabul's throne on 7 August 1839, but so much against the wishes of the Afghan people as to lead to the first Afghan War, which proved disastrous for the British. While Ranjit Singh had learnt of Kandahar's fall in April 1839, news of the capture of Kabul and Ghazni had reached Lahore only after his death on 27 June 1839. The troops for whom Clerk was seeking passage through Punjab were British forces beginning to return from Afghanistan to their positions south of the Sutlej at the end of 1839, although full British withdrawal from Afghanistan would not take place until October 1842.[11]

The request for the passage of troops was not as innocent as it seemed, because the British wished to use the opportunity thus afforded to assess the strength of the Sikh forces. The political agent at Ludhiana, accompanied by a few British officers, while returning from Afghanistan in 1841, had indeed collected detailed information on Sikh troop dispositions for the British High Command, just as Fane, commander-in-chief of the British army in India, had done before him when attending the wedding of Nau Nihal Singh in 1837. But the abuse of hospitality was to be taken still further. When the British requested the Lahore Darbar's help after the rout of the English troops in Kabul in 1841, and the Darbar obliged by sending a force under Gulab Singh, the British tried to buy him and his men over. In the words of Henry Lawrence, who later played a key role in Punjab, 'we need such men as the Raja [Gulab Singh] . . . and should bind them to us, by the only tie they recognize – self interest'.[12] Gulab Singh was more than willing.

As were two other Darbar officers of his ilk, the Brahmins Lal Singh and Tej Singh, who in Kapur Singh's words 'paved the way for the eventual enslavement of the Sikh people'. Their treachery, as will be evident in the following pages, was exceptional even in the annals of such base deals. While the British would have executed such wartime traitors in their own ranks, they were elated at having Tej Singh help them win against the Sikhs by betraying his troops. In the final summing up, British victories in the two Sikh Wars were not won by valour on the battlefield but because the victors were able to persuade their adversary's key men to betray their side.

What was becoming clear to most astute observers was that a showdown between the British and the Sikhs would soon take place; there was no way Sikh pride and self-esteem could be reconciled with the obsessive British desire to bring the whole of India under their control. The two sides were now on a collision course, and the question was when would the collision take place. The hawkish governor-general Lord Ellenborough, who had taken over from the more moderate Lord Auckland, was already preparing to mobilize a sizeable army south of the Sutlej from where Punjab could be invaded. He wrote to the Duke of Wellington on 20 April 1844 that 'we can only consider our relations with Lahore to be those of an armed truce. I earnestly hope nothing will compel us to cross the Sutlej that we may have no attack to repel till November 1845. I shall then be prepared for anything. In the meantime we shall do all we can in a quiet way to strengthen ourselves.'[13]

The political agent of the Lahore Durbar at Ludhiana, a trusted *vakil* (authorized agent), sent some news on British troop movements to Lahore: 'About this time a newsletter was received . . . announcing that in view of the general disorder in the Punjab, the British said that the Sikhs all over Punjab had gone mad and had set their house on fire and that their neighbours feared that the fire might spread to their own house. Consequently the English Company Bahadur [the East India Company] had decided to strengthen the frontier.'[14]

If the British were to attack the Sikh state, 'since appearances had to kept up, the British had to be shown as responding to unprovoked aggression, their moves must convey a sense of *noblesse oblige*'.[15] As so often, accuracy was sacrificed for expediency. The provocation came from Major George Broadfoot, the new British agent at Ludhiana, a man who could not abide the Sikhs and in fact had been hostile towards them for many years. His provocations included constructing cantonments at Ludhiana, Ferozepur, Ambala and Kasauli; assembling materials for pontoon bridges along the Sutlej; and declaring the cis-Sutlej possessions of the Lahore Durbar to be under British protection. Hardinge was quite approving of Broadfoot and said he was 'in his element on the frontier'.

The irrepressible Major's next audacious act was to confiscate, in November 1845, two villages of the Sikh state south of the Sutlej near Ludhiana on the trumped–up charge that they were sheltering criminals. All these moves of the British left the Sikhs in no doubt of the intentions of their adversary. It was once again Cunningham who placed these developments in their true perspective. 'Had the shrewd committees of the [Sikh] armies observed no military preparations on the part of the English, they would not have heeded the insidious exhortations of such mercenary men as Lal Singh and Tej Singh, although in former days they would have marched unenquiringly towards Delhi at the bidding of their great Maharaja . . . [so] when the men were tauntingly asked whether they would quietly look on while the limits of the Khalsa dominion were being reduced . . . they answered that they would defend with their lives all belonging to the commonwealth of Gobind and that they would march and give battle to the invaders on their own ground.'[16]

❦

Broadfoot's scheming to precipitate an armed showdown between the two erstwhile allies was successful. This *agent provocateur* of major's rank, with the full support of Governor-General Hardinge (in the words of Ellenborough, the outgoing governor-general: 'I will not fail to make him [Hardinge] acquainted with your merits and services'[17]), succeeded in provoking the Sikh army to cross the Sutlej – in clear transgression of the Sutlej Treaty – under the command of Tej Singh on 12 December 1845. Hardinge declared war on the Lahore Darbar on 13 December 1845.

This was in line with what the British had planned, and the stage was now set for some of the sleaziest conduct in the history of warfare. To stave off defeat when it stared them in the face, the

British made desperate moves to encourage Tej Singh and Lal Singh – made commander-in-chief and *wazir* or prime minister around 8 November 1845 by the Lahore Durbar – into betraying the Sikhs during critical periods of the fighting. One of the most extraordinary actions by these two, instigated by the British, was to desist from attacking Ferozepur after the Sikh troops had crossed the Sutlej. Ferozepur was stocked with a good deal of military equipment and stores which the British were in no mind to lose to the Sikhs. Accordingly, both Tej Singh, who had already crossed the Sutlej with segments of the army, and Lal Singh, who with some cavalry units was just across the river to support the formations which had crossed over, instead of helping the Sikh troops helped the British by deflecting the Sikh army from attacking where the adversary was most vulnerable.

Lal Singh at first refused to cross the river to help the Sikh formations on the other bank, but his troops compelled him to do so. His own personal agenda as he put it was that he 'had not come to gain a victory over the British; his object was to solicit their goodwill and continue as minister in a dependent Punjab'.[18] He had thoughtfully informed the assistant political agent at Ferozepur on 12 December that he 'desired nothing more than that the Sikh Army be destroyed'.[19]

Tej Singh's own goal was no different. He prevailed on his troops to move towards Mudki, on the pretext that there was much bigger game there than at Ferozepur which lay ahead. To top it all, an assurance was also secretly sent to the British on 16 December 1845 that Ferozepur would not be attacked, this despite the fact that Ferozepur with only 7,000 defenders would have fallen like a house of cards before the Sikh force of 35,000 men, lacking the fortifications to withstand the Sikh heavy artillery.[20]

At Mudki, too, deceit and betrayal were in evidence on 18 December 1845. As a detachment of the Sikhs attacked the British force, Lal Singh deserted his men. Although the outcome of this battle was victory of sorts for the British, 'The success of the English was not so complete as should have been achieved by the victors in so many battles.'[21] The British at this point decided to join forces with Sir John Littler who had been commanding Ferozepur about ten miles from Mudki. Lal Singh persuaded his men that there was more glory to be won by delaying an engagement until they could do battle with the main body of the enemy instead of the isolated garrison at Ferozepur.[22] Had the Sikhs gone ahead and neutralized Littler's force at Ferozepur, the outcome of not only the Battle of Ferozeshahr which followed but of the entire First Sikh War would have been entirely different.

The Battle of Ferozeshahr is not easy to describe. Even with the help of betrayals, the British forces were shaken to the core by the punishment they received. Both sides of this coin, betrayal on one and a drubbing such as the British had not received in a long time on the other, are again described by Cunningham, one of the few objective historians of his time. Writing of the battle between the Sikhs and the British which began on 21 December he wrote that the confident English 'had at last got the field they wanted ... [but] the resistance met was wholly unexpected . . . Guns were dismounted, and their ammunition was blown into the air; squadrons were checked in mid career; battalion after battalion was hurled back with shattered ranks ... the obstinacy of the contest threw the English into confusion; men of all regiments and arms were mixed together; generals were doubtful of the fact or of the extent of their own success, and colonels knew not what had become of the regiments they commanded or of the army of which they formed a part.'[23]

Sir Hope Grant, a British general involved in the Anglo-Sikh Wars, writing of the same night, described it as 'one of gloom and never perhaps in our annals of Indian warfare, has a British army on so large a scale been nearer to defeat which could have involved annihilation. The Sikhs had practically recovered the whole of their entrenched camp; our exhausted and decimated divisions bivouacked without mutual cohesion over a wide area.'[24]

But the conduct of Tej Singh and Lal Singh had still to reach its nadir. At dawn on 22 December, as the Sikh and British forces once again took to the field of battle, Tej Singh also arrived with a well-rested reserve Sikh force, to the utter dismay of the enemy. 'The wearied and famished English saw before them a desperate and, perhaps, useless struggle.'[25] 'The whole ground between Feroze-shahr and the latter place [Sultan-Khan-Wala] appeared, indeed, covered with men; some running, others looking behind them with terror depicted in their faces, the dread of the Sikhs at their heels almost depriving them of the power of motion.'[26] But Tej Singh, 'when the fate of India trembled in the balance', refused to attack the dispirited and devastated British.[27] The extent to which Tej Singh and Lal Singh – each driven by his own selfish agenda – went to ensure British victory and the defeat of the Sikh army is nowhere more graphically highlighted than by the events of 22 December at Ferozeshahr. Once again, had the two commanders who led the Sikh forces on that day been men of integrity the outcome of the momentous engagement on the final day of the Ferozeshahr battle would have been profoundly differ-ent – as might have been the future of India.

Tej Singh bided his time that day until the British were able to regroup their scattered forces and did not move even when the Sikhs under Lal Singh's ineffective leadership were being targeted by the British. His tactics were to skirmish and feint with the British forces instead of taking them head-on wherever they were at their weakest, because he wanted defeat, not victory, for his side. As Gen-eral Sir Henry Havelock, a veteran of that battle, said later: 'another such action ... will shake the Empire'[28] ... 'India has been saved by a miracle.'[29] It was, more accurately, saved by two turncoats.

But even if the British 'won' the day at Mudki and Ferozeshahr,

their losses were unusually high. Among the senior British officers killed were Sir Robert Sale, quartermaster-general, Sir John
McCaskill, divisional commander, Brigadier Bolton, head of the
First Brigade of Sir Harry Smith's division, Brigadier Wallace, staff
officers Herries and Munro, Major George Broadfoot, political
agent at Ludhiana, Major Somerset, military secretary to the governor-general and many others. The British prime minister, Sir
Robert Peel, placed this war in perspective when he spoke in the
House of Commons about the mournfully large losses of British
officers and men in fighting with 'the most warlike [men] in India'.
He was handsome enough to acknowledge the valorous conduct
and courage of the Sikh soldiers so badly led and betrayed. 'We are
astonished at the numbers, the power of concentration and the
skill and courage of the enemy.'

The Royal Army, the Fauj-i-khas, had covered themselves with
glory at Ferozeshar, even British commentators being full of
praise. Osborne noted that its troops could shoot 'with greater
precision and regularity, both volleys and file firing, than any other
troops I ever saw'; and old soldiers from the Napoleonic Wars considered its fire to be 'both better delivered and better aimed than
that of Napoleon's infantry'.[30]

But it was the Sikh artillery, nearly doubled in strength since
Ranjit Singh's death, that inflicted most damage, its units carefully
taking up fortified positions and waiting for the enemy to attack.
Its precision and rapidity of fire were a great surprise to the
British, who had consistently underrated the Sikh artillery. One
English eyewitness recorded its superior rate of fire at Ferozeshahr:
'the Sikhs fired their guns in the ratio of thrice to our twice, which
multiplies most fearfully the battering power of artillery, and raises
the calibre of a six- into a nine-pounder'.[31] Another factor in the
greater destructive power of the Sikh guns was that many of
them were made of heavier metal than their British counterparts,
a Sikh four-pounder, for instance, being the weight of a British

six-pounder and able to use double charges of powder, grape and shot. After the battle it was found that the Sikhs had guns of many different calibres, firing up to 24-pound shot. Hardinge reported in his dispatches that the Sikh artillery was better equipped and manned than the British, possessing 'much superior calibre to the British 9-pounder batteries'.[32]

Realistic as always, the British took deeply serious note of the opening battle of the First Anglo-Sikh War in their inner councils, because it was soon clear to them that a high price indeed had been paid for what was drummed a victory but was 'not very far removed from failure'. Over a fifth of the British force had either died on the battlefield or been wounded, despite the fact that the largest body of armed men the British had ever assembled in India now faced the Sikh army on the Sutlej. Inevitably the situation, in a region of critical importance, led to urgent correspondence between the prime minister, Governor-General Hardinge and the commander-in-chief, Sir Hugh Gough, on the handling of political, military and diplomatic affairs in India. One outcome of these high-level exchanges was very strained relations between the governor-general and the commander-in-chief.

Clearly the next battle could not be far off. Tej Singh, who had a unique opportunity to attack British troops after their cavalry had precipitously retreated, did not do so. Instead, his largely unused force slowly began to follow Lal Singh's battle-weary units as they headed back towards the Sutlej. It is interesting to see how the British looked on this amazing withdrawal of largely 'untouched' Sikh forces: 'The Sikh leader had only to continue to fire from his heavy guns to win an easy victory, for even the British found the trial almost unendurable. Perhaps Tej Singh did know this, for his . . . failure to press home his obvious advantages on the 22nd point[s] to his reported reluctance to see the Khalsa beat the British.'[33]

Continuing to employ his weapon of treachery, on Christmas

Day 1845 Hardinge offered rewards and future pensions to all those who deserted from the Sikh ranks. '*Hindostanee Proclamation* – Whereas the English Government is anxious to reward . . . bravery and fidelity . . . any non-commissioned officer or soldier of the Lahore Government who shall present himself before His Excellency the Governor General, shall be immediately rewarded with the accustomed liberality, and shall have the benefit of invalid pension . . . In fact, every opportunity of favour and cherishment shall at all times be kept in sight by the Government.'[34] This raised double-standards to a new high. The British would have shot their own troops out of hand had they succumbed to such offers.

On New Year's Eve the governor-general issued another proclamation from Ferozepur stating that he had been forced to take steps to punish the Lahore government for their 'unprovoked aggression' and to prevent them from further acts of treason in the future he 'called upon all natives of Hindustan who had taken service under the Lahore Government to quit their service at once, and place themselves under the orders of the Governor-General of India. They were ordered to repair to the British side of the Sutlej and to report themselves to the British authorities. If they failed to comply with this order, they were to be considered as having forfeited all claim to British protection, and to be treated as traitors to their country and enemies of the British Government.'[35]

Few British historians mention the British governor-general's incitement to desertion. While English accounts of events of this period are replete with some real but mostly concocted tales of oriental treachery and barbarities, there is a distinct glossing over of certain facts in order to hide unpalatable truths. For example, in *The Sikhs and the Sikh Wars: The Rise, Conquest, and Annexation of the Punjab State* by Arthur D. Innes and Sir Charles Gough, published in 1891, it is stated that 'the Sikh War is a standing example of one which was forced upon us, willy-nilly, in spite of long continued efforts to avoid collision in the face of serious menace from the Sikhs themselves'. The truth is pretty well the exact opposite. Punjab and the whole North-West Frontier of India being high on their agenda of annexations, to buy time the British entered into treaties, identified traitors, settled the price to be paid for their treachery and tried to bribe or buy anyone they possibly could to achieve their ends. This was the game the East India Company played to establish its hold, and when it became an imperial game with much higher stakes the methods used and the means employed became murkier still. But the air of *noblesse oblige* was maintained with aplomb.

With the opportunity to win the First Sikh War squandered away by the two Brahmin leaders masquerading as Sikhs at Ferozeshahr, the two sides again clashed between the villages of Aliwal and Budri on 28 January 1846. With about 12,000 troops sent by each side into the battle, it was bloody in the extreme. The Sikhs lost almost 3,000 men compared to the British casualties which were around 600. Accounts suggest that Sikh losses were a result of the ferocity with which they fought: 'they knelt to receive the dashing charge of the British Lancers and their Indian comrades; but as these approached, they instinctively rose and delivered their fire. Beneath the charge that followed, they did not yield, nor was it till they had three times been ridden over, that they gave way. After the battle it was found that the ground was more thickly strewn with the bodies of the victorious horsemen than of the beaten infantry.'[36] But the Sikhs lost in the end partly because of the river right behind them, which left them no room for manoeuvre; partly because they were totally outflanked and when they jumped into the river to swim across it was under a 'tempest of shot and shell from the British guns'.

The pinnacle of perfidy was reached at Sabraon during the fourth and last battle of the First Anglo-Sikh War. The parties to the secret deals were Britain's governor-general and the avaricious Gulab Singh of Jammu, who had now become prime minister at the Lahore Durbar. Sabraon, the last Sikh redoubt on the Sutlej, was of critical importance to the two sides: to the Sikhs because its loss would lay the road to Lahore open to the enemy; to the British because without it they could not establish their writ north of the Sutlej. The British stakes were higher since without a decisive victory at Sabraon the myth of British military superiority would be exposed. The battles they had won over the last few days had neither been convincing victories nor an endorsement of Britain's military might. The painstakingly created self-image of the formidable British had been rudely shaken, which had not gone unobserved by a large number of Indians; the carefully built image of themselves would no longer be unquestionably accepted. With the help of Gulab Singh they made sure that the outcome of the Battle of Sabraon would be in their favour.

Gulab Singh had outwitted the equally perfidious Lal Singh by inveigling himself into the good books of Maharaja Dalip Singh's mother, Rani Jindan Kaur. From this position of power he was in close touch with the governor-general on how best to turn the looming battle to their mutual advantage. Confidential records of the government of India, which include the army chief Sir Hugh Gough's dispatches as also Henry Hardinge's papers, 'refer with staggering frankness to . . . the open and avowed treachery of Gulab Singh'.[37]

But this was just the beginning of the many treasonable acts that would follow. '[Hardinge] knew that time was pressing, that the speedy dictation of a treaty under the walls of Lahore was essential to the British. A remedy had to be found that would accomplish this and, at the same time, suit the ends of Gulab Singh, Tej Singh and Lal Singh. It required a policy of discretion allied to shameless treason.'[38] Treason this time would be more than shameless. It would have a different face and would be orchestrated by a different conductor. Lal Singh and Tej Singh were once again given military commands, but this time they would subvert the Sikh army under the direction of Gulab Singh.

The subversion started from the very outset. The thirteen days between the engagements at Aliwal and Sabraon, which should have been used for intensive exercises, manoeuvres and preparations of battlefield positions, were wasted through deliberate inaction. The British were given time to reassemble their forces, which had been in serious disarray since the beginning of the war. On the fateful day of 10 February 1846 when battle was finally joined at Sabraon, the British entered the field with a substantial force – including its Aliwal forces which had been considerably augmented. The battle was fought with daring, with utter disregard for life, and blood was shed as only those men can who have a passionate commitment to their cause. A British military historian, writing of the epochal scene on the battlefield, describes it thus: 'The Sikhs, seeing their right had been broken into, commenced a rush from all parts of their position to retake it in a strong counter-attack delivered with determination. In vain Stacey's brigade tried to withstand the mass of enemy; Wilkinson's brigade was forced back, and even the addition of Ashburnham's reserve failed to restore the earlier successes. Gradually the three brigades were driven back, disputing every inch of ground but unable to maintain themselves, until the Sikhs finally drove them from the batteries and recaptured the guns.'[39]

It should come as no surprise that Tej Singh, commander-in-chief of the Sikh army, fled the scene of battle not long after the fighting began. At the same time, with complete disregard for the Durbar and for his men, Lal Singh with his cavalry headed for Lahore! Despite the valour with which they now fought as always, and the previous victories they had scored against the British, the Sikhs this time were fighting against hopeless odds because of the series of secret understandings that had been reached between Hardinge and Gulab Singh. The latter 'had been in direct communication with the British authorities, assuring them of his loyalty and supplying them information. He was prepared to act as a British agent for the subversion of the State, and the dispersal of the Sikh armies, in return for a British recognition of his independent sovereignty in the hills; and he persistently demanded a reward for his treachery. Henry Lawrence had given him a written assurance on behalf of the British Government, that his interests would be taken into consideration after the termination of hostilities.'[40]

Since the aim of both the British and Gulab Singh was to ensure the decisive defeat of the Sikh army, the Khalsa's forces were fighting on many fronts, including their own formations, their top leaders being determined to ensure the defeat of the men they had been appointed to lead. Such were the odds that faced the Sikh army at Sabraon. Inevitably the road to Lahore was opened for the British by yet another wanton act of treachery. But before coming to that it is important to note the intensity with which the two sides fought for victory at Sabraon, as was testified by the roar of heavy ordnance, howitzers, mortars, batteries of field artillery, rockets and rifle fire which filled the air around the opposed entrenchments. It was difficult to tell which side was winning and which was desperately trying to hold on. But what was never in doubt, judging by the sound of the cannonades and the din of war as men defied death, was that this war was being fought to the finish.

Lal Singh having already left the field for Lahore, it was now the turn of Tej Singh to show his hand. As he fled over the bridge of boats, ostensibly to reach the Sikh forces on the other side of the Sutlej, his game-plan became clear: 'by accident or design' his men sank a boat in the middle of the bridge after he had gone ahead.

> The river had risen nearly seven feet in flood during the night, so that the fords were impassable, and the damaged bridge made retreat difficult for the now broken Sikhs. Steadily advancing, though still violently opposed, the

British troops . . . [pushed] before them the still fighting
defenders towards the impassable river, or [forced] them
into the struggling mass upon the frail, rocking bridge. Suddenly the bridge, overcrowded with guns, horses, soldiers
and arms, collapsed into the rapidly running river. The water
was alive with a mass of struggling men. The guns, quickly
brought up, poured into them a heavy and destructive fire of
grape and shrapnel. Few escaped and none surrendered: by
half-past ten there was not a live Sikh remaining on the left
bank of the Sutlej.[41]

A number of accounts by officers such as Major-General Sir
Harry Smith, Sir James Kempt and others who participated in
the various engagements at Sabraon testify to the resoluteness of
the Sikh forces. In a letter to his sister, Mrs Sargent, Sir Harry
Smith wrote on 25 February 1846: 'by dint of the hardest fighting
I ever saw (except Badajoz, New Orleans and Waterloo) I carried
the [Sikh] entrenchments. By Jupiter! the enemy were within a
hairsbreadth of driving me back . . . and such hand-to-hand
conflict ensued, for twenty-five minutes I could barely hold my
own.'[42] In another account by J.D. Cunningham, 'although
assailed on either side by squadrons of horse and battalions of
foot, no Sikh offered to submit, and no disciple of Gobind asked
for quarter. They everywhere showed a front to the victors . . .
while many rushed singly forth to meet assured death by con-
tending with a multitude. The victors looked with stolid
wonderment upon the indomitable courage of the vanquished.'[43]
Among the high-ranking British officers killed were Sir Robert
Dick, veteran of the Waterloo and Peninsular Wars, Brigadier
Taylor and Brigadier Maclaran.

A particularly moving account of unflinching heroism facing
certain death records a last stand by Sardar Sham Singh Attariwala,
one of the most respected chieftains of the Sikhs. Cunningham

again: 'The traitor, Tej Singh . . . fled on the first assault, and, either accidentally or by design, sank a boat in the middle of the bridge of communication. But the ancient Sham Singh remembered his vow; he clothed himself in simple white attire, as one devoted to death, and calling on all around him to fight for the Guru, who had promised everlasting bliss to the brave, he repeatedly rallied his shattered ranks, and at last fell a martyr on a heap of his slain countrymen.'[44]

One of the best summings-up of the battle was 'under such circumstances of discreet policy and shameless treason was the battle of Sabraon fought'.[45] Even in victory Hardinge was unable to show grace. In a proclamation issued on 14 February 1846 he referred to the crossing of the Sutlej into Punjab as 'having been forced upon him' for the purpose of 'effectually protecting the British provinces and vindicating the authority of the British Government, and punishing the violators of treaties and the disturbers of the public peace'.[46] Thus was 'the authority of the British Government' – which came into existence in India only after the Mutiny of 1857–8 – claimed by the head of a trading company, clothing age-old aims of pilferage and plunder in noble oratory.

The British acquired through the Treaty of Lahore, signed on 9 March 1846, the territories of the Sikh state lying south of the Sutlej; they also gained the entire territory of 11,408 square miles between the Sutlej and Beas; but for a few battalions the Sikh army would be disbanded; the Sikhs would pay an indemnity of £1.5 million for war expenses; Kashmir and Hazara were also taken over by the British. On 5 March Gulab Singh was declared an independent sovereign and vested with the title of Maharaja, of the territories in his possession – and also those which the British might reward him with. And reward him they did. Through a separate agreement signed on 16 March 1846, they sold him Kashmir and Hazara for 7,500,000 rupees or £1 million (but on Gulab Singh's request the British exchanged Hazara for the

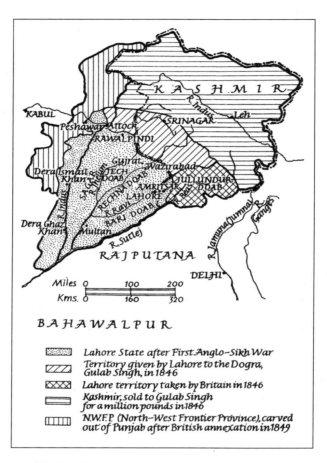

KABUL

KASHMIR

R. Indus — Leh

Peshawar Attock SRINAGAR

RAWALPINDI

Gujrat

Dera Ismail JECH Wazirabad
Khan DOAB
RECHNA DOAB JULLUNDUR
SIND SAGAR DOAB AMRITSAR BIST DOAB
R. Chenab LAHORE
R. Ravi R. Beas
Dera Ghazi BARI DOAB
Khan Multan

R. Indus

R. Sutlej

R. Jamuna (Jumna)

Ganges

RAJPUTANA

DELHI

Miles 0 100 200
Kms. 0 160 320

BAHAWALPUR

Lahore State after First Anglo-Sikh War

Territory given by Lahore to the Dogra,
Gulab Singh, in 1846

Lahore territory taken by Britain in 1846

Kashmir, sold to Gulab Singh
for a million pounds in 1846

N.W.F.P. (North-West Frontier Province), carved
out of Punjab after British annexation in 1849

THE DISMANTLING OF THE SIKH EMPIRE
IN THE 1840S

Jammu–Jhelum belt). Thus was the state of Jammu and Kashmir formed and treason rewarded by the grateful British. Cunningham describes Gulab Singh's investiture as sovereign of his new territories on 15 March. 'On this occasion "Maharaja" Gulab Singh stood up, and, with joined hands, expressed his gratitude to the British viceroy – adding, without however any ironical meaning, that he was indeed his *Zurkharid*, or gold-boughten slave!'[47]

The British, too, did well out of the entire deal. 'Half a million, the total expenses of the war to the E.I. Co.,' read a cryptic comment by Hardinge to Ellenborough when he submitted the Statement of War Charges to London. The figure was arrived at thus: the cost of the sixty days Sutlej campaign was £2 million, of which a million was earned by selling Kashmir to Gulab Singh, and another half a million came in the form of indemnity from the Lahore Durbar. 'From a financial point of view, the First Sikh War was one of the cheapest . . .' What this arithmetic did not indicate was how high the Company's profit actually was. It was clearly a great deal, since the treaty gave the British more than one-third of the Sikh empire's territory and added an annual revenue of 3 million rupees to the revenues of the Company, and good deals were what trading companies – and empire-builders, too – revelled in.

A sad footnote to the Kashmir deal was provided by the celebrated Urdu poet Hafiz Jullundari:

> *Loot li insaan ki qismat pachattar lakh mein*
> *Bik gayee Kashmir ki jannat pachattar lakh mein.*

'A beautiful heritage was sold for 750,000 rupees. The paradise of Kashmir was given away for 750,000 rupees.'

৶

The unstated aim of the First Treaty of Lahore was to consolidate British control of the Sikh state, to be followed in time by outright annexation. The new governor-general who arrived in January

1848 to take over from Hardinge was the Marquis of Dalhousie, variously described as 'ever-excitable' and 'over-strung'. He was hardly of a temperament suited to implementing statesmanlike policies to sustain a sensible relationship with the most turbulent part of the subcontinent. The man who had already been appointed to oversee Punjab's administration from 1 January 1847 was Henry Lawrence, the British resident at Lahore. He began by reinstating Lal Singh and Tej Singh as prime minister of the Sikh state and commander-in-chief of its army. He turned a blind eye to Lal Singh's arbitrary confiscation for himself of several *jagirs* belonging to the Khalsa. Lal Singh, who also wished to replace the governor of Multan with his own brother but couldn't, over-reached himself by trying to get the Lahore Durbar's representative in Kashmir to refuse to hand over the province to Gulab Singh. The British felt he had gone far enough and expelled him from Punjab. Tej Singh was also removed and created Raja of Sialkot on 7 August 1847.

The British now became busy entrenching themselves in Punjab. Relentlessly, and with a clear sense of purpose, they were tightening their hold on Punjab; familiarizing themselves with every stratum of this region with its extraordinary diversity of people, religions, languages, natural resources and beliefs. To make their hold more secure the British insisted on a Second Treaty of Lahore, signed at Bhyrowal on 22 December 1846, which made the once-powerful Sikh empire a virtual protectorate of the British.

When the stakes are high there can be no squeamishness about means and methods. The British showed none when it came to Ranjit Singh's last son and heir. Dalip Singh was separated from his mother, the Regent Jindan Kaur, in 1847 at the age of eight when she was exiled from Lahore and placed under the guardianship of Sir John Login, governor of the Lahore Citadel, in 1849. He was banished from the Punjab in February 1850 for fear of some of Punjab's resentful Sikhs rallying around him and sent to

Fatehgarh in Central India. On 8 March 1853, at the age of fifteen, he was quietly converted to Christianity at Fatehgarh. The governor-general's role in not only uprooting and banishing him from the land of his forefathers but also in his conversion is best summed up in Dalhousie's words. In a letter to Dalip Singh he wrote: 'I earnestly hope that your future life may be in conformity by the precepts of that religion, and that you may show to your countrymen in India an example of a pure and blameless life, such as is befitting a Christian prince.'[48] Although publicly Dalhousie went out of his way to stress that Dalip Singh had converted by his own free will, in a letter to Sir George Couper he wrote: 'Politically, we would desire nothing better, for it destroys his influence for ever.'[49]

Dalip Singh departed for Britain on 19 April 1854, and that was the last he saw of the land of his birth. At the time of his death in exile, in an insignificant hotel in Paris on 22 October 1893, he was alone and thousands of miles away from the magnificent setting from which he had been forcibly exiled by the British – their way of erasing all that remained of their once worthy foe and his empire. A newspaper report of his death commented: 'When the son and heir to Ranjit Singh died, there was no one with him to close his eyes.'[50]

⁓

The government of the Sikh realm, some face-saving devices aside, was now in British hands. In the very year of the fall of the Sikh empire a British writer gave this assessment of the situation: 'The Government of Lahore may be said to be annihilated. In appearance, it exists: there is a king, a prime minister, and an army. But one and all are dependent on the British power! The capital of the country is not garrisoned by Sikhs. It is entirely in the hands of the paramount power, whose soldiers are lent for a time to preserve the semblance of a government, but in reality to keep possession of the advantages already gained, until the season of the year shall enable the Governor-General to annex the whole country to the British possessions.'[51]

Considering the mixed bag of district commissioners, revenue collectors, political agents, engineers, troop commanders and traders who had fanned out across the sprawling Sikh domain, sparks could be expected to fly, given the volatile nature of the Sikhs and the domineering ways of the British. And so it transpired in Multan at the end of 1847, where by April 1848 a small disturbance had developed into a major rebellion. Diwan Mulraj, the able governor of Multan whose father Diwan Sawan Mal had also been a capable and admired governor of this strategically important region, was for various reasons eased out by the British. The troops of the Lahore Durbar did not take kindly to this, and a flashpoint was reached on 20 April when the two British officers who were accompanying Mulraj's replacement were killed by resentful Sikh soldiers. The killing coincided with, or triggered off, a major rebellion in Multan.

The new resident at Lahore, Sir Frederick Currie, who had taken over from John Lawrence on 6 March 1848, held the Lahore Durbar responsible for the mutiny, whereas the Sikh view was that it had been precipitated by the Company's clumsy handling of the situation in its early stages. But the British would not take the blame for it. Currie continued to hold the Durbar responsible for events at Multan and, furthermore, demanded that its Sikh troops put it down. The result of this mindless order was that the rebellion began to spread, with more and more Sikh soldiers rallying around Mulraj, to be joined even by those who had been earlier disbanded from the Sikh army.

From the time the two British officers were killed, the situation at Multan deteriorated to the point where many felt it to be a prime cause of the Second Sikh War. By June 1848 the Sikhs were forced to retreat inside the fort. On 4 September a trainful of British troops from the Sutlej arrived, and an attack on the city was launched five days later. On 14 September events took a dramatic turn when Raja Sher Singh Attariwala, a Sikh chieftain who was also a good friend of the British, was sent to Multan with a contingent of Durbar troops to help quell the rebellion there. But within days of his arrival things got out of hand. Rebellious Sikh troops not only swung the Darbar troops to their side but brought out the simmering anger in Sher Singh which had been ignited by aspersions cast on his father Sardar Chattar Singh Attariwala, governor of Hazara, a man highly regarded both by the Sikhs and the British resident. An excitable political assistant, Captain James Abbott – described as a 'suspicious little autocrat' – had not only spread unworthy reports about Chattar Singh but also mounted an expedition against him. Governor-General Dalhousie, even more excitable and erratic than Abbott, supported him. It was in this inflammable environment of anger and outrage that Chattar Singh's son Sher Singh was sent to Multan.

In a manifesto issued by Sher Singh under his seal, he declared: 'In the first place, they [the English] have broken the treaty, by imprisoning, and sending away to Hindostan, the Maharanee [Rani Jind Kaur], the mother of her people. Secondly, the race of Sikhs, the children of the Maharajah [Ranjit Singh], have suffered so much from their tyranny, that our very religion has been taken away from us. Thirdly, the kingdom has lost its former repute. By the direction of the holy Gooroo, Raja Sher Singh and others, with their valiant troops, have joined the trusty and faithful Dewan Moolraj, on the part of Maharajah Duleep Sing, with a view to eradicate and expel the tyrannous and crafty Feringees.'[52]

Instead of showing serious concern at the way things were going, Dalhousie announced that 'we have without hesitation resolved that Punjab can no longer be allowed to exist as a power and must be destroyed!' Not content with this brash statement, even more coarsely, he wrote in a letter to London on 8 October 1848: 'I have drawn the sword and have this time thrown away the scabbard. If the Sikhs, after this is over, arise again, they shall intrench themselves behind a dunghill, and fight with their finger-nails, for if I live twelve months they shall have nothing else to fight with.'[53]

As the fighting in Multan escalated, on 16 November 1848 the British commander-in-chief Sir Hugh Gough crossed the Ravi to confront Sher Singh. A week later, at Ramnagar on the River Chenab, a major battle was under way. The Company's force

> of over 104,000 men, about 60,000 supported by 45 guns, converged to give battle to the Sikhs, whose strength was around 23,000 men, drawn from the Hazzara, Peshawar, Tank and Bannu garrisons, and including Sher Singh's own contingent. Because the British had for over two years systematically dismantled the Sikh army, sending some of its finest fighting men back to their villages, disbanding its generals and appropriating or destroying its guns, a force of 92,000 men, 31,800 cavalry and over 384 guns was now reduced to a few thousand. Moreover, unlike the British, the heavily outnumbered Sikhs had no reinforcements to fall back upon, as even their unarmed comrades from the Majha and Malwa regions were stopped at river crossings and fords and prevented from joining them. After the British – helped by Pathan horsemen – had taken over the lightly defended fort at Attock, the prospects of Sikh troops from Peshawar joining Chattar Singh's force at Hazara were also slim.[54]

In this first battle of the Second Anglo-Sikh war at Ramnagar on 22 November 1848 the British were decisively defeated. The heavily outnumbered Sikh forces under Sher Singh took a major toll of the enemy whose two cavalry commanders, Brigadier Cureton and Colonel Havelock, were killed. Gough, who tried to make this defeat appear as a victory for the British, got some caustic comments for his pains. While the governor-general said he would rather 'reserve salutes for real victories which this is not',[55] the president of the Company's board of directors said that 'it is no wonder that all confidence in Lord Gough, if it was ever entertained, should have been entirely lost'.[56]

The second major battle of the Second Sikh War was fought at Chillianwala on 13 January 1849. Once again the Sikhs were outnumbered in the field when their force of 10,000 men faced a far bigger army. But even then the enemy lost 2,446 men, including 132 officers. Few historians have tried to gloss over the devastating defeat suffered by the British at Chillianwala:

> advancing British infantrymen were mowed down by the terrific fire of the Sikh musketry. The Sikh *ghorcharas* . . . in successive onslaughts broke up the British cavalry line and cut down their horsemen . . . suddenly to their amazement the enemy took to their heels . . . galloping over their own horse artillery and turning it topsy-turvy leaving their comrades to be slaughtered by the Sikhs. At another site from within the jungle the guns opened up with devastating effect. Lieut. Col. Brookes leading the 24th Foot was killed between the enemy guns. Trapped, the brigade turned to flee in the face of destructive fire of shot and shell. In yet another engagement a large body of Sikhs surrounded the Second Infantry Brigade. Now Gilbert's Force [Sir Walter Gilbert was divisional commander] had neither the cover of guns nor the support of cavalry. In the hand

to hand fight, the brigade was repulsed and driven
back with heavy loss.[57]

By an extraordinary coincidence this historic engagement took
place at nearly the same site where 2,175 years earlier King Porus
had fought his battle against the Macedonians under Alexander.
This time it was the intruder on Indian soil who was soundly
beaten. The irrepressible Gough once more claimed victory for
the British at Chillianwala – a claim his own governor-general dismissed as 'poetical'. Dalhousie's comment on the 'victory' at
Chillianwala was that 'another such would ruin us'. The conster-
nation in London at this setback found expression in many
different ways, ranging from the eighty-year-old Wellington's offer
to go to India to set things right to demands for Gough's immediate recall.

But Dalhousie was planning to turn the Chillianwala defeat
to his advantage. He would use it to demand the complete annexation of Punjab, erase the Sikh state from the face of India
and establish British rule over the entire subcontinent. 'As he
knew himself to be always in the right and those who differed
from him always in the wrong,' a late nineteenth-century English
historian comments, 'he naturally desired to shape the growth
towards a restricted autonomy of the province, which was the
first fruit of his policy of all India for the English.'[58] Since expansion was very much in vogue in the higher echelons of power in
Britain at that time, Dalhousie's was a welcome assertion of
Britain's sense of its own destiny, even though there were several
men of influence in London, including Auckland, Ellenbrough,
Hardinge and Henry Lawrence, who were against the annexation
of Punjab.

The above-quoted historian further observes: 'It was Henry
Lawrence's refusal to recognise that [the Battle of] Gujrat had
destroyed all old title-deeds, and given us a clean slate whereon to

inscribe our own sovereign will and pleasure, which soon after-wards caused the final breach between him and the self-willed autocrat [Dalhousie] then guiding our destinies in India.'[59] Dalhousie was not easily deterred, and since he was the man on the spot he decided to make the Battle of Gujrat the clincher of the Second Sikh War. Many historians hold that for no other single battle had the British assembled such a formidable force of infantry, horsemen, armour and field artillery of every size, range and destructive power. As for the number of men who confronted each other at 7.30 that morning of 21 February 1849, the British had 56,636 infantry and 11,569 cavalry, while the entire Sikh force facing them consisted of 20,000 men.

The battle was fought with unbelievable ferocity since each side knew what the ultimate significance of the Battle of Gujrat was: if the British won they would complete their control of India. Thus, even though the Sikhs were outnumbered, outgunned and unable to replenish their supplies as the British could, they fought with passionate intensity for the honour of the Sikh empire, the hal-lowed teachings of their Gurus and for the sanctity of the very soil of Punjab. When on 14 March 1849 Chattar Singh and Raja Sher Singh Attariwala surrendered to General Gilbert near Rawalpindi, it was the saddest day in the history of a proud and zestful people who had lived and fought all their lives according to their beliefs and with a rare sense of confidence and self-esteem.

There is a moving account which captures the moment of Sikh grief and deep inner hurt when an old veteran of the Sikh army threw down his sword in disgust at the surrender ceremony with the words '*Aaj Ranjit Singh mar gaya*', 'Ranjit Singh has finally died today.'

❧

Britain's dealings with the Sikhs in the ten years after Ranjit Singh's death, and with the Lahore Durbar in particular, increasingly lacked a moral focus. Even appearances, so beloved of the British, were forgotten except for the platitudes which provided more moral comfort to them than they did to those they were directed at. The overriding purpose of the British during the years 1839–49 was to subjugate India to the status of yet another colony of the British Empire. The officers of the East India Company had shrewdly assessed the extraordinary wealth of India from the moment of their arrival in the subcontinent. But even more important was the untold wealth India could produce with British technology and India's vast natural resources and skilled manpower. Britain was in no doubt about the significance of this new jewel in its crown.

Its ultimate agenda for India was to structure the land as a great hub for generating immense revenues for centuries to come. Global events, of course, would at last put an end to this dream, but not before Britain had managed to siphon off a huge quantity of India's treasures, ranging from jewels and rare works of art to the wealth produced by India's inexhaustible pool of labour, minerals, ores and manufacturing skills, in addition to its trained military manpower and much else.

British aims in the period following annexation of the Sikh state in 1849 lay clearly in sequestration of its wealth. There were various channels for the acquisition of precious objects. A huge array of priceless antiquities, gold, jewels, precious stones, paintings and sculptures, textiles, gold-decorated arms and armour was seized and shipped to Britain as spoils of war. A very large number of art treasures have remain unaccounted for, either going into the imperial treasury, joining the crown jewels or entering the vaults of a vast number of museums or becoming part of private collections – especially of those involved with ruling India.

Thanks to the high value the British placed on meticulous paperwork, some valuable insights are provided by their *Press Lists of Old Records in the Punjab Secretariat*. In the ransacking of Sikh treasures the British were methodical as ever, not stopping

at the revered relics of the Gurus, as this letter from the governor-general's office dated 11 June 1851 shows: 'Adverting to
Government letter No. 2903, dated 18 December 1850, the Secretary to the Government of India requests that the golden chair
and the arms of Guru Gobind be sent to the Government
Toshakhana [the British treasury] at Simla proper precautions
being taken for their safety on the road, and that a document
certifying the arms and recording the facts or traditions established regarding them, be forwarded at the same time, in
triplicate, signed by Misr Meg Raj, or whoever may be authority
for the traditions.'[60]

The governor-general made sure of a fair share for his sovereign. 'The Secretary to the Government of India forwards a copy
of the two lists of articles which the Governor-General recently
selected for Her Majesty Queen Victoria and the Hon'ble Court
of Directors from the arms and armour in the Toshakhana at
Lahore, and conveys His Lordship's request that the articles be
carefully packed and transmitted by a safe opportunity to Bombay,
thence to be forwarded to the Court of Directors overland according to their orders. Also requests the Board to preserve in the
Toshakhana the Muhammadan relics, the arms of the Guru, the
golden chair, and the silver bungalow until orders are received
regarding them from the Court of Directors.'[61]

The loot of Sikh treasures was indulged in from the highest to
the lowest levels of the occupying power, from the topmost officials and echelons of power to the soldiery. 'Captain J.M. Drake,
Officiating Deputy Judge Advocate-General, Lahore, requests to
be furnished with information on certain points connected with
the robberies committed in the Toshakhana at Lahore by European soldiers in July, November and December 1849.'[62]

Barely two months after the annexation of the Punjab in 1849
Dr J.S. Login, officer in charge of the Public Establishment in
Lahore, with a letter dated 24 May 1849 addressed to the secretary

of the Board of Administration, Punjab, forwarded 'a list of gold articles in the Toshakhana at Lahore' and suggested that 'as the state of the market is favourable, they might be sold off at once'. Came the reply: 'the Secretary to the Board of Administration authorizes Dr Login to sell off the gold by instalments so as not to glut the market. [He] states that the gold coins called *Boodkees* might be expended in paying up establishments who would have to receive them at the market rates.'[63]

While the above correspondence pertains to Ranjit Singh's state treasury, the following letter dated 9 August 1850 is equally interesting, showing how little time was being wasted in taking over Ranjit Singh's personal wealth. 'The Secretary to the Board of Administration acknowledges the receipt of letter No. 1300, dated 19th July 1850, from the Secretary to the Government of India, and states that a list of jewels has been furnished to Government, but the Board will direct a further examination of them to discover such as are likely to be prized in Europe, and report the result for communication to the Most Noble the Governor-General; that they will also communicate with the Governor-General's Agent at Benares regarding the jewels of the Maharani Chunda [Jindan]. Details of the manner in which it is proposed to dispose of the gold and silver in the Toshakhana, i.e., of the gold by sale at Lahore if a good price can be obtained for it, and of the silver by despatch to Bombay with the rupees of Native [Nanakshahi] currency now being collected for recoinage.'[64]

Further insights into British handling of the contents of the Toshakhana after the takeover of the Punjab are provided in the correspondence of Lady Login, wife of the above-mentioned senior official Sir John Login, appointed Maharaja Dalip Singh's guardian and governor of the citadel on 6 April 1849. Her cousin Robert Adams briefly visited Lahore in that year and writes to Lady Login in England:

Citadel, Lahore
Nov. 2nd, 1849.

My dear Cousin,

I scarcely regret that I have been detained here by illness a
few days, as it has given me an opportunity of seeing all the
multifarious wonders, animal and mineral, over which your
worthy husband keeps guard within the Citadel, and of
telling you before I leave this, how well his really responsible duties have agreed with him. . . . I wish you could walk
through the Toshkhana and see its wonders! the vast
quantities of gold and silver, the jewels not to be valued, so
many and so rich! the Koh-i-Noor, far beyond what I had
imagined; and, perhaps above all, the immense collection
of magnificent Cashmere shawls, rooms full of them,
laid out on shelves, and heaped up in bales – it is not to be
described!

Your affectionate cousin,
ROBERT R. ADAMS.

P.S. – The enclosed rough memorandum will amuse you.

Memorandum of Memorabilia, under charge of
JOHN SPENCER LOGIN,
In the Citadel of Lahore,
April 6th, 1849.

– THE DIAMOND (KOH-I-NOOR).
– The State jewels and treasures in gold, silver, and
precious stones; dishes, plates, cups, cooking pots,
and gurrahs of gold and silver.
– The vast store of Cashmere shawls, chogas, & c.
– Runjeet's golden chair of State; his silver summer-
house; gold and silver poled, tents and camp-equipage

of rich Cashmere; arms and armour, very magnificent.
– Shah Sooja's State pavilion, gorgeously embroidered.
– Relics of the Prophet; his shoes, walking-stick,
shirt, cap, and pyjamas; his book of prayers in the
Kufic character; several locks of his hair.
– The Kulgee 'plume' of the last Guru (Govind).
– The sword of the Persian hero Roostum, taken
from Shah Sooja by Runjeet Singh.
– The sword of Wuzeer Fathie Khan, founder of the
Baruksye family at Cabul and Candahar.
–The sword of Holkar (an old Spanish blade).
– The armour worn by the warriors and Sirdars of
note, many of them stained with their blood.
– The wedding garment of Maha Singh.
– Besides these, many valuable curiosities and relics
of all kinds, too numerous to note.[65]

Credit must be given to Lady Login for nailing the British government for continuing its tradition of sequestering the wealth of
its adversaries and allies alike on the simple premise that 'might is
right': 'The Government has never accounted to the Maharajah
[Dalip Singh] for the money received for the sale of the house, nor
has he received anything in respect of the value of the land, though
the papers show that the whole was purchased out of his money,
nor any compensation in respect of the contents of the house,
which were destroyed at the Mutiny.'[66]

In addition to appropriating the wealth of the Sikh empire without a qualm of conscience, a new administrative system was also
structured to increase revenues and funnel them into the British
treasury. As one of the present writers has described elsewhere: 'The
Punjab was divided into seven Commissionerships and 27 Districts,
and by 1 June 1849 the new administrative system had been set up
in most areas. The District Officer's job was collection of revenue,

keeping the peace, the dispensation of justice, and the economic development of his District. Revenue in Punjab was collected from water rates, land revenue, *malikana* (fees for recognizing proprietary titles), and various other forms of duties, rents and cesses. When it came to constructing canals, however, the cost of their development was largely financed by the Punjabis rather than the colonial administration although the revenue collected went to its treasury, and from there to the British exchequer as charges for administering India.'[67]

The general goal of development projects – railroads, post and telegraph systems, agricultural production – was the creation of stable conditions in which the human resources of Punjab could be harnessed to generate wealth which British banks, trading houses, shippers and other businesses could exploit. First the foundation and then the skilful administration of institutions established on sound economic foundations provided a key means for the systematic funnelling of India's wealth out of the country.

The British got what they wanted to a substantial degree. And so did many others who either through deceit or treachery enriched themselves at the expense of a state created by the political genius of one man out of a sense of mission given to him and its population by a new faith. But in the end responsibility for the fate that overtook the Sikhs, and the furthermost reaches of their proud state, rested not with Brahmins, Dogras, the British or countless baggage-carriers, mountebanks and mercenaries but with the Sikhs themselves, who frittered away the unique legacy bequeathed to them. Perhaps the very richness of this legacy proved the undoing of those who inherited it, belief in their own infallibility making them indifferent to the many hostile forces around them.

As Chapter 7 of this book will have made clear, Ranjit Singh himself was in part responsible for the destruction of the edifice he had so energetically and enthusiastically built. He failed to assess the far-reaching implications of founding a monarchy, whose creation was in stark contradiction to the fundamental tenets of the Khalsa. The commonwealth of the Khalsa was founded on republican tradition, with no place for any hierarchies. In it everyone was equal in the eyes of God and by definition equal in the eyes of each other. Equality was the cornerstone of the faith: its inspiration, strength, source of self-renewal, its essential dynamic.

The monarchy established by Ranjit Singh weakened the Sikh faith. The very concept of monarchical rule was anathema to the Sikhs because it signified the dictates of a paramount power, and paramountcy was alien to the concept of the Khalsa. As a self-assertive people, the Sikhs could be contentious, and when a medley of aspiring individuals laid claim to power at the Lahore Durbar after Ranjit Singh's death contentions multiplied and spawned conspiracies, attempted coups and conflicts within the backbone of the state, the army.

Ranjit Singh, with his rare insights into men and his extraordinary qualities of leadership, handled his monarchy with the same flair as he did the many different roles he played in life, but those who came after him possessed none of his genius. The wasting of his legacy was a very great loss to his successors and all Sikhs, because they produced a leader such as rarely emerges in the galaxy of great leaders.

> Courage transcends knowledge. It springs from motivation, from duty, from devotion to one's fellows, patriotism, belief in a cause. These overcome fear of death itself, and make men ready to die for what they believe in.
>
> I.F STONE, *The Trial of Socrates*

MAHARAJA RANJIT
SINGH'S FAMILY TREE

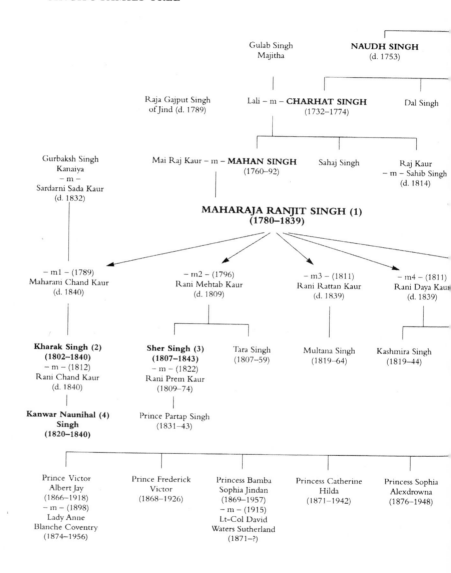

Gulab Singh
Majitha

NAUDH SINGH
(d. 1753)

Raja Gajput Singh
of Jind (d. 1789)

Lali – m – **CHARHAT SINGH**
(1732–1774)

Dal Singh

Gurbaksh Singh
Kanaiya
– m –
Sardarni Sada Kaur
(d. 1832)

Mai Raj Kaur – m – **MAHAN SINGH**
(1760–92)

Sahaj Singh

Raj Kaur
– m – Sahib Singh
(d. 1814)

MAHARAJA RANJIT SINGH (1)
(1780–1839)

– m1 – (1789)
Maharani Chand Kaur
(d. 1840)

– m2 – (1796)
Rani Mehtab Kaur
(d. 1809)

– m3 – (1811)
Rani Rattan Kaur
(d. 1839)

– m4 – (1811)
Rani Daya Kaur
(d. 1839)

Kharak Singh (2)
(1802–1840)
– m – (1812)
Rani Chand Kaur
(d. 1840)

Sher Singh (3)
(1807–1843)
– m – (1822)
Rani Prem Kaur
(1809–74)

Tara Singh
(1807–59)

Multana Singh
(1819–64)

Kashmira Singh
(1819–44)

Kanwar Naunihal (4)
Singh
(1820–1840)

Prince Partap Singh
(1831–43)

Prince Victor
Albert Jay
(1866–1918)
– m – (1898)
Lady Anne
Blanche Coventry
(1874–1956)

Prince Frederick
Victor
(1868–1926)

Princess Bamba
Sophia Jindan
(1869–1957)
– m – (1915)
Lt-Col David
Waters Sutherland
(1871–?)

Princess Catherine
Hilda
(1871–1942)

Princess Sophia
Alexdrowna
(1876–1948)

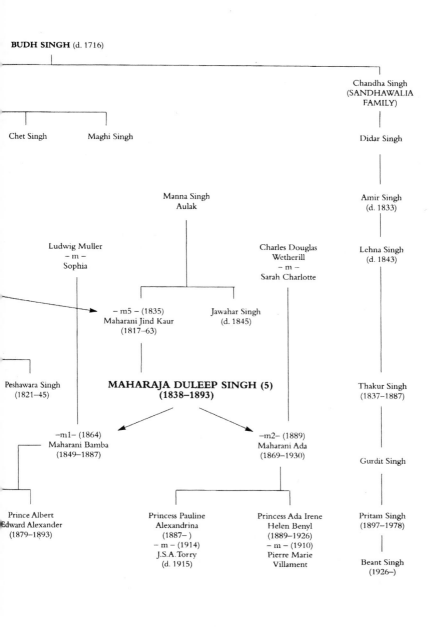

BUDH SINGH (d. 1716)

Chandha Singh
(SANDHAWALIA
FAMILY)

Chet Singh   Maghi Singh

Didar Singh

Manna Singh
Aulak

Amir Singh
(d. 1833)

Ludwig Muller
– m –
Sophia

Charles Douglas
Wetherill
– m –
Sarah Charlotte

Lehna Singh
(d. 1843)

– m5 – (1835)
Maharani Jind Kaur
(1817–63)

Jawahar Singh
(d. 1845)

Peshawara Singh
(1821–45)

Thakur Singh
(1837–1887)

**MAHARAJA DULEEP SINGH (5)
(1838–1893)**

–m1– (1864)
Maharani Bamba
(1849–1887)

–m2– (1889)
Maharani Ada
(1869–1930)

Gurdit Singh

Prince Albert
Edward Alexander
(1879–1893)

Princess Pauline
Alexandrina
(1887–)
– m – (1914)
J.S.A. Torry
(d. 1915)

Princess Ada Irene
Helen Benyl
(1889–1926)
– m – (1910)
Pierre Marie
Villament

Pritam Singh
(1897–1978)

Beant Singh
(1926–)

$\mathscr{N}otes$

CHAPTER 1: The Legacy That Made the Sikhs Proud

1 Syad Muhammad Latif, *History of the Punjab* [originally published 1891], Kalyani Publishers, New Delhi, 1989, p. 65.

2 Major H.M.L. Lawrence, *Adventures of an Officer in the Punjab* [1846], 2 vols, Panjabi University (Languages Department), Patiala, Vol. 1, 1970 reprint, pp. 30–31.

3 The name Punjab derives from the Persian words *punj* (five) and *ab* (rivers).

4 Syad Muhammad Latif, *History of the Punjab*, Preface, 1989, p. iii.

5 His father was an accountant for a Rajput landowner, a convert to Islam, and a Muslim midwife brought Nanak into the world.

6 Guru Granth Sahib, Raj Bhairon, p. 1136.

7 Included in the Guru Granth Sahib, Asa, p. 471.

8 This original edition was known as the Adi Granth, while the final edition, the Guru Granth, was given its form by the tenth and last Guru Gobind Singh who added to it the hymns of the ninth Guru, Tegh Bahadur.

9 In India the word 'secular' has its own special meaning, a 'secular' society being one in which each citizen believes firmly in his or her own religious faith, with no one being prevented from holding or practising his or her own faith, no majority faith imposed on anyone and no discrimination on grounds of faith or preference for co-religionists. The secular principle laid down by the Gurus

was to be scrupulously followed by Ranjit Singh during his reign.

10 *Tuzuk-i-Jahangiri or Memoirs of Jahangir*, trans. Alexander Rogers, ed. Henry Beveridge, Munshiram Manoharlal, New Delhi, 1968, pp. 72–3.

11 Max Arthur Macauliffe, *The Sikh Religion: Its Gurus, Sacred Writings and Authors* [1909], 6 vols, Oxford University Press, Oxford, 1995, Vol. 3, p. 99.

12 Ibid.

13 Max Arthur Macauliffe, *The Sikh Religion*, Vol. 4, p. 305.

14 Saqi Mustad Khan, *Maasir-i-Alamgir (A History of the Emperor Aurangzeb-Alangir, 1650–1707)* [1947], trans. Jadunath Sarkar, Munshiram Manoharlal, New Delhi, 1986, pp. 51–2.

15 Duncan Greenless, *The Gospel of the Guru Granth Sahib*, Theosophical Publishing House, Madras, 1952, p. 87.

16 *Akbarat-i-Darbari-Mualla* [Persian], Royal Asiatic Society, London, Vol. 1: *1677–1695*.

17 See note 9, Chapter 1.

18 Harbans Singh, *Guru Gobind Singh*, Sterling Publishers, New Delhi, 1979, pp. 46–7.

19 Dalip Singh, *Guru Gobind Singh and Khalsa Discipline*, Singh Brothers, Amritsar, 1992.

20 Harbans Singh, *Guru Gobind Singh*, p. 58.

21 Harpreet Brar, 'Guru Gobind Singh's Relations with Aurangzeb', pp. 17–33, *The Punjab Past and Present* (biannual journal), Panjabi University, Patiala, April 1983, 19.

22 Ganda Singh, 'Guru Gobind Singh: The Last Phase', ibid., p. 2.

23 K.S. Duggal, *Ranjit Singh: A Secular Sikh Sovereign*, Abhinav Publications, New Delhi, 1989.

24 Khafi Khan, 'Muntakhab-ul-Lubab', in H. M. Elliot and J. Dowson (eds), *The History of India as Told by Its Own Historians*, Vol. VII, Kitab Mahal, Allahabad, 1972 (reprint), p. 415.

25 William Irvine, 'Political History of the Sikhs', *The Asiatic Quarterly*, January–April 1894, pp. 420–31, and 'Guru Gobind

Singh and Bandah', *Journal of the Asiatic Society*, January–April 1894, pp. 112–43.

26 'Akhbar-i-Darbar-i-Mualla: Mughal Court News Relating to the Punjab, AD 1707–1718', *The Punjab Past and Present*, Panjabi University, Patiala, October 1984, p. 141.

27 Bikrama Jit Hasrat, *The Life and Times of Ranjit Singh: A Saga of Benevolent Despotism*, V.V. Research Institute Book Agency, Hoshiarpur, 1977, p. 311.

28 These figures are extrapolated from census figures for 1881.

29 Hari Ram Gupta, *History of the Sikhs* (5 vols), Munshiram Manoharlal, New Delhi, Vol. II, 1978, pp. 255–6.

30 These figures are taken from Bhagat Singh, *A History of the Sikh Misals*, Punjabi University, Patiala, 1993, p. 55.

CHAPTER 2: Drumbeat of a School Drop-out

1 C.H. Payne, *A Short History of the Sikhs*, Thomas Nelson and Sons, London, 1915, p. 114.

2 Captain Leopold Von Orlich, *Travels in India including Sinde and the Punjab*, 2 vols, [London, 1845], Usha Publications, New Delhi, 1985, Vol. 1, p. 172.

3 Sir Gokul Chand Narang, *Transformation of Sikhism*, New Book Society, Lahore, 1912, p. 317.

4 Joginder Singh Kapur, 'Birthplace of Maharajah Ranjit Singh – Gujranwala or Badrukhan?', www.sikhstudies.org/periodicals.

5 *District and State Gazetteers of the Undivided Punjab* (prior to independence) (4 vols) [Gujranwala District, 1935], Low Price Publications, New Delhi, 1993, Vol. 1, p. 342.

6 General Sir John J.H. Gordon, *The Sikhs* [1904], Panjab University (Languages Department), Chandigarh, 1988, p. 84.

7 Sir Gokul Chand Narang, *Transformation of Sikhism*, p. 317.

8 Hari Ram Gupta, *History of the Sikhs*, Vol. 5, 1991, p. 14.

9 Teja Singh (ed.), *Maharaja Ranjit Singh: First Death Centenary Memorial* [1939], Deepak, Amritsar, 1993, p. 100.

10 See Chapter 1, note 9.

11 Major G. Smyth, *A History of the Reigning Family of Lahore* [1847], Nirmal Publishers and Distributors, New Delhi, 1987, p. 14.

12 Hari Ram Gupta, *History of the Sikhs*, Vol. 5, p. 10.

13 Sir Lepel Griffin, *Rulers of India: Ranjit Singh* [1911], S. Chand and Co., New Delhi, 1967, p. 98.

14 Ibid. pp. 79–80.

15 Bikrama Jit Hasrat, *The Life and Times of Ranjit Singh: A Saga of Benevolent Despotism*, V.V. Research Institute Book Agency, Hoshiarpur, 1977, p. 35.

16 Hari Ram Gupta, *History of the Sikhs*, Vol. 5, p. 16.

17 Henry T. Prinsep, *The Origin of the Sikh Power in the Punjab and Political Life of Muha-Raja Runjeet Singh* [1834], Military Orphan Press, Calcutta, 1965, p.180.

18 Ibid.

19 Syad Muhammad Latif, *History of the Punjab*, p. 352.

20 Hari Ram Gupta, *History of the Sikhs*, Vol. 5, p. 448.

21 K.K. Khullar, *Maharaja Ranjit Singh*, Prominent Printers, New Delhi, 1980, p. 184.

22 Hari Ram Gupta, *History of the Sikhs*, Vol. 5, p. 22.

23 Based on 1881 census figures which placed Punjab's population at 22 million.

24 Baron Charles Hugel, *Kashmir and the Punjab* [1845], Light and Life Publishers, Jammu, 1972, p. 288.

25 General Sir John J.H. Gordon, *The Sikhs* [1904], Panjab University (Languages Department), Chandigarh, 1988, pp. 86–7.

26 Harbans Singh, *Guru Gobind Singh*, Sterling Publishers, New Delhi, 1979, pp. 46–7.

27 Fauja Singh and A.C. Arora, *Maharaja Ranjit Singh: Politics, Society and Economy*, Panjabi University, Patiala, 1984, p. 316.

28 K.K. Khullar, *Maharaja Ranjit Singh*, p. 50.

CHAPTER 3: Emergence of the Sikh Kingdom

1 Teja Singh (ed.), *Maharaja Ranjit Singh: First Death Centenary Memorial*, p. 218.

2 Henry T. Prinsep, *Origin of the Sikh Power in the Punjab*, p. 179.

3 W.G. Osborne, *The Court and Camp of Runjeet Sing*, Henry Colburn, London, 1840, pp. 113–14.

4 K.K. Khullar, *Maharaja Ranjit Singh*, p. 201.

5 G.L. Chopra (quoting from the *Risala-i-Sahib Numa* by Ganesh Das), *Maharaja Ranjit Singh: First Death Centenary Memorial*, p. 121.

6 Hardit Singh Dhillon, *Maharaja Ranjit Singh: First Death Centenary Memorial*, p. 123.

7 W.L. McGregor, *History of the Sikhs* [1846], 2 vols, Rupa, New Delhi, 2007, Vol. 1, p. 220.

8 Sir Alexander Burnes, *Cabool: A Personal Narrative of a Journey to, and Residence in That City, the Years 1836–1838* [1841], Indus Publications, Karachi, Vol. 2, 1986, p. 28.

9 Captain Leopold Von Orlich, *Travels in India Including Sinde and the Punjab* [1845], 2 vols, Vol. 1, Usha Publications, New Delhi, 1985, pp. 171–2.

10 Charles Metcalfe, Despatch No. 25, 1 October 1808, quoted in Bikrama Jit Hasrat, *The Life and Times of Ranjit Singh: A Saga of Benevolent Despotism*, V.V. Research Institute Book Agency, Hoshiarpur, 1977, p. 314.

11 Philip Woodruff, *The Men Who Ruled India*, Jonathan Cape, London, Vol. 1: *The Founders*, 1953, p. 200.

12 S.S. Thorburn, *The Punjab in Peace and War* [1883], Panjab University (Languages Department), Chandigarh, 1989, p. 3.

13 Ibid., p. 4.

14 Bikrama Jit Hasrat, *Life and Times of Ranjit Singh*, p. 320.

15 Ian Heath, *The Sikh Army 1799–1849*, Osprey Publishing, Oxford, 2005, p. 7.

16 Sita Ram Kohli, 'The Army of Maharaja Ranjit Singh', *Journal of*

Indian History, Vols 1–5, 1921–6; cited by Heath, ibid., p. 14.

17 Quoted in Ian Heath, *The Sikh Army 1799–1849*, p. 34.

18 W.G. Osborne, *The Court and Camp of Runjeet Singh*, p. 54.

19 Henry Steinbach, *The Country of the Sikhs* [1846], KLM Book House, New Delhi, 1978, p. 69.

20 W.G. Osborne, *The Court and Camp of Runjeet Singh*, p. 55.

21 *Records of the Ludhiana Agency* (Punjab Government Press) [1911], Sang-e-Meel Publications, Lahore, 2006, Preface, p. i.

22 Victor Kiernan, *Metcalfe's Mission to Lahore (1808–1809)*, Punjab Government Record Office, Lahore, Monograph No. 1, 1950, p. 4.

23 Patwant Singh, *The Sikhs*, John Murray, London, 1999, pp. 111–12.

24 Bikrama Jit Hasrat, *The Life and Times of Ranjit Singh*, pp. 80–81.

25 Gurmukh Nihal Singh, 'A Note on the Policy of Maharaja Ranjit Singh Towards the British', *Maharaja Ranjit Singh: First Death Centenary Memorial*, p. 163.

26 Quoted in K.K. Khullar, *Maharaja Ranjit Singh*, p. 119

27 Patwant Singh, *The Sikhs*, p. 119

28 Monisha Bharadwaj, *Great Diamonds of India*, India Book House, Mumbai, 2002, p. 24.

29 Iradj Amini, *Koh-i-Noor*, Roli Books, New Delhi, 1994, p. 27.

30 Hari Ram Gupta, *History of the Sikhs*, Vol. 5, p. 102.

31 'This gun was made in 1757. It is 14 ft long and of 9-in. bore, and was forged under the orders of Ahmad Shah Abdali, after collecting brass & copper vessels from the homes of the Hindus of Lahore as a punishment . . .' Gopal Singh, *A History of the Sikh People (1469–1978)*, World Sikh University Press, New Delhi, 1979, p. 452.

32 Ahmed Nabi Khan, *Multan: History and Architecture*, Institute of Islamic History, Culture and Civilization, Islamabad, 1983, p. 141.

33 J.S. Grewal, 'From the Treaty of Amritsar to the Conquest of Multan: The Evidence of Umdat-ut-Tawarikh', in Fauja Singh and A.C. Arora (eds), *Maharaja Ranjit Singh: Politics, Society and Economy*, Panjabi University, Patiala, 1984, pp. 15–16.

34 Hari Ram Gupta, *History of the Sikhs*, Vol. 5, p. 128.

35 Charles Baron Von Hugel, *Kashmir Under Maharaja Ranjit Singh* [1845], Atlantic Publishers and Distributors, New Delhi, 1984, p. iv.

36 *Gazetteer of the Peshawar District 1897–98*, Sang-e-Meel Publications, Lahore, 1989, p. 65.

37 Ibid., p. 73.

38 Ahmad Hasan Dani, *Peshawar: Historic City of the Frontier*, Sang-e-Meel Publications, Lahore, 1995, p. 15.

CHAPTER 4: Campaigns, Conquests and Consolidation

1 Hari Ram Gupta, *History of the Sikhs*, Vol. 5, pp. 387–8.

2 Joseph Davey Cunningham, *A History of the Sikhs: From the Origins of the Nation to the Battles of the Sutlej* [1849], S. Chand and Co. New Delhi, 1966, p. 153.

3 Sir Lepel Griffin, *Rulers of India: Ranjit Singh*, p. 127.

4 Ibid., p. 115.

5 Sir Lepel Griffin, *The Punjab Chiefs* [1890], Civil and Military Press, Lahore, Vol. 1, 1909, p. 260.

6 W.G. Osborne, *The Court and Camp of Runjeet Sing*, pp. 74, 75.

7 Sir Lepel Griffin, *The Punjab Chiefs*, Vol. 1, p. 296.

8 K.K. Khullar, *Maharaja Ranjit Singh*, pp. 39–40.

9 Joseph Davey Cunningham, *A History of the Sikhs*, p.185.

10 Ibid., p. 184.

11 R.R. Sethi, *The Mighty and the Shrewd Maharaja*, S. Chand and Co., New Delhi, p. 136.

12 Henry T. Prinsep, *Origin of the Sikh Power in the Punjab*, pp. 166, 167–8.

13 Bikrama Jit Hasrat, *The Life and Times of Ranjit Singh*, p. 150.

14 Ibid., p. 168.

15 Teja Singh (ed.), *Maharaja Ranjit Singh: First Death Centenary Memorial*, p. 40.

16 Hari Ram Gupta, *History of the Sikhs*, Vol. 5, p. 262.

17 Henry T. Prinsep, *Origin of the Sikh Power in the Punjab*,
p. 183.

18 Bikrama Jit Hasrat, *The Life and Times of Ranjit Singh*, p. 364.

19 *Records of the Ludhiana Agency* [1911], Sang-e-Meel Publications,
Lahore, 2006, pp. 279–82.

CHAPTER 5: The Unabashed Sensualist

1 Fakir Syed Waheeduddin, *The Real Ranjit Singh*, Panjabi
University, Patiala, 1981, p. 171.

2 Henry T. Prinsep, *Origin of the Sikh Power in the Punjab*,
pp. 84–5.

3 Baron Charles Hugel, *Kashmir and the Punjab*, p. 311.

4 Captain Leopold von Orlich, *Travels in India Including Sinde and
the Punjab*, Vol. 1, p. 173.

5 Joseph Davey Cunningham, *A History of the Sikhs*, p. 159.

6 Ibid., p. 160.

7 Fakir Syed Waheeduddin, *The Real Ranjit Singh*, pp. 170,
171, 172.

8 Ibid., p. 169.

9 Lala Sohan Lal Suri, *Umdat-Ut-Tawarikh (Chronicle of the Reign of
Maharaja Ranjit Singh)* [1889], Daftar-III, Parts 1–5, S. Chand and
Co. New Delhi, 1961, p. 99.

10 Syad Mohammad Latif, *Lahore: Its History, Architectural
Remains and Antiquities*, Sang-e-Meel Publications, Lahore, 1892,
pp. 249, 250.

11 W.G. Osborne, *The Court and Camp of Runjeet Sing*, pp. 96–7.

12 Fakir Syed Waheeduddin, *The Real Ranjit Singh*, p. 175.

13 W.G. Osborne, *The Court and Camp of Runjeet Sing*, pp. 85–6.

14 Ibid., pp. 198, 199.

15 Henry Edward Fane, *Five Years in India* [1842], Deepak, Gurgaon,
Vol. 1, 1989, p. 170.

16 Hari Ram Gupta, *History of the Sikhs*, Vol. 5, pp. 537, 538.

17 Fakir Syed Waheeduddin, *The Real Ranjit Singh*, p. 165.

18 Sir Lepel Griffin, *The Punjab Chiefs*, Civil and Military Gazette Press, Lahore, 1890, p. 388.

19 C.H. Payne, *A Short History of the Sikhs*, Thomas Nelson and Sons, London, 1915, p. 99.

20 Syad Mohammad Latif, *History of the Punjab*, p. 423.

21 Ibid.

22 A gold coin then worth 15 rupees.

23 Lala Sohan Lal Suri, *Umdat-ut-Tawarikh*, pp. 331–2.

24 Syad Muhammad Latif, *History of the Punjab*, p. 480.

25 Ibid., p. 481.

26 Harbans Singh (ed.), *The Encyclopedia of Sikhism* (4 vols), Panjabi University, Patiala, Vol. 2, 1996, p. 9.

27 Joseph Davey Cunningham, *A History of the Sikhs*, p. 193.

28 K.K. Khullar, *Maharaja Ranjit Singh*, p. 151.

29 Ibid.

30 Ibid., p. 154.

31 Ibid.

32 Ibid.

CHAPTER 6: Patron of the Arts and Minter Extraordinary

1 W.G. Archer, *Paintings of the Sikhs*, Her Majesty's Stationery Office, London, 1966, pp. 19, 26.

2 Mulk Raj, Anand (ed.), *Maharaja Ranjit Singh as Patron of the Arts*, Marg Publications, Bombay, 1981, p. 96.

3 Lieutenant William Barr, *Journal of a March from Delhi to Cabul* [1844], Panjabi University (Languages Department), Patiala, 1970, p. 57.

4 Mulk Raj, Anand (ed.), *Maharaja Ranjit Singh as Patron of the Arts*, p. 54.

5 Patwant Singh, *The Golden Temple*, Time Books International, New Delhi, 1989, pp. 102–3.

6 Lala Sohan Lal Suri, *Umdat-Ut-Tawarikh*, Daftar-III, Parts 1–5 [1839], S. Chand and Co. New Delhi, 1961, p. 435.

7   T.S. Randhawa, *The Sikhs: Images of a Heritage*, Prakash Books, New Delhi, 2000, p. 23.

8   F.S. Aijazuddin, *Sikh Portraits by European Artists*, Sotheby Parke Bernet Publications, London, 1979, p. 21.

9   Lieutenant William Barr, *Journal of a March from Delhi to Cabul*, p. 65.

10 Ganda Singh, *The Punjab in 1839–40*, Panjabi University, Patiala, 1952, p. 17.

11 W.G. Archer, *Paintings of the Sikhs*, p. 9.

12 W.L. McGregor, *The History of the Sikhs* [1846], Rupa, New Delhi, 2007, Vol. 1, p. 223.

13 Baron Charles Hugel, *Kashmir and the Punjab*, pp. 302–3.

14 Ibid., p. 304.

15 *Journal of the Asiatic Society of Bengal*, December 1909, Vol. 5 (new series).

16 Syad Muhammad Latif, *Lahore: Its History, Architectural Remains and Antiquities*, p. 224.

17 British Parliamentary Papers, *Report Relating to a Gold Currency for India*, Resolution No. 1325, Financial Department, Government of India, Simla, 12 July 1864 (published 1865).

18 What Major Edwards does not make clear in his covering note to the resident at Lahore is that Raja Sher Singh Attariwala did not desert to the enemy (the remnants of Ranjit Singh's army were by no means 'the enemy') and that 'the real interests' of Maharaja Dalip Singh were hardly served by the British exiling him from the land of his birth and his heritage.

19 *Papers Relating to the Punjab, 1847–9*, Inclosure No. 1 in No. 39, p. 376, Harrison and Son, London.

20 R. Bosworth Smith, *Life of Lord Lawrence*, Smith, Elder and Co., London, Vol. 1, 1883, pp. 307–8.

21 Press lists of old records in the *Punjab Secretariat Supplementary*, 5 April 1849–10 February 1853.

CHAPTER 7: Flouting the Republican Tradition

1 Bhagat Singh, *A History of the Sikh Misals*, Panjabi University, Patiala, 1993, p. 81.

2 Henry Steinbach, *The Country of the Sikhs* [1846], KLM Book House, New Delhi, 1978, p. 14.

3 General Sir John J.H. Gordon, *The Sikhs*, pp. 116–17.

4 C.H. Payne, *A Short History of the Sikhs*, pp. 133–4.

5 Henry T. Prinsep, *Origins of the Sikh Power*, p. 214.

6 Joseph Davey Cunningham, *A History of the Sikhs*, p. 200.

7 Max Arthur Macauliffe, *The Sikh Religion: Its Gurus, Sacred Writings and Authors* [1909], Oxford University Press, Oxford, Vol. 5, 1995, pp. 243–4.

8 Kapur Singh, *Parasaraprasna or the Baisakhi of Guru Gobind Singh: An Exposition of Sikhism*, Hind Publishers, Jullundar, 1959, p. 366.

9 Kapur Singh, *Parasaraprasna*, Guru Nanak Dev University, Amritsar, 1989, pp. 59–60.

10 Ibid., p. 43.

11 Translation of a verse attributed to the Sikh historian Bhai Rattan Singh Bhangu, author of *Pracin Panth Prakas*, 1841, quoted in Kapur Singh, *Parasaraprasna*, p. 41.

12 Patwant Singh, *The Sikhs*, p. 148.

CHAPTER 8: The Decadent and Deceitful

1 Major G. Smyth, *A History of the Reigning Family of Lahore*, p. 25.

2 For example, Syad Muhammad Latif, *History of the Punjab* [1891], p. 498.

3 Bikrama Jit Hasrat, *Life and Times of Ranjit Singh*, p. 217.

4 Fauja Singh, *Maharaja Kharak Singh*, Panjabi University, Patiala, 1977, p. xliv.

5 Major G. Smyth, *A History of the Reigning Family of Lahore*, p. 36.

6 Ibid., p. 36.

7 Joseph Davey Cunningham, *A History of the Sikhs*, p. 209.

8 Syad Muhammad Latif, *History of the Punjab*, p. 502.

9 Major G. Smyth, *A History of the Reigning Family of Lahore*, p. 38.
10 Syad Muhammad Latif, *History of the Punjab*, pp. 505–6.
11 Ibid, p. 506.
12 Ganda Singh, *The Punjab in 1839–40*, p. 17.
13 Syad Muhammad Latif, *History of the Punjab*, p. 507.
14 Hari Ram Gupta, *Panjab on the Eve of the First Sikh War*, Panjab University, Chandigarh, 1956, p. 39.
15 C.H. Payne, *A Short History of the Sikhs*, p. 114.
16 Ibid., p. 144.
17 Emily Eden, *Up the Country* [1930], Curzon Press, London, 1978, p. 22.
18 Bikrama Jit Hasrat, *Life and Times of Ranjit Singh*, pp. 223–4.
19 Harbans Singh, *The Heritage of the Sikhs*, Manohar Publications, New Delhi, 1985, p. 199.
20 Bikrama Jit Hasrat, *Life and Times of Ranjit Singh*, p. 201.
21 Michael Alexander and Sushila Anand, *Queen Victoria's Maharajah: Duleep Singh 1838–93*, Weidenfeld and Nicolson, London, 1980, p. 2.
22 C.H. Payne, *A Short History of the Sikhs*, p. 146.

CHAPTER 9: Twilight of an Empire

1 S.S. Thorburn, *The Punjab in Peace and War*, p. 2.
2 Major Evans Bell, *The Annexation of the Punjab and Maharajah Duleep Singh* [1882], Nirmal Publishers and Distributors, New Delhi, 1986, pp. 9–10.
3 Barbara W. Tuchman, *Sand Against the Wind: Stilwell and the American Experience in China 1911–45*, Macmillan, London, 1971, p. 436.
4 Donald Featherstone, *At Them with the Bayonet: The First Sikh War*, London, Jarrolds, 1968, p. x.
5 Viscount Hardinge, *Rulers of India*, Clarendon Press, Oxford, 1900, p. 28.
6 Ibid., pp. 49–50.

7   S.S. Thorburn, *The Punjab in Peace and War*, p. 4.

8   Joseph Davey Cunningham, *A History of the Sikhs*, p. 279.

9   Bikrama Jit Hasrat, *Life and Times of Ranjit Singh*, p. 251.

10 Bikrama Jit Hasrat, *Anglo-Sikh Relations, 1799–1849*, V.V. Research Institute, Hoshiarpur, 1968, p. 189.

11 Hari Ram Gupta, *Punjab, Central Asia and the First Afghan War*, Panjab University, Chandigarh, 1943, p. 271.

12 Harbans Singh, *Heritage of the Sikhs*, p. 198.

13 Bikrama Jit Hasrat, *The Punjab Papers (1836–1849)*, V.V. Research Institute, Hoshiarpur, 1970, p. 72.

14 Dewan Ajudhia Parshad, *Waqai Jang-i-Sikhan [Events of the (First) Anglo-Sikh War – 1845–46]*, Punjab Itihas Prakashan, Chandigarh, 1975, pp. 11–12.

15 Patwant Singh, *The Sikhs*, p. 153.

16 Joseph Davey Cunningham, *A History of the Sikhs*, pp. 257–8.

17 Sita Ram Kohli, *Sunset of the Sikh Empire*, Orient Longman, New Delhi, 1967, p. 103, n. 2.

18 Ibid., p. 106.

19 Joseph Davey Cunningham, *A History of the Sikhs*, p. 292.

20 Donald Featherstone, *At Them with the Bayonet*, p. 46.

21 Joseph Davey Cunningham, *A History of the Sikhs*, p. 265.

22 Sita Ram Kohli, *Sunset of the Sikh Empire*, p. 106.

23 Joseph Davey Cunningham, *A History of the Sikhs*, p. 266.

24 Khushwant Singh, *The Fall of the Kingdom of Punjab*, Orient Longman, New Delhi, 1962, p. 99.

25 Joseph Davey Cunningham, *A History of the Sikhs*, p. 267.

26 W.L. McGregor, *The History of the Sikhs*, Vol. 2, p. 120.

27 Donald Featherstone, *At Them with the Bayonet*, p. 90.

28 Sita Ram Kohli, *Sunset of the Sikh Empire*, p. 106.

29 Donald Featherstone, *At Them with the Bayonet*, p. 101.

30 Quoted in Ian Heath, *The Sikh Army 1799–1849*, p. 13.

31 Quoted ibid., p. 22.

32 'The Return of Ordnance', in *Despatches of Lord Hardinge, Lord*

Gough and Sir Harry Smith and Other Documents, Oliver and Ackerman, London, 1846, p. 36.

33 Donald Featherstone, *At Them with the Bayonet*, p. 99.

34 Major G. Smyth, *A History of the Reigning Family of Lahore*, p. xxvi.

35 Syad Muhammad Latif, *History of the Punjab*, p. 544.

36 Sita Ram Kohli, *Sunset of the Sikh Empire*, p. 112.

37 Bikrama Jit Hasrat, *Anglo-Sikh Relations 1799–1949*, p. 284.

38 Donald Featherstone, *At Them with the Bayonet*, pp. 134–45.

39 Ibid., p. 143.

40 Bikrama Jit Hasrat, *Anglo-Sikh Relations 1799–1849*, p. 284.

41 Donald Featherstone, *At Them with the Bayonet*, pp. 145–6.

42 Ibid., p. 146.

43 Joseph Davey Cunningham, *A History of the Sikhs*, p. 284.

44 Ibid.

45 Ibid, p. 279.

46 Donald Featherstone, *At Them with the Bayonet*, p. 153.

47 Joseph Davey Cunningham, *A History of the Sikhs*, p. 289.

48 E. Dalhousie Login, *Lady Login's Recollections: Court Life and Camp Life 1820–1904*, Panjabi University (Languages Department) Patiala, 1970, p. 95.

49 Bikrama Jit Hasrat, *Anglo-Sikh Relations 1799–1849*, p. 359.

50 *The Tribune*, 25 October 1893.

51 W.L. McGregor, *The History of the Sikhs*, Vol. 2, p. 256.

52 *Papers relating to the Punjab, 1847–9*, Inclosure No. 32 in No. 38, Harrison and Son, London.

53 Bikrama Jit Hasrat, *Anglo-Sikh Relations 1799–1849*, p. 323.

54 Patwant Singh, *The Sikhs*, pp. 168–9.

55 Bikrama Jit Hasrat, *Anglo-Sikh Relations 1799–1849*, p. 328.

56 Ibid., p. 332.

57 Ibid., pp. 335–7.

58 S.S. Thorburn, *The Punjab in Peace and War*, p. 142.

59 Ibid., pp. 139–40.

60 Press lists of old records in the Punjab Secretariat: 'From the Secretary to the Government of India to the Board of Administration for the affairs of the Punjab', p. 277 (11 June 1851).

61 Ibid., p. 223.

62 Ibid., 'From Captain J.M. Drake, to P. Melvill, Secretary to the Board of Administration, Punjab', p. 130 (24 May 1849).

63 Ibid., Vol. XII, 'Board of Administration, Punjab, 5 April 1849 to 10 February 1853', p. 31.

64 Ibid., Vol. 11, 'From the Secretary to the Board of Administration, Punjab, to the Secretary to the Government of India', p. 180 (19 July 1850).

65 Lady Login, *Sir John Login and Duleep Singh (1809–1886)* [1889], Panjab University (Languages Department), Chandigarh, 1970, pp. 179–83.

66 Ibid., p. 548.

67 Patwant Singh, *The Sikhs*, p. 176.

Further Reading

BOOKS, GAZETTEERS AND ARTICLES

Ahluwalia, M.L., *Life and Times of Jassa Singh Ahluwalia*, Panjabi University, Patiala, 1989

Ahuja, Roshan Lal, *Maharaja Ranjit Singh*, Punjab Writers' Cooperative Society, New Delhi, 1983

Aijazuddin, F.S., *Historical Images of Pakistan*, Ferozsons, Lahore, 1992

Aijazuddin, F.S., *Lahore: Illustrated Views of the Nineteenth Century*, Mappin, Ahmedabad, 1988

Aijazuddin, F.S., *Lahore Recollected – an Album*, Sang-e-Meel Publications, Lahore, 2003

Aijazuddin, F.S., *Sikh Portraits by European Artists*, Sotheby Parke Bernet Publications, London, 1979

Alexander, Michael and Sushila Anand, *Queen Victoria's Maharajah Duleep Singh 1838–93*, Weidenfeld and Nicolson, London, 1980

Ali, Shahamat, *The Sikhs and Afghans* [1849], Nirmal Publishers and Distributors, New Delhi, 1986

Allan, J.M.A., *The Cambridge Shorter History of India*, S. Chand and Co., New Delhi, 1964

Archer, W.G., *Paintings of the Sikhs*, Her Majesty's Stationery Office, London, 1966

Baillie, F. Alexander, *Kurrachee: Past, Present and Future*, Oxford University Press, Karachi, 1997

Baqir, M., *Lahore: Past and Present* [1952], Low Price Publications, Delhi, 1993

Barr, Lieutenant William, *Journal of a March from Delhi to Cabul* [1844], Panjabi University (Languages Department), Patiala, 1970

Bell, Major Evans, *The Annexation of the Punjaub and Maharajah Duleep Singh* [1882], Nirmal Publishers and Distributors, New Delhi, 1986

Bhatia, H.S., *Rare Documents on Sikhs and Their Rule in the Punjab*, Deep and Deep Publications, New Delhi, 1992

Burnes, Sir Alexander, *Cabool: A Personal Narrative of a Journey to, and Residence in That City, the Years 1836–1838* [1841], Indus Publications, Karachi, 1986

Chaudhry, Nazir Ahmad, *Lahore Fort: A Witness to History*, Sang-e-Meel Publications, Lahore, 1999

Chaudhry, Nazir Ahmad (ed.), *The Maharaja Duleep Singh and the Government: A Narrative*, Sang-e-Meel Publications, Lahore, 1999

Cole, John Jones, *A Sketch of the Siege of Mooltan* [1849], Sang-e-Meel Publications, Lahore, 1999

Cotton, J.S., *Rulers of India: Mountstuart Elphinstone* [1896], Clarendon Press, Oxford, 1896

Court, Henry, *History of the Sikhs* [1888], Longmans, Calcutta, 1959

Cunningham, Alexander, *The Ancient Geography of India* [1871], Indological Book House, Varanasi, 1979

Cunningham, Joseph Davey, *A History of the Sikhs: From the Origins of the Nation to the Battles of the Sutlej* [1849], S. Chand and Co., Delhi, 1966

Dani, Ahmad Hasan, *Peshawar: Historic City of the Frontier*, Sang-e-Meel Publications, Lahore, 1995

Data, Piara Singh, *The Sikh Empire*, National Book Shop, Delhi, 1986

Douie, Sir James, *The Panjab, North-West Frontier Province and Kashmir* [1916], Low Price Publications, Delhi, 1994

Duggal, K.S., *Ranjit Singh: A Secular Sikh Sovereign*, Abhinav Publications, New Delhi, 1989

Elliott, Captain A.C., *The Chronicles of Gujrat* [1902], Nirmal
   Publishers and Distributors, New Delhi, 1986

Fane, Henry Edward, *Five Years in India* [1842], 2 vols, Deepak,
   Gurgaon, 1989

Featherstone, Donald, *At Them with the Bayonet: The First Sikh War*,
   London, Jarrolds, 1968

Garrett, H.L.O., *The Punjab a Hundred Years Ago*, Nirmal Publishers
   and Distributors, New Delhi, 1986

Garrett, H.L.O. and G.L. Chopra, *Events at the Court of Ranjeet Singh
   1810–1817* [1935], Amar Prakashan, New Delhi, 1979

Gazetteer of the Amritsar District, 1883–84 [1892], Civil and Military
   Gazette Press, Lahore, 1892

Gazetteer of the Dera Ghazi Khan District, 1893–97 [1898], Civil and
   Military Gazette Press, Lahore, 1898

Gazetteer of the Dera Ismail Khan District, 1883–84 [1884], Civil and
   Military Gazette Press, Lahore, 1884

Gazetteer of the Hazara Khan District, 1883–84 [1884], Civil and Military
   Gazette Press, Lahore, 1884

Gazetteer of the Kangra District, 1924–25 [1926], Kangra Cultural
   Society, Dharamsala, 1995

Gazetteer of the Peshawar District, 1897–98 [1898], Civil and Military
   Gazette Press, Lahore, 1989

Gazetteers of the District and States of the Undivided Punjab (prior to
   Independence) [1904, 1914], 4 vols, Low Price Publications, Delhi, 1993

Gill, Avtar Singh, *Lahore Darbar and Rani Jindan*, Central Publishers,
   Ludhiana, 1983

Gordon, Sir John J.H., *The Sikhs* [1904], Panjab University (Languages
   Department), Chandigarh, 1988

Goswamy, B.N., *Piety and Splendour: Sikh Heritage in Art*, National
   Museum, New Delhi, 2000

Gough, Sir Charles and Arthur D., *The Sikhs and the Sikh Wars:
   The Rise, Conquest and Annexation of the Punjab State* [1897],
   Deepak, Gurgaon, 1993

Grewal, J.S., *Maharaja Ranjit Singh*, Guru Nanak Dev University, Amritsar, 1982

Grewal, J.S. and Indu Banga, *Early Nineteenth Century Panjab*, Guru Nanak Dev University, Amritsar, 1975

Grey, C. and H.L.O. Garrett, *European Adventurers of Northern India, 1785 to 1849* [1929], Asian Educational Services, Madras, 1993

Griffin, Sir Lepel H., *The Punjab Chiefs* [1890], Civil and Military Gazette Press, Lahore, 1909

Griffin, Sir Lepel H., *The Rajas of the Punjab*, Trubner and Co., London, 1873

Griffin, Sir Lepel H., *Rulers of India: Ranjit Singh* [1911], S. Chand and Co., Delhi, 1967

Gupta, Hari Ram, *History of the Sikhs*, 5 vols, Munshiram Manoharlal, New Delhi, 1991

Gupta, Hari Ram, *Later Mughal History of the Punjab*, Sang-e-Meel Publications, Lahore, 1996

Gupta, Hari Ram, *Marathas and Panipat*, Panjab University, Chandigarh, 1961

Gupta, Hari Ram, *Punjab, Central Asia and the First Afghan War*, Panjab University, Chandigarh, 1987

Gupta, Hari Ram, *Punjab on the Eve of First Sikh War*, Panjab University, Chandigarh, 1956

Hardinge, Viscount Charles, *Rulers of India*, Clarendon Press, Oxford, 1900

Hasrat, Bikrama Jit, *Anglo-Sikh Relations, 1799–1849: A Reappraisal of the Rise and Fall of the Sikhs*, V.V. Research Institute Book Agency, Hoshiarpur, 1968

Hasrat, Bikrama Jit, *Life and Times of Ranjit Singh: A Saga of Benevolent Despotism*, V.V. Research Institute Book Agency, Hoshiarpur, 1977

Hasrat, Bikrama Jit, *The Punjab Papers (1836–1849)*, V.V. Research Institute Book Agency, Hoshiarpur, 1970

Henry, G.A., *Through the Sikh War* [1921], Panjab University (Languages Department), Chandigarh, 1970

Honigberger, John Martin, *Thirty-Five Years in the East* [1852], Sundeep Prakashan, New Delhi, 1995

Hugel, Baron Charles, *Kashmir and the Punjab* [1845], Light and Life Publishers, Jammu, 1972

Hugel, Baron Charles, *Kashmir Under Maharaja Ranjit Singh* [1845], Atlantic Publishers and Distributors, New Delhi, 1984

Hutchison, J. and J.P. Vogel, *History of the Punjab Hill States* [1933], 2 vols, Department of Language and Culture, Simla, 1982

Ibbetson, Sir Denzil, *A Glossary of the Tribes and Castes of the Punjab and North-West Frontier Province* [1883], 3 vols, Panjab University (Languages Department), 1989

Irvine, William, *Later Mughals* [1922], 2 vols, Oriental Books, New Delhi, 1971

Johar, Surinder Singh, *The Heritage of Amritsar*, Sundeep Prakashan, New Delhi, 1978

Johar, Surinder Singh, *The Secular Maharaja: A Biography of Maharaja Ranjit Singh*, Manas Publications, New Delhi, 1985

Kapur, Prithpal Singh and Dharam Singh (eds), *Maharaja Ranjit Singh Commemoration Volume*, Panjabi University, Patiala, 2001

Kaur, Madanjit, *The Golden Temple, Past and Present*, Guru Nanak Dev University, Amritsar, 1983

Khan, Ahmad Nabi, *A History of the Saddozai Afghans of Multan*, Research Society of Pakistan, Lahore, 1977

Khan, Ahmad Nabi, *Multan: History and Architecture*, Institute of Islamic History, Culture and Civilization, Islamabad, 1983

Khan, F.A., *The Princess Bamba Collection (Antiquities of the Sikh Period)*, catalogue, Ministry of Education and Scientific Research, Karachi, 1961

Khan, Khan Mohammad Waliullah, *Sikh Shrines in West Pakistan*, Ferozsons, Karachi, 1962

Khullar, K.K., *Maharaja Ranjit Singh*, Prominent Printers, New Delhi, 1980

Kiernan, Victor G., *Metcalfe's Mission to Lahore (1808–1809)*, Punjab Government Record Office, Monograph No. 1, Lahore, 1950

Kirpa, Ram Diwan, *Gulabnama: History of Maharaja Gulab Singh of Jammu and Kashmir*, Light and Life Publishers, New Delhi, 1977

Kohli, Sita Ram, *Sunset of the Sikh Empire*, Orient Longman, New Delhi, 1967

Kohli, Sita Ram, *The Trial of Diwan Mulraj*, Panjabi University (Languages Department), Patiala, 1971

Lafont, Jean-Marie, *French Administrators of Maharaja Ranjit Singh*, National Book Shop, New Delhi, 1988

Lafont, Jean-Marie, *Maharaja Ranjit Singh: Lord of the Five Rivers*, Oxford University Press, New Delhi, 2002

Lal, Mohan, *Travels in the Punjab, Afghanistan, and Turkistan* [1834], Nirmal Publishers and Distributors, New Delhi, 1986

Latif, Syad Mohammad, 'The Early History of Multan' [1891], *Calcutta Review*

Latif, Syad Mohammad, *History of the Panjab from the Remotest Antiquity to the Present Time* [1891], Kalyani Publishers, New Delhi, 1989

Latif, Syad Mohammad, *Lahore: Its History, Architectural Remains and Antiquities*, [1892] Sang-e-Meel Publications, Lahore, 1994

Lawrence, Major H.M.L., *Adventures of an Officer in the Punjab* [1846], 2 vols, Panjabi University (Languages Department), Patiala, 1970

Leigh, M.S., *The Punjab and the War*, Sang-e-Meel Publications, Lahore, 1997

Login, E. Dalhousie, *Lady Login's Recollections: Court Life and Camp Life 1820–1904* [1916], Panjabi University (Languages Department), Patiala, 1970

Login Lady, *Sir John Login and Duleep Singh (1809–1886)* [1889], Panjab University (Languages Department), Patiala, 1970

Macauliffe, M.A., *The Sikh Religion* [1909], Vol. 6, Oxford University Press, Oxford, 1995

Malcolm, Lieutenant Colonel, *Sketch of the Sikhs* [1812], Asian
Educational Services, 1986

Mulk Raj, Anand (ed.), *Maharaja Ranjit Singh as Patron of the Arts*,
Marg Publications, Bombay, 1981

Masson, Charles, *Narrative of Various Journeys in Balochistan,
Afghanistan and the Punjab, 1826 to 1838* [1842], 3 vols, Munshiram
Manoharlal, New Delhi, 1997

McGregor, W.L., *The History of the Sikhs* [1846], Rupa, New Delhi, 2007

Mehra, Parshotam, *North-western Frontier and British India, 1839–42*,
2 vols, Panjab University, Chandigarh, 1982

Moin, Major S., *Chillianwala: Some Aspects of Leadership*, National
Publishing House, Lahore, n.d.

Moorcroft, William and George Trebeck, *Travels in the Himalayan
Provinces of Hindustan and the Punjab in Ladakh and Kashmir; in
Peshawar, Kabul, Kunduz, and Bokhara, 1819–1825*, John Murray,
London, 1837

Murray, W.M., *History of the Punjab and of the Rise, Progress, and
Present Condition of the Sect and Nation of the Sikhs* [1846], 2 vols,
Deepak, Gurgaon, 1993

Narang, Sir Gokul Chand, *Transformation of Sikhism*, New Book
Society, Lahore, 1912

Nayyar, G.S., *Life and Accomplishments of Sardar Hari Singh Nalwa,
Marshal of the Khalsa*, Harinder Singh Khalsa Publishers, Amritsar,
1993

Orlich, Captain Leopold von, *Travels in India Including Sinde and the
Punjab* [1845], 2 vols, Usha Publications, New Delhi, 1985

Osborne, W.G., *The Court and Camp of Runjeet Sing*, Henry Colburn,
London, 1840

Parshad, Dewan Ajudhia, *Waqai Jang-I-Sikhan [Events of the (First)
Anglo-Sikh War – 1845–6]*, Punjab Itihas Prakashan, Chandigarh,
1975

Payne, C.N., *A Short History of the Sikhs*, Thomas Nelson, London, 1915

Pearse, Major Hugh, *Memories of Alexander Gardner (Colonel of*

Artillery in the Service of Maharaja Ranjit Singh) [1898], Deepak, Gurgaon, 1993

Political Diaries: Delhi Residency and Agency Records, 1807 to 57, Vol. 1, Pioneer Press, Allahabad, 1911

Political Diaries: Ludhiana Agency Records, 1808 to 1815, Vol. 2, Pioneer Press, Allahabad, 1911

Political Diaries of the Resident at Lahore and His Assistants, 1846 to 1849, Vols 3–5 (Lahore Political Diaries), 1911

Prinsep, Henry T., *Origin of the Sikh Power in the Punjab and the Political Life of Muha-Raja Runjeet Singh* [1834], Military Orphan Press, Calcutta, 1965

Randhawa, T.S., *The Sikhs: Images of a Heritage*, Prakash Books, New Delhi, 2000

Raza, Hanif M., *Lahore Through Centuries*, Colorpix, Islamabad, 1996

Rehatsek E., 'A Notice of the Zafarnama-I-Ranjit-Singh of Kanihayya Lal', *The Indian Antiquary* (Bombay), 1887–8

Rehmani, Dr Anjum, *Masterpieces of Lahore Museum*, Lahore Museum, Lahore, 1999

Ross, David, *The Land of the Five Rivers and Sindh*, Nirmal Publishers and Distributors, New Delhi, 1970

Saggar, Balraj, *Who's Who in the History of Punjab (1800–1849)*, National Book Organization, New Delhi, 1993

Seetal, Sohan Lal, *The Sikh Misals and the Punjab*, Lahore Book Shop, Ludhiana, 1981

Sethi, R.R., *Trial of Raja Lal Singh (The Lahore Minister)*, Nirmal Publishers and Distributors, New Delhi, 1986

Sidhu, Colonel Kuldip Singh, *Ranjit Singh's Khalsa Raj and Attariwala Sardars*, National Book Shop, New Delhi, 1994

Singh, Bhagat, *A History of Sikh Misals*, Panjabi University, Patiala, 1993

Singh, Fauja, *Maharaja Kharak Singh*, Panjabi University, Patiala, 1977

Singh, Fauja, *Sirhind Through the Ages*, Panjabi University, Patiala, 1984

Singh, Fauja and A.C. Arora, *Maharaja Ranjit Singh: Politics, Society and Economy*, Panjabi University, Patiala, 1984

Singh, Ganda, *A Bibliography of the Punjab*, Panjabi University, Patiala, 1966

Singh, Ganda, *History of the Gurdwara Shahidganj, Lahore, from Its Origin to November 1935*, self-published, Amritsar, 1935

Singh, Ganda, *Life of Banda Singh Bahadur*, Panjabi University, Patiala, 1990

Singh, Ganda, *The Punjab: Past and Present*, Panjabi University, Patiala, 1983

Singh, Ganda, *Sardar Jassa Singh Ahluwlia*, Panjabi University, Patiala, 1990

Singh, Gopal, *A History of the Sikh People, 1469–1978*, World Sikh University Press, New Delhi, 1979

Singh, Harbans, *The Heritage of the Sikhs*, Manobar Publications, New Delhi, 1985

Singh, Kapur, *Parasharprasna or the Baisakhi of Guru Gobind Singh: An Exposition of Sikhism*, Hind Publishers, Jullundur, 1959

Singh, Khushwant, *The Fall of the Kingdom of Punjab*, Orient Longman, New Delhi, 1962

Singh, Khushwant, *A History of the Sikhs*, 2 vols, Princeton University Press, New Jersey, 1963

Singh, Khushwant, *Ranjit Singh: Maharajah of the Punjab, 1780–1839*, George Allen and Unwin, London, 1962

Singh, Mohinder and Rishi Singh, *Maharaja Ranjit Singh*, UBS Publishers' Distributors/National Institute of Panjab Studies, New Delhi, 2002

Singh, Patwant, *The Golden Temple*, Times Books International, New Delhi, 1989

Singh, Patwant, *The Sikhs*, John Murray, London, 1999

Singh, Sohan, *Life and Exploits of Banda Singh Bahadur*, Panjabi University, Patiala, 1915

Singh, Teja (ed.), *Maharaja Ranjit Singh: First Death Centenary Memorial* [1939], Deepak, Amritsar, 1993

Smith, Bosworth R., *Life of Lord Lawrence*, 2 vols, Smith, Elder and Co., London, 1883

Smyth Major G., *A History of the Reigning Family of Lahore* [1847], Nirmal Publishers and Distributors, New Delhi, 1987

Steinbach, Henry, *The Country of the Sikhs* [1846], KLM Book House, New Delhi, 1978

Stronge, Susan, *The Arts of the Sikh Kingdoms*, Victoria and Albert Museum Publications, London, 1999

Suri, Lala Sohan Lal, *Umdat-Ut-Tawarikh*, Daftar III [1889], Parts 1–5, S. Chand and Co., New Delhi, 1961

Thackwell, Edward Joseph, *Narrative of the Second Sikh War in 1848–49* [1851], Nirmal Publishers and Distributors, New Delhi, 1986

Thorburn, S.S., *Musalmans and Money Lenders in the Punjab*, Mittal Publications, New Delhi, 1983

Thorburn, S.S., *The Punjab in Peace and War* [1883], Panjab University (Languages Department), Chandigarh, 1989

Vigne, G.T., *Travels in Kashmir: Ladak, Iskardo* [1842], 2 vols, Indus Publications, Karachi, 1987

Waheeduddin, Fakir Syed, *The Real Ranjit Singh*, Panjabi University, Patiala, 1965

DOCUMENTS ON THE PUNJAB, 1847–9

Press Lists of Old Records in the Punjab Secretariat:
Volume IX: Lahore Agency and Residency, 1846–47
Volume X: Correspondence of the Resident to the Governor-General, 1848–49
Volume XI: Board of Administrationnjab, 1849–53
Volume XII: Board of Administration, Punjab, 1849–53
Report on the Select Committees on Indian Territories, 1852
Report on the Select Committees on Indian Territories, Vol. X

General Report upon the Administration of the Punjab Proper,
1849–51

'The Return of Ordnance', in *Despatches of Lord Hardinge, Lord Gough
and Sir Harry Smith and Other Documents*, Oliver and Ackerman,
London, 1846

BOOKS AND PAPERS ON SIKH NUMISMATICS

British Parliamentary Papers, *Accounts and Papers, Vol. XXXIX*, 1865

British Parliamentary Papers, *Accounts and Papers, Vol. XLII*, 1864

British Parliamentary Papers, *Accounts and Papers, Vol. XLIII*, 1857–8

British Parliamentary Papers, *Accounts and Papers, Vol. XLV*, 1856

British Parliamentary Papers, *Accounts and Papers, Vol. LXXI*, 1870

British Parliamentary Papers, *Report Relating to a Gold Currency for
India*, 1865

British Parliamentary Papers, *Report of the Committee to Enquire into
Indian Currency*, London, 1899

Herrli, Hans, *The Coins of the Sikhs*, Munshiram Manoharlal, New
Delhi, 2004

Rai, Jyoti, 'Unidentified Sikh Mints: Proof of the Existence of the Mint
at Nimak', *Newsletter of the Oriental Numismatic Society* (United
Kingdom), No. 143, 1995

Rai, Jyoti, 'Rediscovering Sikh Mints: Peshawar, Dera, Rawalpindi',
Newsletter of the Oriental Numismatic Society (United Kingdom),
No. 146, 1995

Rodgers, C. J., *Coins of Ahmad Shah Abdali*, Vol. LIV, Royal Asiatic
Society of Bengal, Calcutta, 1885

Rodgers, C. J., *On the Coins of the Sikhs*, Vol. L, Royal Asiatic Society of
Bengal, Calcutta, 1881

Singh, Saran, 'The First Coins of the Sikhs', *Newsletter of the Oriental
Numismatic Society* (United Kingdom), No. 144, 1995

Thornton, Thomas, *The East India Calculator*, London, 1823

Epilogue

BY JYOTI M. RAI

The Lion of Punjab is dead, leaving the Sikh Empire in the hands of weak and incapable successors. Their advisers are ambitious, unscrupulous and self-serving nobles. In addition, the British are waiting and conspiring to take over the empire so that the whole of sub-Himalayan India will be in their hands. This was the situation ten years after the death of Maharaja Ranjit Singh. What might have happened had he lived longer?

The face of India changed when it became part of the British Empire in 1858. Maharaja Ranjit Singh was a mountain that could not be moved or reduced in size. At the end of the eighteenth century India had been controlled by a medley of fractious princely rulers, a weak Mogul emperor and independent states such as those of Mysore, the Marathas and the Sikhs. Ambitious European trading companies did their best to get a firm foothold in this land of riches. The Honourable East India Company, breaking all trade agreements, felt no compunction in seizing the territories, holdings, wealth and armies of a number of ruling rajahs. With this additional military power and arsenal the Company took on the last remaining strongholds. In the south the mighty Tipu Sultan, the Tiger of Mysore, finally fell after a valiant fight in 1799. The Peshwas (Marathas) in the west acceded to the British in 1818. This left the Sikhs, the only remaining independent kingdom, under Maharaja Ranjit Singh in the north. For the British it was crucial to have control of Punjab. Without this vast region's riches, agricultural potential, military manpower and strategic place on the map, total domination over India was impossible.

The Lion of Punjab was a formidable ruler who built and governed his empire with an iron fist. No one dared oppose him or even contemplated invading his territories. His strategic treaties and well-trained army kept his neighbours watchful but at bay. From any historical survey of Punjab it is clear that the full process of disintegration of the Sikh Empire got under way immediately after the death of Maharaja Ranjit Singh in 1839. If he had lived another ten years or so the subsequent face and history of India would very possibly have been significantly different.

The British would then have had to contend with a tough and astute Ranjit Singh rather than his weak successors and treacherous nobles. While he remained alive and in full possession of his faculties the Sikhs would have abided by their treaty with the British and would never have been provoked to cross the Sutlej under any pretext as they did in 1845. Consequently the two Anglo-Sikh Wars of 1846 and 1849 would not have taken place and Punjab would have remained at this point a powerful independent state.

This brings up another interesting question. Without the Punjab, would the East India Company have come out of the Mutiny of 1857 as the victors? Without the support of Punjab's economic power and skilled Sikh regiments, would the Company have had enough muscle to suppress the spreading uprising? Furthermore, the Sikhs, given a chance to rid themselves of a powerful foreign neighbour, would in all likelihood have joined hands with the rebels, causing a domino effect in the sequence of events. Other subjugated princes would have taken advantage of this golden opportunity and joined in the fray, their major aim being to throw the foreigners out and to reclaim their power and kingdoms. The turmoil could have extended throughout India, making it impossible for the Company to fight on all fronts. It relied heavily on Indian soldiers to fight alongside its British troops, and without their help its forces would have been hopelessly outnumbered.

It is improbable that India would have become a subject of the British Empire in 1858 if the East India Company had been defeated in the Mutiny. British powers, military and otherwise, would have been seriously diminished. There would have been no glorious reign of the British Raj, no Lutyens's Delhi, no Durbars, no Viceroys, no struggle for independence. There would have been no Partition of India in 1947; East and West Pakistan would not have existed; the post-1947 chaos, the displacement, massacres and anguish of millions of people would not have taken place. Not being placed under an alien rule, with its riches and resources being sent home to its imperial masters, India with its wealth intact would have experienced a different future. The importance of Ranjit Singh to the Sikhs is well known, but his importance and contribution to India has not been sufficiently recognized. While he was alive he held the British, Afghans and other factions at arm's length. As long as Punjab remained impregnable the possibility of any foreign power taking over and controlling India was remote.

When considering some of the problems currently facing India that have roots in the past, the first to come to mind is Kashmir. The once beautiful land of lakes and gardens has been the chief bone of contention between India and its neighbour Pakistan for nearly seven decades. Talks between the two countries come to a grinding halt the moment Kashmir and its ownership is brought up. Why Kashmir? Why not some other state? To answer this it is necessary to look back to Ranjit Singh's era. The Sikhs took Kashmir from the Afghans in 1819, which was no mean feat, but it was done and the Afghans were pushed back to Afghanistan. The region remained in Sikh hands until 1846 when it was transferred to the wily Gulab Singh Dogra, Raja of Jammu.

After the First Anglo-Sikh War of 1845–6, apart from the ceding of territories it was decided that the Lahore Durbar pay the victors an indemnity of £1.5 million sterling for war expenses. When the Sikhs ran short of the amount the ever-helpful Gulab Singh was at hand. For his invaluable support and insider help during the First Sikh War the grateful British sold him Kashmir and Hazara for £1 million. This was achieved in a separate treaty in March 1846, but before that he was declared an independent ruler and awarded the title of Maharaja by the British. Finding the hilly region of Hazara, situated nearer Afghanistan, unsuitable, the newly created Maharaja persuaded his benefactors to grant him Jammu instead, which was contiguous with Kashmir. This was easily done, and Hazara was returned to the Lahore Durbar in lieu of Jammu, in complete disregard of the 1846 Treaty. The fortunate Maharaja of Jammu and Kashmir was given permission to pay in instalments.

It is important to have the facts in mind about how Jammu and Kashmir got separated from the rest of Punjab. Acknowledging allegiance to the British, the state was awarded the status of a separate kingdom. This included its right to coin, and in later years it was honoured with the right to conduct a 21-gun salute. A century later, at Partition in 1947, Maharaja Hari Singh of Jammu and Kashmir was in a dilemma. A Hindu ruler with mainly Muslim subjects, he had a choice of siding with either India or Pakistan. He kept dallying, preferring to be independent. This gave way to conflict within the state and infiltration from Pakistan. In October that year he finally signed the Instrument of Accession and ceded to India, but the skirmishes between Indian and Pakistani troops continued well into the following year. The United Nations finally brokered a ceasefire on 1 January 1949. With Pakistan holding on to part of Kashmir, conflicts took place between the two countries in 1965 and 1999. Had Maharaja Ranjit Singh lived longer it would seem to have been impossible for

Gulab Singh to have shown his true colours or for the British to have dared carve up his kingdom. Kashmir would have continued as part of Punjab and been treated as such, very possibly with a proportional increase in its Sikh population, and the seven-decade discord would never have arisen.

At this point the history of the Koh-i-Noor becomes especially symbolic. The priceless Golconda diamond had a chequered career of its own, as described earlier in this book. The incomparable Koh-i-Noor was the first jewel Maharaja Ranjit Singh coveted and felt he had to have at any cost. The one jewel he enjoyed wearing on ceremonial occasions, it was his prized possession. Lying sick in bed just before he passed away in June 1839, he told his ministers that he would like to gift the Koh-i-Noor to the Hindu temple Jagannathpuri in Orissa. Some accounts say that he wanted to offer the stone to the Sikh temple of Guru Ram Das. He certainly asked for it to be brought to him so that he could throw water on it, signifying that he had made a behest. After pretending to send for the Koh-i-Noor, his ministers lied to him by saying it was not at Lahore but in the royal treasury at Amritsar. Dhian Singh Dogra, together with several of the Maharaja's trusted ministers, keeping their own ambitions in mind, did not wish the jewel to leave Lahore. The story of the Koh-i-Noor would have taken a dramatic turn if Maharaja Ranjit Singh's dying wish had been carried out.

The Koh-i-Noor remained in the Lahore Durbar treasury and was worn by Maharaja Ranjit Singh's successors, Kharak Singh, Sher Singh and Dalip Singh, in turn. The legend goes that whoever owns the diamond rules the kingdom, and this still holds true in principle today. After the annexation of the Punjab the prized stone came under tremendous scrutiny; the major objective being to transport it to England as soon as possible and to present it to the Queen. Lengthy discussions took place on how exactly it should be presented and by whom. Finally it was decided that the young Dalip Singh as the successor to Maharaja Ranjit Singh would do the honours. In 1851 the thirteen-year-old ex-Maharaja of Punjab was removed from his native Punjab and three years later, in England, made to hand over the prized heirloom that had been in his family for decades.

The Koh-i-Noor was the highlight of the Great Exhibition in London of the same year. Prince Albert was disappointed with the appearance of the stone and in 1852 ordered it to be recut. For centuries the unusual cut of the Golconda diamond distinguished it from other diamonds, its facets being specially cut to give a soft glow so that they enhanced the beauty of the wearer and not the other way round. Now this unique 186-carat jewel appeared just like any other large commercial diamond and retained none of its natural characteristics or shape, reduced to a mere 105 carats and losing 42 per cent of its weight. It was first worn by the Queen as a brooch but later set as the centrepiece of her royal crown. The Koh-i-Noor was the personal property of Maharaja Ranjit Singh. By treating it and other treasures belonging to him as state property a grave injustice was done in the process of annexation of the Punjab by a trading company that had no legal or moral right to do so.

Had Maharaja Ranjit Singh lived longer the history of India, together with that of the Punjab, might have proved markedly different. Punjab would have remained a powerful kingdom for many more years, possibly giving the Maharaja's heirs time to be more effective. Both Maharajas Sher Singh and Kharak Singh were proficient generals and headed many successful campaigns. Under different circumstances they might have made successful rulers. Things unquestionably would have been different for young Maharaja Dalip Singh, having come of age and being in a position – with the support of his more than capable mother Rani Jindan – to exercise control over his Empire and subjects and so keep the British on their side of the border just as his father had done, halting Britain's ambitions of a grand takeover. One cannot imagine an India without its British Raj. But for the early demise of a diminutive, pockmarked, one-eyed, uneducated Sikh ruler who happened to be a statesman of genius this would have been entirely possible.

Jyoti M. Rai
New Delhi
April 2013

$\mathscr{O}\!\mathit{ndex}$

For consistency and to preserve the general usage in the text, names of non-European historical personages are all indexed by the first element.

Peter Owen Publishers
81 Ridge Road
London N8 9NP
UK

T + 44 (0)20 8350 1775
F + 44 (0)20 8340 9488
E info@peterowen.com
www.peterowen.com
@PeterOwenPubs

Independent publishers since 1951

SOME AUTHORS WE HAVE PUBLISHED

James Agee • Bella Akhmadulina • Tariq Ali • Kenneth Allsop • Alfred Andersch
Guillaume Apollinaire • Machado de Assis • Miguel Angel Asturias • Duke of Bedford
Oliver Bernard • Thomas Blackburn • Jane Bowles • Paul Bowles • Richard Bradford
Ilse, Countess von Bredow • Lenny Bruce • Finn Carling • Blaise Cendrars • Marc Chagall
Giorgio de Chirico • Uno Chiyo • Hugo Claus • Jean Cocteau • Albert Cohen
Colette • Ithell Colquhoun • Richard Corson • Benedetto Croce • Margaret Crosland
e.e. cummings • Stig Dalager • Salvador Dalí • Osamu Dazai • Anita Desai
Charles Dickens • Bernard Diederich • Fabián Dobles • William Donaldson
Autran Dourado • Yuri Druzhnikov • Lawrence Durrell • Isabelle Eberhardt
Sergei Eisenstein • Shusaku Endo • Erté • Knut Faldbakken • Ida Fink
Wolfgang George Fischer • Nicholas Freeling • Philip Freund • Dennis Friedman
Carlo Emilio Gadda • Rhea Galanaki • Salvador Garmendia • Michel Gauquelin
André Gide • Natalia Ginzburg • Jean Giono • Geoffrey Gorer • William Goyen
Julien Gracq • Sue Grafton • Robert Graves • Angela Green • Julien Green
George Grosz • Barbara Hardy • H.D. • Rayner Heppenstall • David Herbert
Gustaw Herling • Hermann Hesse • Shere Hite • Stewart Home • Abdullah Hussein
King Hussein of Jordan • Ruth Inglis • Grace Ingoldby • Yasushi Inoue
Hans Henny Jahnn • Karl Jaspers • Takeshi Kaiko • Jaan Kaplinski • Anna Kavan
Yasunuri Kawabata • Nikos Kazantzakis • Orhan Kemal • Christer Kihlman
James Kirkup • Paul Klee • James Laughlin • Patricia Laurent • Violette Leduc
Lee Seung-U • Vernon Lee • József Lengyel • Robert Liddell • Francisco García Lorca
Moura Lympany • Dacia Maraini • Marcel Marceau • André Maurois
Henri Michaux • Henry Miller • Miranda Miller • Marga Minco • Yukio Mishima
Quim Monzó • Margaret Morris • Angus Wolfe Murray • Atle Næss • Gérard de Nerval
Anaïs Nin • Yoko Ono • Uri Orlev • Wendy Owen • Arto Paasilinna • Marco Pallis
Oscar Parland • Boris Pasternak • Cesare Pavese • Milorad Pavic • Octavio Paz
Mervyn Peake • Carlos Pedretti • Dame Margery Perham • Graciliano Ramos
Jeremy Reed • Rodrigo Rey Rosa • Joseph Roth • Ken Russell • Marquis de Sade
Cora Sandel • George Santayana • May Sarton • Jean-Paul Sartre
Ferdinand de Saussure • Gerald Scarfe • Albert Schweitzer • George Bernard Shaw
Isaac Bashevis Singer • Patwant Singh • Edith Sitwell • Suzanne St Albans • Stevie Smith
C.P. Snow • Bengt Söderbergh • Vladimir Soloukhin • Natsume Soseki • Muriel Spark
Gertrude Stein • Bram Stoker • August Strindberg • Rabindranath Tagore
Tambimuttu • Elisabeth Russell Taylor • Emma Tennant • Anne Tibble • Roland Topor
Miloš Urban • Anne Valery • Peter Vansittart • José J. Veiga • Tarjei Vesaas
Noel Virtue • Max Weber • Edith Wharton • William Carlos Williams • Phyllis Willmott
G. Peter Winnington • Monique Wittig • A.B. Yehoshua • Marguerite Young
Fakhar Zaman • Alexander Zinoviev • Emile Zola